DAVID M. STONE

GUERCINO
MASTER DRAFTSMAN

WORKS FROM NORTH AMERICAN COLLECTIONS

Harvard University Art Museums

Nuova Alfa Editoriale

For my Teachers
especially my parents
Daniel and Ann Plaat Stone

Published on the occasion of an exhibition organized
by the Harvard University Art Museums with funds provided by a
generous grant from the National Endowment for the Arts, a Federal Agency

Exhibition dates:
Arthur M. Sackler Museum, Harvard University Art Museums, Cambridge, 15 February - 31 March 1991
National Gallery of Canada / Musée des Beaux-Arts du Canada, Ottawa, 3 May - 16 June 1991
Cleveland Museum of Art, 27 August - 13 October 1991

Designed by Maurizio Armaroli and David Stone
Printed and bound in Italy by
Bertoncello Arti Grafiche
Cittadella (Padua)

Cover illustration: see cat. no. 48

Nuova Alfa Editoriale
Elemond Editori Associati
ISBN 88-7779-263-9

Contents

Lenders to the Exhibition

Achenbach Foundation for Graphic Arts,
The Fine Arts Museums of San Francisco

Allen Memorial Art Museum, Oberlin College

Arkansas Arts Center

The Art Institute of Chicago

The Chrysler Museum, Norfolk, Virginia

Cleveland Museum of Art

Fogg Art Museum, Harvard University

The J. Paul Getty Museum

Honolulu Academy of Arts

University of Iowa Art Museum

Los Angeles County Museum of Art

The Metropolitan Museum of Art, New York

University of Michigan Museum of Art

Philadelphia Museum of Art

The Pierpont Morgan Library, New York

The Art Museum, Princeton University

National Gallery of Art, Washington, D.C.

National Gallery of Canada / Musée des
Beaux-Arts du Canada, Ottawa

The Nelson-Atkins Museum of Art

Saint Louis Art Museum

Seattle Art Museum

The Snite Museum of Art,
University of Notre Dame

Vassar College Art Gallery

Worcester Art Museum

Mr. and Mrs. Benton Case, Jr.

Dr. Carlo M. Croce

Lisa Donneson and Henry Weisburg

Evalyne S. Grand

Mr. and Mrs. Morton B. Harris

Jak Katalan

Dr. Hilary Koprowski

Michael and Margaret Korda

J. F. McCrindle

Robert and Bertina Suida Manning

Janet Mavec

Elmar W. Seibel

Mrs. Richard L. Selle

William D. Shorey

and eight anonymous Private Collections

Foreword

This catalogue and the exhibition it accompanies commemorate the 400th anniversary of the birth of Giovanni Francesco Barbieri, called il Guercino (1591 - 1666), one of the greatest draftsmen and painters of the seventeenth century. The first major loan show in North America devoted to his work, the exhibition presents a splendid survey of ninety-two drawings, supplemented by two prints, selected from twenty-four museums and twenty-two private collections in the United States and Canada. More drawings survive by Guercino than by any other Italian Baroque master of the first rank, and North American collections have yielded an impressive group that includes famous and lesser known sheets. The appendix to the catalogue lists virtually every known Guercino drawing in the United States and Canada, thus providing an idea of the extent and history of North American holdings of his work.

The drawings exhibited here reveal the extraordinary range of subjects and functions that characterize Guercino's oeuvre. While the exhibition emphasizes the fascinating design process that led up to the creation of his altarpieces and cabinet pictures, biblical, mythological, and historical themes, it also incorporates finished drawings, models for prints, nudes, genre scenes, portraits, caricatures, and landscapes—nearly the entire scope of the master's output.

We are deeply grateful to Dr. David Stone, Assistant Professor of Art History at the University of Delaware, who initiated the exhibition, selected the drawings, and wrote the catalogue. Thanks to Professor Stone's exhaustive investigation of North American collections and to his profound knowledge of the artist, the show brings to light a number of rarely exhibited drawings. With its wealth of new insights and information, the catalogue makes a substantial contribution to the Guercino literature.

The exhibition has been organized by the Harvard University Art Museums, and our thanks go to several staff members who helped realize this project. Edgar Peters Bowron, former director of the Harvard University Art Museums, enthusiastically supported the show during its initial stages. Penley Knipe, Curatorial Assistant in the Drawings Department, expertly coordinated the curatorial aspects of the exhibition and lent valuable assistance to Professor Stone. William Robinson, Ian Woodner Curator of Drawings, with the help of Miriam Stewart, Assistant Curator of Drawings, supervised the organization of the show. We are also particularly grateful to Maureen Donovan, Associate Registrar, who adeptly managed the incoming loans and the tour. Craigen Bowen, Philip and Lynn Straus Conservator of Works of Art on Paper, and Anne Driesse, Assistant Conservator of Works of Art on Paper, of the Center for Conservation and Technical Studies performed the necessary conservation work and prepared several of the sheets for exhibition. Thanks also go to Danielle Hanrahan, Administrator for Design and Installation, and to Peter Walsh, Director of Communications.

In Ottawa, the exhibition was coordinated by Mimi Cazort, Curator of Prints and Drawings, and in Cleveland, by Michael Miller, Assistant Curator, Department of Prints and Drawings. We gratefully acknowledge their help and enthusiasm.

We also wish to express our warmest thanks to Nuova Alfa Editoriale, Bologna, and especially to Maurizio Armaroli for producing the handsome catalogue.

This exhibition is funded by a generous grant from the National Endowment for the Arts, a Federal Agency. We are deeply grateful for their continuing support.

Last, but far from least, we thank all the lenders, without whose generosity this wonderful exhibition could not have taken place.

Marjorie B. Cohn, Acting Director, Harvard University Art Museums

Dr. Shirley Thomson, Director, National Gallery of Canada, Ottawa

Dr. Evan Turner, Director, The Cleveland Museum of Art

Acknowledgements

This exhibition and catalogue could not have been brought to light if it had not been for the support of a large number of scholars, curators, museum directors, registrars, art dealers, collectors, photographers, editors, software specialists, fax machines, overnight mail couriers, a great Bolognese dentist, as well as many long-suffering and dear friends. I thank them all.

That I might someday have the chance to organize the first major Guercino exhibition to be held in North America never occurred to me when I was a graduate student at Harvard studying with Sydney J. Freedberg and Konrad Oberhuber. Though my dissertation on Guercino and Seicento theory was deeply concerned with drawings, it was not until the study was finished that I realized that I had not completely explained some of my ideas about Guercino's design methods and that I would have to try again. I hope that the patient readers of my thesis will find that I have sharpened my concepts in the meantime. To my advisors, "master teachers" to whom I will always owe an immense debt, I offer sincere thanks.

It was the former director of the Harvard University Art Museums, Edgar Peters Bowron, who gave me his cooperation and support to do a Guercino show when everyone else said it would be impossible to organize and too expensive. His interest in the material itself was the key (it always is) and I am obliged to him for taking on this important project. I also thank the directors of the National Gallery of Canada and the Cleveland Museum of Art, as well as their curators, respectively Mimi Cazort and Michael Miller, for their willingness to participate in the tour. William Robinson, Ian Woodner Curator of Drawings, Miriam Stewart, Assistant Curator, and Penley Knipe, Curatorial Assistant in the Drawings Department did everything and more a guest curator could hope for in the way of providing scholarly advice, moral and technical support, and superb coordination of all the bureaucratic matters that go into an exhibition with 46 different lenders from as far away as Honolulu and Arkansas and an exhibition catalogue with some 300 illustrations published in Italy. Penley more than anyone else was responsible for helping me with the loan requests and photo orders. She deserves special thanks for all her hard work as well as for her patience when "talking me down" from her telephone in the control tower on those not so rare days when everything went wrong. I would also like to gratefully acknowledge the help of Marjorie Cohn, Acting Director of the Harvard University Art Museums, Maureen Donovan of the Registrar's office, and Peter Walsh, Director of Communications.

The National Endowment for the Arts, a Federal Agency, favored our project with a generous grant just when we needed it most. The College of Arts and Sciences of the University of Delaware, Helen Gouldner, Dean, provided me with a General University Research Grant which I used to spend a valuable summer in the drawing cabinets of Europe in the summer of 1989. For this, as well as for other funds made available to me by my University for photographs published in the Supplement, I am truly grateful. I would also like to thank my chairman, Dr. William I. Homer, and all of my colleagues and students in the Department of Art History at the University of Delaware for their understanding and encouragement.

For scholarly advice, I am greatly indebted to the master of Guercino studies, Sir Denis Mahon, who on numerous occasions made himself available to me for consultations in London and Bologna—even when in the throes of organizing what will undoubtedly be his crowing achievement, the great Guercino *mostra* that will open in Bologna and Cento in September of 1991. Sir Denis's Windsor partner, Mr. Nicholas Turner, Assistant Keeper in the Department of Prints and Drawings at the British Museum, contributed more to the content of the exhibition and catalogue than anyone. His generosity in helping me weed out unworthy sheets and in providing me with knowledge of proper substitutes or additional connected drawings in Europe and America (most of which he had discovered himself) is much appreciated. One awaits with great anticipation the unveiling of his new Guercino *scoperte* in the British Museum exhibition he has expertly organized of Guercino drawings in British collections slated for the summer of 1991. To my friend Prof. Luigi Salerno, whose catalogue raisonné of Guercino's paintings is cited on virtually every page of this book, I once again offer my thanks for the many kindnesses he and his publisher Patrizio Busiri Vici have extended to me over the past eight years. The assistance of many other scholars and curators should also be mentioned, among them: David Acton, Jacob Bean, Veronika Birke, Jonathan Bober, Suzanne Boorsch, Fred den Broeder, Barbara Butts, Richard Campbell, Victor Carlson, Bruce Davis, Diane DeGrazia, Cara Denison, Andrea Emiliani, Marzia Faietti, Larry Feinberg, Mary Frisk, Laura Giles, George Goldner, Fausto Gozzi, Richard Harprath, Jefferson Harrison, Chiyo Ishikawa, Jay Jensen, Robert Flynn Johnson, Rebecca Lawton, Judith Weiss Levy, Stéphane Loire, Suzanne Folds McCullagh, George McKenna, Nancy Ward Neilson, Ann Percy, Barbara Ross, Jennifer Saville, John Seyller, Stephen Spiro, Carel van Tuyll, Wendy Watson, Stephanie Wiles, Carolyn Wood, and Townsend Wolf. We are obviously much obliged to all the curators and their staffs who allowed us access to their Guercino drawings and who provided technical information, references, and photographs.

Three people who saw me through the writing of the book deserve special mention. Whatever clarity of thought may have graced the following pages is probably due to the advice of Dr. Linda Pellecchia. She read over most of the entries and offered many valuable suggestions. I cannot repay her for all the time and energy she has given to this project. Mary Brantl, my technical editor and assistant, was responsible for the bibliography and the final editing of entries. For all her time, good humor, and expertise, I am truly grateful. My great friend and Bolognese book dealer, Fabio Paltrinieri of Libreria Leonardo, who for nearly a decade has made my trips to Italy a joy, was unstinting in this time of need. He allowed me to turn his small apartment into an office and his bookstore into a research library. I cannot thank him enough.

Maurizio Armaroli, Director of Nuova Alfa Editoriale in Bologna followed the design and printing of the catalogue from beginning to end and deserves great praise. Tiziana Antonacchio of the Linotipia Nettunia expertly impaginated the entire book.

There is not space or time to thank all the other people who contributed to my research and the publication of the catalogue, and so I must apologize for being haphazard in mentioning a few more names. Among art dealers and drawing experts: Francis Russell and Hugo Chapman of Christie's, Julien Stock and Elizabeth Llewellyn of Sotheby's, Mark Brady, Yvonne Tan Bunzl, Stephen Ongpin of Colnaghi's, Margot Gordon, Mary Jane Harris, formerly of Corsini Galleries, Gabriel Naughton of Agnew's, Stephen Pepper, Kate de Rothschild, Alan Salz, Mia Weiner, and Eunice Williams. For additional help, I would like to acknowledge: Elizabeth Bickley, Grazia Biscaretti, Elizabeth Stone Charlson, Aroldo Greco, Toby Jurovics, Rodney Nevitt, and Christopher K. Nissen.

We are extremely grateful to the generous lenders to the exhibition. Without their participation, we would never have arrived at so high a level of quality.

David M. Stone

Introduction

Quà vi è un giovane di patria di Cento, che dipinge con somma felicità d'invenzione. E gran disegnatore, e felicissimo coloritore: è mostro di natura, e miracolo da far stupire chi vede le sue opere. Non dico nulla: ei fa rimaner stupidi li primi pittori: basta il vedrà al suo ritorno (Ludovico Carracci, 1617).[1]

Few Baroque painters are as well-known and appreciated for their drawings as for their canvases. Giovanni Francesco Barbieri, called il Guercino ("the squinter"), is one of these truly exceptional artists. From the very beginning of his career, as Ludovico Carracci was quick to recognize, Guercino demonstrated prodigious skills as a draftsman. Since that time, his drawings have been highly prized and widely collected, particularly in eighteenth-century England, where so many of his sheets (nearly a thousand, if one includes the drawings now assigned to Guercino's School and imitators) found a permanent home in the Royal Library at Windsor Castle. American collections boast far fewer examples but are equally rich—perhaps surprisingly so—when it comes to quality, diversity (of subjects, techniques, and media), and chronological range. It has thus been possible to organize a virtually complete survey of Guercino's graphic production with loans from the United States and Canada. The exhibition and catalogue presented here on the occasion of the 400th anniversary of the artist's birth, serve not only as opportunities to celebrate a great draftsman and to put forward several new ideas concerning the function of his drawings and his design process, they also provide the perfect context to make better known the wealth of Guercino material currently in North American public and private collections, much of it acquired in the last twenty-five years and published now for the first time.

*   *   *

Guercino was baptized on 8 February 1591 in Cento, a small town situated between Ferrara and Bologna in northern Italy. Malvasia, Guercino's biographer, reports that the boy, age nine, was sent by his parents to a *pittore da guazzo* (probably not much more than a house decorator) to learn how to paint, but that after a short time he returned home and practiced on his own.[2] The author also mentions a short apprenticeship with Paolo Zagnoni, a *quadratura* specialist active in Bologna.[3] In 1607, when Guercino was sixteen, he was sent to the studio of the Centese artist Benedetto Gennari, Senior (1563-1610). Supposedly, after only a year as an assistant, Guercino became an active collaborator with Gennari in various projects in Cento; however, no works by the latter or by the two artists working together have been identified.[4]

Provincial artistically, Cento received its first altarpiece in the new Baroque style in the very year of Guercino's birth, 1591: *The Holy Family with St. Francis, Two Angels and Donors* by Ludovico Carracci (1555-1619), originally in the Chiesa dei Cappuccini and now in the Cento Pinacoteca.[5] Through this animated, colorful, and naturalistic painting, the modern, anti-Mannerist style of Bologna created over the course of the previous decade by Ludovico and his cousins, the brothers Annibale (1560-1609) and Agostino (1557-1602), reached Cento and transformed local taste in art. Guercino—all the Seicento sources tell us—took Ludovico's altarpiece as his point of departure.[6] Although his early paintings reflect the influence of several important sources in Ferrarese art (Scarsellino especially),[7] Guercino's style and ideas owe more to the Carracci and their illustrious students (such as Guido Reni, Domenichino, Schedone, Cavedone, and Spada) than to any other tradition.

Apparently without ever actually attending the Carracci Academy that had been founded in c. 1582 in Bologna (a city renowned for its great university and intellectual life),[8] the wildly talented Guercino learned the secrets of their naturalistic and expressive style simply by studying their paintings, drawings, and prints. It is in a sense a great tribute to the effectiveness of the Carracci's anti-Mannerist campaign (they sought to replace the aestheticism and abstraction of later sixteenth-century religious art with legible narrative and realistic treatment of color, light, and the human figure) that a largely self-taught painter from an artistic backwater could understand what they had to say and was able to carry their style forward.

Guercino could not have succeeded, however, without also following the Carracci's drawing exercises and design methods. These had been developed as part of an innovative, comprehensive curriculum taught at the Academy that stressed the importance of drawing after the live nude model and encouraged the production of countless composition and figure studies, genre sketches, landscapes, and caricatures (a Carracci invention). Guercino was devoted to this well-established drawing practice, which was initially intended as an antidote to the artificiality and preciousness of Mannerist draftsmanship, and added new and significant dimensions to it, especially in the area of preparatory drawings. We will describe Guercino's drawings—their various techniques and functions; their relationship to his pictures—momentarily, after first providing an outline of Guercino's career and stylistic development as a painter.

Following the production of several important altarpieces (e.g., the *S. Agostino* altar of c. 1616 now in Brussels)[9] and palace decorations in Cento between 1613 and 1617 (see cat. no. 2), Guer-

V

II

IV

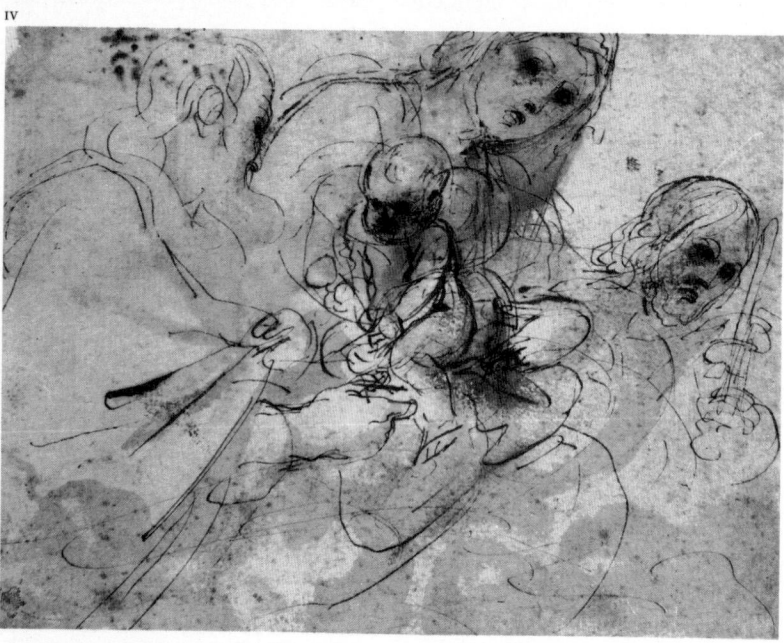

III: recto

cino was called to Bologna, where in 1617-1618 he painted four canvases for Cardinal Alessandro Ludovisi, Archbishop of Bologna, who was soon to ascend the papal throne.[10] Guercino's success was now guaranteed and it was surely this group of paintings which caught Ludovico Carracci's attention and prompted his enthusiastic missive to Don Ferrante Carlo cited above. Works like the *Return of the Prodigal Son* of 1617 (Turin, Galleria Sabauda),[11] perhaps the most dramatic picture done for Cardinal Ludovisi, demonstrate Guercino's phenomenal talent for bringing narrative to life. Rather than forcing the story to fit into a pre-existing compositional formula, Guercino designs his painting according to the requirements of the subject. The originality of his ideas is due in part to the intensity of the preparatory process, in which Guercino considers the characters and their interaction over and over again in quick sketches, each time in a different configuration.[12]

A short visit to Venice in early 1618 may have been the inspiration for Guercino's Titianesque picture of *Apollo Flaying Marsyas* made later that year for the Grand Duke of Tuscany and now in the Pitti Palace in Florence.[13] The romantic quality of the illumination—a brilliant moonlight set against a deep blue sky—and the monumentality of the fleshy nude Apollo shown with a dark red cape flying over his shoulder document Guercino's seduction by Venetian painting at a pivotal moment in his development.[14] The coloristic poetry achieved in this work is coupled with a new, highly sophisticated treatment of composition as an abstract formal language in pictures like the *Raising of Lazarus* in the Louvre (fig. 7a),[15] one of several powerful, tightly structured images executed by Guercino at Ferrara in 1619-1620 for the Papal Legate of that city, Cardinal Jacopo Serra (see cat. nos. 7-8). A two-week sojourn at Mantua in early 1620 gave Guercino access to the prestigious Gonzaga collections, which included important pictures by Domenico Fetti, Rubens, and Caravaggio. The Rubensian character of two Guercino paintings of half-length figures completed in 1621, the *Capture of Christ* in the Fitzwilliam Museum, Cambridge[16] and its pendant, the *Incredulity of St. Thomas* in the National Gallery, London (fig. 10a) for which we have discovered the only known preparatory sketch (cat. no. 10), shows how quickly and masterfully Guercino could absorb new ideas and adapt them for his own purposes.

The crowning achievement of Guercino's early period is the large altarpiece of the *Investiture of St. William of Aquitaine* (fig. 9a) painted for S. Gregorio in 1620 and now in the Bologna Pinacoteca. This was his first commission for a Bolognese church and it seems that the pressure of so significant an opportunity induced him to make an unprecedented number (dozens and dozens) of preparatory sketches for its design. A sample group of these drawings (figs. I - V) is described below; see also under cat. no. 9.

Guercino's most celebrated works were made in Rome between 1621 and 1623, where he again served Alessandro Ludovisi, now Pope Gregory XV, and his Cardinal nephew, Ludovico Ludovisi. Two commissions in particular, the *Aurora* ceiling fresco of 1621 in the Casino Ludovisi (fig. VI)[17] and the colossal *Burial and Reception into Heaven of St. Petronilla*, an altarpiece completed in the spring of 1623 for St. Peter's and now preserved in the Capitoline Museum in Rome (fig. IX),[18] stand out as landmarks in the creation of the High Baroque and surely influenced such major figures as Bernini and Pietro da Cortona.

Pope Gregory's abrupt death on 8 July 1623 ended Guercino's hopes of ever painting the Loggia della Benedizione of St. Peter's, a commission Malvasia believed had been designated for Guercino when the Ludovisi invited the artist to Rome some twenty-five months earlier.[19] The realization that he had lost his main protector and Maecenas was probably the cause of Guercino's immediate departure for Cento in the late summer of 1623.

The years between 1623 and 1629 are generally recognized as Guercino's "transitional period." In contrast to the two-year sojourn in Rome, which had been for him a period of intense activity and rapid growth (he had been inspired by the heroic classicism of the late Annibale Carracci at the Farnese Gallery and by the dramatic, illusionistic productions of Caravaggio, particularly the Vatican *Entombment*), the pace and developments of the mid-1620s were somewhat relaxed and less focussed on a single artistic goal or ideal. One senses that for the first time in his mature career, Guercino was not entirely certain how to proceed. This may have been partly due to the fact that the kinds of projects he had executed in Rome—illusionistic, hyperbolic tours-de-force for the Ludovisi pontificate—were now unavailable to him in Cento and difficult to obtain even in the larger cities of Emilia, the name given to this region of Italy. The one exception might be the stirring altarpiece of 1624-1625 representing the *Crucifixion with Saints* that Guercino made for the huge church of the Madonna della Ghiara at Reggio Emilia (fig. 12a). This work draws liberally upon the experience of the *St. Petronilla* of 1623, and is a rare reoccurrence in these years of the grandiosity that had characterized Guercino's Roman style (see cat. nos. 12-13). More typical and forward-looking are the restrained compositions of small works like the dazzlingly beautiful *Presentation of Christ at the Temple*, a picture on copper of late 1623 in the Mahon Collection now on loan to the National Gallery, London.[20] In this important painting, the placement of figures is calculated to form a measured, fully classical structure. The human forms and draperies, more frontal and planar than in the past, move with insistent, precise rhythms, as if beating time in concert with a metronome. The strong chiaroscuro and bold color contrasts of the early period have now **xiii**

VI

xiv

given way to brighter, purer tones and more evenly distributed illumination. The mathematical stringency of this picture, which depends on the Raphaelism of Domenichino's Roman style, did not, however, become a real trend in Guercino's art. It was a temporary interest whose intellectuality did not completely satisfy or suit him. Its style will be supplanted within a few years by the more suave and gentle aesthetic of Guido Reni, whose *grazia* (gracefulness) of design and *bellezza* (beauty) of color and line were then the most favored aspects of painting among Guercino's Emilian patrons.

Guercino oscillates between the extremes represented by the Ghiara *Crucifixion* and the Mahon *Presentation* until he undertakes the fresco decorations of the great cupola of Piacenza Cathedral between 1626 and 1627 (for a complete account, see cat. nos. 19-21). The dark colors, bulky figures, and turbulent compositions of his early works (e.g., the *St. Albert* of 1618, fig. 4a) are now a distant memory. His new style—particularly noticeable in the elaborate, ornamental draperies he designed for the Prophets and Sibyls in the cupola and lunettes—begins here in earnest to take on the elegance and idealization of Reni. The lyricism and sweetness of his conception of the airborne angels and, especially, of the tender putti that make up a frieze below the lunettes may have been inspired by renewed contact with the great frescoes at Parma by Correggio, the High Renaissance master whose altarpieces (at Modena) and red-chalk drawings Guercino undoubtedly knew since his earliest days. An example of the radiant style forged at Piacenza may be seen in the Morgan Library *Holy Family* (cat. no. 23), a drawing not connected with the Piacenza cupola project but one which seems to sum up everything that Guercino had accomplished there. In the *Risen Christ Appearing to the Virgin* of 1628-1630 (Cento, Pinacoteca)[21] and the Giroldo Chapel laterals for the Cathedral of Reggio Emilia of 1627-1632 (see figs. 24a-25a and cat. nos. 24-26), the transformation into a Reniesque idiom is complete. A superb red-chalk drawing of two figures (*SS. John the Baptist and John the Evangelist*) of 1631-1632 in the Los Angeles County Museum of Art (cat. no. 27) evinces the new luminosity and sensitivity in Guercino's draftsmanship. The subtle modulations of light and shadow achieved here with the help of stumping (a technique in which the chalk is rubbed and smoothed across the page with a blunt leather tool) correspond to the silvery, pastel tonalities found in many of Guercino's later paintings.

Though he may have regretted leaving Rome in 1623, Guercino's fame did not diminish in Cento. His return to his native city gave rise to the foundation of an astonishingly successful mail-order workshop with an international clientele. Gregory's successor, Pope Urban VIII Barberini, as well as Marie de' Medici of France, Charles I of England, Francesco I d'Este of Modena, and many other important European rulers and art-collectors sought Guercino's talents.

Proof of his prosperity may be found in the *Libro dei Conti*, the account book begun in 1629 by Guercino's brother, the still-life painter Paolo Antonio Barbieri (1603-1649), who faithfully recorded receipts of payment for virtually all the pictures he and Guercino executed.[22] After Paolo Antonio's death, the book was continued by Guercino and other members of his household until the master's own death on 22 December 1666. From this precious document we learn of the breadth and magnitude of Guercino's production and of his rigid pricing system, something we have commented on several times in the text of the Catalogue. He charged by the figure, half-figure, and head and was not apt to alter his fees for anyone.[23] This pricing method had ramifications for the actual designs of his paintings. The case of the *Vision of St. Philip Neri* (fig. 52a) is particularly telling. The picture was commissioned by Padre Guerra in 1646 for Santa Maria in Galliera at Bologna. It originally showed Philip Neri—supported by two angels (see cat. no. 52)—looking upwards at clouds, putti, and the Dove of the Holy Spirit. Most of the upper half of this large altarpiece was empty. Apparently, Padre Guerra could only afford to give St. Philip a cut-rate vision (and even then it took the church two years to pay their bill). However, as the *Libro dei Conti* indicates, in 1662, a Madonna and Child was added by Guercino to the upper left corner of the altarpiece. Luckily for the church, Count Ettore Ghisiglieri, one of Guercino's patrons, had recently renounced worldly life and had joined the Oratorian brotherhood at Santa Maria in Galliera. "Fra" Ghisiglieri paid Guercino to add the figures and to clean and retouch the whole painting. The asymmetry of the composition as one sees it today is due to the fact that Guercino had designed the picture for only three figures: there was not enough room in the upper center for the Madonna and Child, and they had to be placed off to one side.

Rather than order a high-quality altarpiece with a restricted number of life-size figures executed by the master himself, some of Guercino's patrons—especially when the projected work was to be set up in a minor church—elected for reasons of economy to have a painting with a full complement of figures done by the workshop. This seems to have been the case when Cardinal Girolamo Colonna, Archbishop of Bologna from 1632 to 1645, decided to favor the church of San Barnaba at Marino Laziale, a Colonna *feudo* near Rome, with a large altarpiece (4.0 x 3.3 m.) of the *Martyrdom of San Barnaba* (fig. XIV),[24] still *in situ* in the apse. The picture was not made by Guercino but by his assistant Bartolomeo Gennari (1544-1661), the brother of Guercino's brother-in-law Ercole.

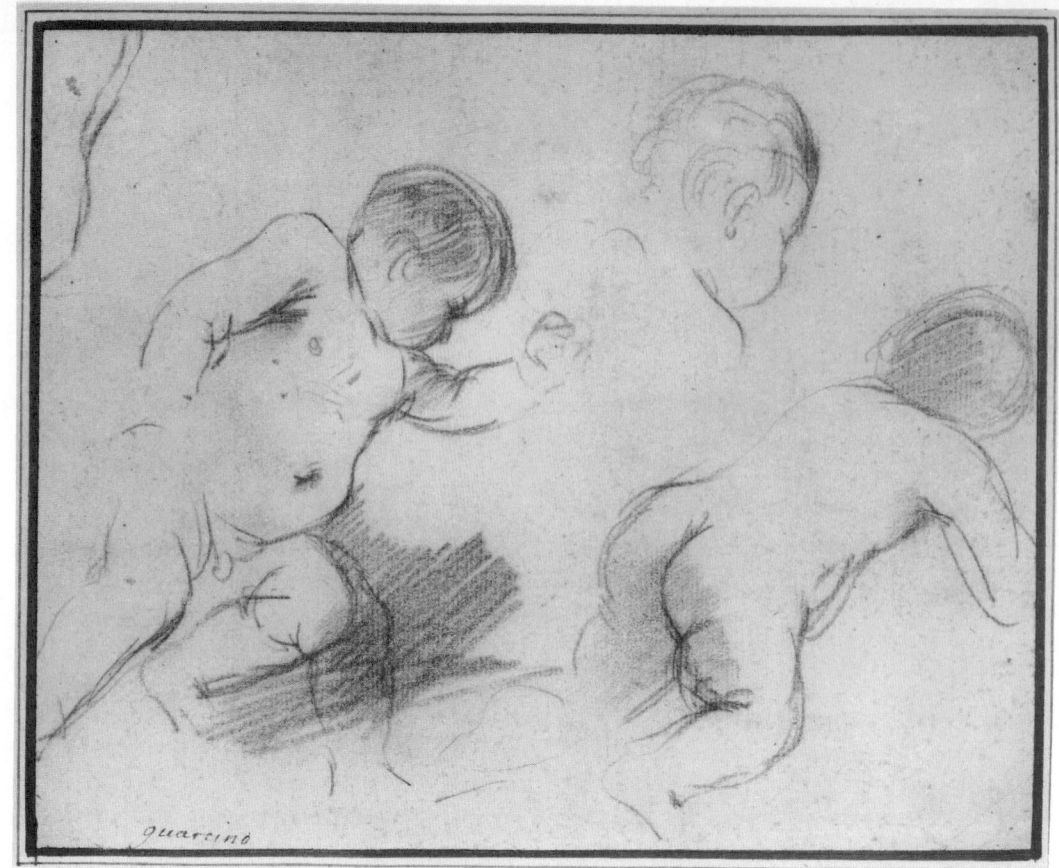

VII

VIII

The Cardinal's motivation for sending a large Bolognese painting to a provincial church must have been obvious to everyone. His donation of a picture in the recognizable style of Guercino, by this time the leader of the Bolognese school, inevitably reminded the Colonna's subjects in Marino of the Cardinal's exalted status as Archbishop of Bologna. Since a primary function of the commission was diplomatic, it did not necessarily matter whether the painting was autograph or by the workshop; the main requirement was that it look like a Guercino. Colonna's frugality in employing Gennari instead of Guercino, therefore, made financial sense (Colonna, who on other occasions patronized Guercino directly, was hardly poor). In a similar move, Colonna employed Giacinto Campana to copy Guercino's *Martyrdom of St. Bartholomew* (see cat. nos. 32-35) from the original altarpiece at Siena. The copy (fig. 32a) eventually found its way to the church of San Barnaba at Marino, where it still hangs, not far from Gennari's painting.

Four recently discovered documents preserved at the Colonna Archive in Rome confirm what has often been suspected (but rarely illustrated in such detail) about Guercino's role as a designer for workshop productions.[25] They also provide a new date for the San Barnaba commission. The work, previously assigned to c. 1660,[26] turns out to have been completed in 1645. A receipt of 27 May 1645 in the hand of Bartolomeo Gennari (Doc. B) acknowledges payment of 250 lire on account for the picture. Guercino's letter to Colonna of 28 October 1645 (Doc. D) states that the work has just been finished.

From a letter of 7 January 1643 written at Bologna by Guercino to Archbishop Colonna (Doc. A), we learn that the artist made a drawing of the *Martyrdom of San Barnaba* after consulting the *Golden Legend* by Jacobus da Voragine (the classic medieval text describing the legends of the saints)[27] and that he sent it to the Cardinal's attention. Guercino makes reference to what must have been by now an all-too-familiar issue with the Cento master's patrons, that of the quantity of figures, and implicitly demonstrates his awareness of the danger in large pictures of not including enough figures to fill up the space: ". . . et ho cercato di farlo copioso di figure perche dovendo la misura del quadro essere assai grande, magiorm.te resterà pieno il sito del quale andrano colorite le figure...." Guercino goes on to say that when his assistant, Gennari, executes the painting—obviously from Guercino's designs—he (Guercino) will not fail to give him as much help and guidance as necessary to make the work a success: ". . . e quando il S. Gennaro farà l'opera non restarò di darli ogni havertim.to et haiutto per maggiorm.te servire V.E.R. . . ."

Two years and seven months later, on 5 July 1645, Guercino reports (Doc. C) that the picture is coming along well and that Gennari, who has repeatedly been sick in bed with malarial fever ("certe febre terzane che lo fanno stare in letto")—probably an explanation for the long delay in the execution of the work—will continue to make every effort to produce a fine painting. Guercino, who by this time has undoubtedly been put on the spot about the tardiness of the commission and who has almost certainly been questioned about Gennari's competence (and physical ability) to get the picture done, is quick to acquiesce to his patron, confirming that he will go outside stated norms of practice and retouch the figure of the Saint in those parts which are lacking: "In tanto confermo a V.E.R. la mia buona volontà che ho di servirLa e non ho mancato sino ad hora, di dar al medesimo Gennari alcuni havertim.ti così finito che havrà l'opra, ritocherò il Santo in quelle parte che occorerà, ancorche da qualche tempo in quà, io costummi di non ritocar quadri, per molti rispetti, non meno che per le mie continoue occupationi."

The idea generally shared by Guercino scholars that the master did not retouch the products of the workshop, is stated here in plain words. We suspect that the offer to retouch the Saint was a diplomatic gesture intended to calm the patron; nothing in the painting as it appears today would suggest that Guercino actually intervened. Guercino's statement that he was too busy with his own projects to retouch pictures made by others seems wholly accurate.

An unpublished drawing in pen and reddish wash in the National Museum, Warsaw (fig. XV) has recently been identified as an autograph compositional study for the *Martyrdom of San Barnaba*.[28] This may very well be the sheet sent to Cardinal Colonna, since it seems to precede the decision—probably made when Guercino learned exactly where the work was to be hung—to make the picture horizontal rather than vertical in orientation (the drawing mentioned in the 1643 letter is very clearly the first sent to the Cardinal and it may have been he who pointed out to Guercino that the site was better served by a picture in a landscape format).[29] Further studies by Guercino were likely made to adapt the Warsaw composition to the new orientation.

The exhibition contains two drawings of a type comparable to that of the Warsaw sheet, that is, drawings made by Guercino which were designed for pictures executed by assistants. Both sheets (cat. nos. 17-18) served Antonio Bonfanti for his painting of *Christ Among the Doctors* (fig. 17a) of c. 1625-1627. A third exhibited drawing, cat. no. 39, *St. Joseph with the Flowering Staff*, is the likely source for a painting (fig. 39a) attributed to Bartolomeo Gennari. However, this type of picture may not have been commissioned but made on speculation. One suspects, therefore, that the drawing might have been made by Guercino for his own use and later given to Gennari to work up into a painting.

By 1645, the date when Guercino wrote two of the letters mentioned above, he had already been a resident of Bologna for some three years. In 1642, during a moment in which the War of Castro had threatened to overtake Centese territory and only months after the death of Guido Reni, he had moved to Bologna, replacing Reni as *caposcuola* and inheriting many of his patrons. Though no immediate effect of the transfer of the workshop to Bologna can be observed in Guercino's paintings, the period from roughly 1645 to 1656 contains a remarkable number of master-pieces, in their own way comparable to the achievements of the Roman years. Bologna challenged the artist, and he responded by recapturing the intensity of his involvement with pictorial problems that had characterized his early works. From the grand, neoclassical rhetoric displayed in canvases like the *Hersilia Separating Romulus and Tatius* in the Louvre (fig. 50a), a picture commissioned in 1645 by the French Secretary of State, M. La Vrillière, to the subtle, meditative poetry spoken in the Chicago *Entombment* of 1656 (fig. 61a), Guercino proved himself one of the greatest exponents of Baroque classicism in Europe. Pictures such as the *Suicide of Cleopatra* of 1648 now in the Palazzo Rosso, Genoa (fig. XII),[30] for which we would like to mention a remarkably fine unpublished preparatory sketch in red chalk in an American private collection (fig. XIII),[31] offer an unmatched sensuousness of form and meticulousness of execution. The grandeur of the theatrical, parted curtains in this painting would surely have made Rigaud and Le Brun rise to their feet and applaud. Right up to the time of his death in 1666, Guercino never failed to use his art to ennoble humanity and to inspire Christian faith.

* * *

Drawings played an essential role in the stylistic development and professional career we have just described. Like Picasso, Guercino's mind and hand were never idle. He lived to draw. The Cento master may indeed have been the most prolific Italian draftsman of the entire century. Though the vast majority of his drawings served utilitarian purposes—mainly the preparation of paintings—no other artist of the period made so many sheets for his own delight and the enjoyment of others. Guercino was truly a pioneer in treating drawings as independent works of art. The extraordinary survival of so many of his sheets may have been partly due to the fact that he (and later his heirs) regarded them as a record of his genius and creativity and not merely as the by-products of painting and fresco projects.

His preferred drawing medium throughout his life was pen or pen and wash, typically applied to antique laid paper. Sheets like cat. no. 5 of *Hercules Slaying the Hydra* of 1618 demonstrate the velocity with which Guercino could use his pen to "attack" his subject on the sheet: the quick succession of pentimenti in this drawing would have been difficult if not impossible to realize in any other medium. Guercino's calligraphy can often be very brash and economical, as in the lower areas of Christ's drapery in cat. no. 10 (*Christ and St. Thomas*), a sheet, incidentally, which employs three different tones of wash (brown, gray, and green-blue). The rounded, continuous swirls characteristic of the pen lines in the early period are sometimes accompanied or altogether replaced by broken, jagged strokes in the later years, as in the handsome sheet at Iowa of *Saint Jerome and the Angel* of c. 1640 (cat. no. 45). The staggering of linear trajectories by seemingly random ticks of the pen in such sheets tends to slow movement and bring the forms to the surface (rather than allowing them to merge deeply into the picture space). This later style of draftsmanship has a marvelous ornamental quality and soft texture that is lacking in the earlier Guercino. Note also how successfully the master is able to bring out certain features of his design by contrasting two different kinds of linear treatment on the same sheet: in opposition to the short and uneven strokes used to define St. Jerome's elderly arm, Guercino makes one long, brilliant contour for the outside edge of the youthful angel's upraised arm. The finesse of this tightly controlled, razor-sharp bent line is worthy of Raphael.

Especially before 1640 but also afterwards, Guercino employed washes in varying strengths (usually made from brown ink) to set his figures into relief and to create dramatic, often spectacular lighting effects. Sheets like the *Three Studies for a Crucifixion* of 1624-1625 (cat. no. 12) and the *Vision of St. Francis* of c. 1645 (cat. no. 44) achieve a high degree of pictoriality as a consequence of this technique. At his best, as in the sublime *Sisyphus* of 1636 (cat. no. 38) and the *Landscape with a Volcano* (cat. no. 74)—his only landscape done entirely with the brush—Guercino's virtuosity is unrivalled.

His second favorite medium was red chalk. He frequently employed it in the middle and later stages of the design process when, for example, it would become necessary to go beyond the mere blocking out of forms conceived in earlier compositional pen studies and he had to begin planning the actual, detailed look of anatomies and draperies. It was often in red-chalk drawings that modelling according to a specific angle of illumination was first considered with any real precision. At Piacenza, because of the exigencies of working on a large scale in true fresco, such drawings became even more essential and were made in a variety of formats according to very specific functions (see cat. nos. 19-21). In the later 1640s and 1650s (see cat. nos. 57-58), red chalk—which so perfectly predicted the abstraction and delicate pastel tonalities of his paintings—became Guercino's medium of choice.

X

XX XI 13

A fine example of Guercino's sensitive, Correggesque red-chalk technique may be seen in a previously unpublished sketch in the Morgan Library of *Three Putti* (fig. VII).[32] We would like to propose it here as a preparatory study for two or three of the playful *amorini* capturing birds amongst tall cypress trees (fig. VIII) in the *Aurora* fresco of 1621 (fig. VI). This wonderful sheet, whose monumental style is not improperly compared to Annibale's studies for the Farnese Gallery, would plausibly have come just after a partial compositional study in pen at Windsor (M-T, no. 18) and a more general sketch, also drawn in red chalk but in a slightly looser manner, in the Mahon Collection, London (*Disegni*, no. 83).

The exhibition provides a fine array of Guercino's red-chalk drawings and it will perhaps not serve the Reader for us to generalize about them further. Important examples, besides those already mentioned, are cat. nos. 19, 35, 48, 54, 56, 60-61. Cat. no. 23, which employs several different colored chalks including red, is unique in the Guercino corpus and must have been made for a special occasion, perhaps as a gift or "presentation" drawing.

Guercino—in his early days, although not exclusively—was also fond of using oiled black chalk or charcoal, called *carboncino*. This greasy chalk, which typically results in a pitted or granular black surface as it skips over depressions and irregularities in the paper, was employed mostly for large academic nude studies such as the three shown in the exhibition (see cat. nos. 63-65). It allows for near photo-like gradations in tone. In the later 1620s, at about the same time that red chalk became so predominant at Piacenza, this medium seems to have stopped being used by Guercino. In the 1640s and 1650s, Guercino returned to black chalk but only for certain subjects like head studies and sketches of putti (see cat. nos. 49 and 55). These were usually drawn with *carboncino*, although Guercino sometimes used a hard, graphite-like *matita nera* as he seems to have done in cat. no. 62.

Passing now from the question of medium and technique to that of function, we should like to point out that several sections of the exhibition are dedicated specifically to those types of drawings which Guercino made for his own recreation or to give away as presents. Landscapes (cat. nos. 66-74), genre scenes (cat. nos. 77-84), and caricatures (cat. nos. 85-92)—three of the most important categories of drawing routinely practiced in the Carracci Academy—make up a significant portion of Guercino's total graphic output and must have been a great source of pleasure to him and to his family and friends. Each of these types, as well as his academic nude studies (cat. nos. 63-65) and drawings he designed for prints (cat. nos. 75-76), have been properly introduced in the corresponding sections of the Catalogue.

The first and largest section of the exhibition is devoted to Guercino's preparatory studies for paintings—by far the most important and plentiful category of his existing body of work as a draftsman. This group has been organized chronologically in four parts following the general stages of the artist's development. Certain unconnected figure studies and narrative scenes, some of which may have been made as independent works have also been included, since these, no less than the preparatory drawings, were essential elements of Guercino's draftsmanship and illustrate his stylistic *percorso* over a fifty-year period.

More than his predecessors and contemporaries in Bologna and Rome, the Cento master utilized his preparatory drawings for intellectual and artistic discovery. Ideas seem to have come to him most readily as he worked. In one sketch after another, we witness an endless search for gestures, narrative groupings, costumes, and facial expressions. He was never content. The most finished and seemingly perfect drawings are often the least related to the compositions of the paintings they purportedly prepare. Guercino habitually made at least one or two sketches in a design sequence in reverse to the compositions studied in all the other drawings. The more ideas he drew and discarded, it seems, the closer he came to the scheme he would ultimately paint. In many ways the process was subtractive.

Given his highly personal, experiential design methods, it is really not so hard to understand why even the most distinguished of Guercino's patrons often met with obstacles when they requested previews of the paintings they had ordered. Guercino would not willingly dispatch to them so much as a quick sketch, because, as he said, he reserved the right to make changes at any stage of the process in order to improve the work.[33] This is what he somewhat tepidly communicated on 23 November 1661 to Don Antonio Ruffo of Messina (see cat. no. 62), who had made the mistake, apparently not for the first time, of nagging the artist for a drawing of a painting's composition:

> In quanto poi, al continuar pure in cotesti SS[ori] il desiderio vedere un mio disegno del opera che brameno, io (come già li scrissi) non uso far disegni ad alcuno perchè non mi posso, nè voglio legar l'arbitrio nel opera, tutta volta però per condescendere al piacere di V.S. Illma fanonne uno acciò in certo modo vedino ove penderà il pensiero senza però intendermi obligarmi al detto perchè voglio poter cangiar conforme il bisogno per meglioramento del opera.[34]

Guercino's preparatory drawings can be roughly divided into separate types according to function. An important class are the general compositional sketches, most often in pen or pen and wash, like the dramatic *Jacob's Blessing* in the Art Institute of Chicago of 1620 (cat. no. 8). In the later period, such studies were also made in red chalk (e.g., cat. no. 57: recto). Another cate- **xxi**

XIII

XII

gory, one especially well-represented in the exhibition (e.g., cat. nos. 12, 18, 26: recto), is made up of partial compositional sketches. These typically isolate one group of figures from the overall scene and develop their relative placement, costumes, and actions. A previously unconnected but highly important pen-and-wash sketch in the Cooper-Hewitt Museum, New York of *Four Figures* (fig. X) for the principal group of mourners at the *Burial of St. Petronilla* of 1623 (fig. IX), is a vigorous, albeit badly damaged example of this kind of study.[35] It logically followed much more complete compositional studies like the large drawing in the Thorvaldsen Museum, Copenhagen, which deals with the entire lower zone of the painting (fig. XI).[36]

Perhaps the most extensively documented design sequence in all of Guercino's oeuvre is that for the 1620 *Investiture of St. William of Aquitaine* (fig. 9a). After making general compositional studies like the stately work in the Louvre illustrated here (fig. I),[37] Guercino went on to consider and reconsider virtually every element of his picture—even, apparently, after he had begun to paint it.[38] Our entry for cat. no. 9 discusses several of the problems to which Guercino assiduously addressed himself while working on this project. In addition, we should like to draw attention to a fascinating sequence of partial compositional studies for the Holy Family and a Male Saint (St. James ?) who occupy the upper zone of the canvas. This charming group of figures is already competently arranged in the general sketch in the Louvre. But Guercino—who was hardly ever content with something realized on the first or second try—went on in several other sheets, including those in the Albertina, Vienna (fig. II),[39] the Teylers Museum, Haarlem (fig. III: recto),[40] and the Brera, Milan (fig. IV),[41] to experiment with the figures' placement and attitudes.[42] To the drawings just mentioned, which were part of an impressive series shown in Bologna in 1968, should be added an extremely abbreviated pen-and-wash sketch in the Graphische Sammlung, Stuttgart (fig. V).[43] This small sheet, traditionally given to the circle of Luca Cambiaso, was recently reassigned to the Genoese School of the first third of the Seicento.[44] It is a perfectly genuine Guercino drawing which records better than most the swiftness of the artist's design process. It took him just a second or two, after drawing a mere circle on the right side of the sheet in an attempt to locate the head of St. James (?), to realize that he could not use this design and that there was no point in working up the figures any further. The—to us—arbitrariness of Guercino's stage-managing of these heads may at first seem humorous, but in each of these studies Guercino is reaching for symmetries, dialogues, connections with the lower zone of the picture, and many other concepts. His creative decisions were obviously not worked out in advance, but took place on an ongoing basis as the actual physical activity of

drawing led him to new problems to which he could then supply new solutions. As he matured this experimental process became less open-ended. However, it is quite remarkable that even in the late period, as in the exhibited studies for the *Vision of St. Philip Neri* (cat. no. 52) and the *Entombment* (cat. no. 61), Guercino's energy to invent sequentially persisted.

Works such as the *Esther before Ahasuerus* formerly in the collection of Curtis O. Baer (cat. no. 41) conform in type to what some Rembrandt specialists call a "conversation" drawing,[45] a quick sketch illustrating a Biblical passage with emphasis on speech and its accompanying gestures.[46] Guercino frequently made such studies, which might be said to make up a special subcategory of the partial compositional sheets. They often embark on iconographic paths extraneous to his stated purpose in more complete sketches and the final painting. Unlike those sketches we have just reviewed for the *St. William* and *St. Petronilla,* they often do not seem to be concerned with fitting into the basic structure of a general pictorial design established by earlier drawings. These rapid graphic notations are often referred to as *primi pensieri* (first thoughts) drawings. In Guercino's case, they were frequently made well into the design process, and were often "second thoughts."

Guercino used these sheets as vehicles for brainstorming, for developing new motifs and psychologically revealing expressions for his actors. He is not preoccupied in these studies with formal structure, fussy details of architecture and props, or the integration of all the figures into a seamless unity. In short, though they frequently serve a significant role in the preparation of paintings, these sketches do not undertake their design. It is, therefore, quite understandable why certain groups of Guercino's sketches seem so bold and spontaneous, whereas the paintings which derive from them—especially those projects made after 1630—appear so restrained and balanced (e.g., the Seattle *Ecstasy of St. Teresa* shown as cat. no. 31 and the final work now at Aix-en-Provence, reproduced as fig. 31a).

The *conversation* or *primi pensieri* drawings are not "blueprints" for the style of the paintings they study. We should perhaps correct ourselves and say that they are studying the "subjects" of the paintings and not necessarily the paintings themselves. They are intellectual "time-outs" in which the artist gives himself the freedom to invent, to delve into the *istoria,* without having to worry about such tedious issues as the size of the canvas, the number of figures he must eventually squeeze into the composition, or even the format of the picture, whether horizontal or vertical. One has the sense that Guercino entered so deeply and intensely into design/narrative issues that he often got carried **xxiii**

XV

XIV

xxiv

away and kept on drawing, sometimes moving on to subsequent moments of a story. In this way he generated new designs for future projects.

A comparison between Rembrandt's and Guercino's drawings of this type may help clarify a particular point we wish to make about the Cento master's design process. In a perceptive study of Rembrandt's drawings, William Robinson explains that the Dutch painter's history sketches, invariably more detailed and complete than analogous works by Guercino, were not connected to specific projects.[47] They were made as independent drawing exercises. The practice aided Rembrandt in his exploration–both psychological and visual–of the Bible. His history sketches set an example for the Dutch master's numerous pupils, who were encouraged to draw Biblical episodes (often quite obscure episodes) from their imagination. At the end of his essay, Robinson queries whether Guercino's sketches served the same function and might provide a precedent for Rembrandt's unusual practice. Guercino drawings of Biblical "conversations," such as cat. no. 41, do, in fact, predict some aspects of Rembrandt's history sketches, but unlike those made by the Dutch master, they are almost always tied to a commissioned work. Looking at the question from a more philosophical perspective, this contrast in practice between the two titans of Seicento draftsmanship is really not so great. It should not obscure the fact that the ultimate goal of their drawings—an increased ability to bring religious and historical narrative to life—is something they share. Over the years, Guercino's motif-seeking "conversation" drawings and partial compositional studies—even if they served a more immediately practical purpose than in similar sketches made in Rembrandt's studio—amounted to a similar exploration of historical and literary narrative.

We should mention in conclusion several other types of preparatory drawings made by Guercino. "Close-up" studies of half-figures in pen or chalk are often concerned with costume, hair, and the shading of the figure's face. Cat. no 50 is a fine example of this type of sheet which became increasingly common, it seems, after the artist's return to Cento in 1623. Guercino also made numerous sheets of single heads, typically in red or black chalk, such as cat. nos. 49 and 56, and studies of putti, such as cat. nos. 54-55. The only category of drawing not represented in the exhibition (cat. no. 23 is a close substitute) are the chalk drapery studies of the type he made at Piacenza (see above and cat. nos. 19-21).

As described in great detail in the relevant entries of the Catalogue, Guercino's design process was not strictly linear. It did not necessarily begin with general compositional sketches and move in logical steps of increasingly greater detail toward "close-ups" and costume studies. Guercino sometimes worked from the inside out,

starting with one or two figures in conflict or conversation and then developing his overall scheme around them.

* * *

Guercino's drawings have always been popular. As the provenances of many of the sheets in the exhibition establish, there was a true passion for Guercino among the English in the eighteenth century. It is unlikely that so many of the master's sheets would have come down to us—and in such fine condition—if it had not been for this fact.

Another dimension of the appreciation of Guercino's drawings was the fashion of imitating and in some cases forging his sheets. This practice was greatly facilitated by the importation into England of great numbers of Guercino drawings through purchases made by Richard Dalton, Royal Librarian to George III, at Bologna in the 1760s. Dalton acquired hundreds of sheets from Carlo Gennari (1712-1790), the grandson of one of Guercino's nephews and heirs Cesare Gennari (1637-1688). The arrival in England at about this same time of the Florentine engraver Francesco Bartolozzi also added to the diffusion of Guercino's drawing style.[48] Bartolozzi made scores of reproductions of the Windsor sheets. Many of these prints were used by a deceptive forger to make his copies and pastiches after Guercino.[49]

Another large group of drawings from the Casa Gennari collection came to England after first being sold to a dealer named Francesco Forni (not Formi as previously believed),[50] who was probably responsible for laying the sheets down on so-called "Casa Gennari" mounts such as that framing an unpublished caricature in pen and brown ink (traces of wash) of a *Morose Man,* recently acquired by the Metropolitan Museum of Art, New York (fig. XVIII).[51] As Denis Mahon has shown in his thorough study of this particular provenance (see Mahon, "Casa Gennari," 1968), the group owned by Forni was quickly snapped up by the Hon. Edward Bouverie, probably at the end of the 1760s. In the early nineteenth century, the collection passed into the hands of Mr. Hervey, apparently Bouverie's nephew, who then sold it to the first Earl of Gainsborough. The Earl of Northwick also obtained some these sheets, either from Hervey or from Gainsborough. Over the years much of the Gainsborough collection was sold. The largest group of Gainsborough Guercinos was sold at auction in London in 1922. Many of the drawings in the exhibition, in particular those from the collections of Sir Robert Witt (he purchased one of the five lots) and Princeton's benefactor and America's first true Guercino collector, Dan Fellows Platt, came from the 1922 sale. Platt purchased most of his nearly 200 sheets (many are by the school) from E. Parsons & Sons, London, who had acquired two of the five Gainsborough lots. The Bouverie-Gains-

XVII

XVI

XXVI

borough sheets were also the sources of prints and imitations, both before and after they went to England (see cat. no. 46).

Copies sometimes served a purely practical function. In cat. no. 50, we refer to a copy (Vienna, Albertina) after Guercino by Bartolozzi that may have been made for the purposes of making a reproduction. But there are also cases, as the example we are about to discuss illustrates, in which an artist from the Settecento copied the works of a famous artist of the Seicento as an act of homage and as a serious learning exercise.

In the Weld Collection at Lulworth Manor, Dorset, there is a pen-and-ink copy of Guercino's exhibited *Angel Sheathing the Flaming Sword, with SS. Roch and Sebastian in a Landscape,* a Casa Gennari-Bouverie-Witt drawing which we have recently traced to the collection of the University of Notre Dame's Snite Museum (cat. no. 30). The Weld drawing (fig. XVI) is a fastidious and knowing imitation of Guercino's style.[52] It is especially curious because it bears the stamp (L. 2432, lower left recto) of Sir Joshua Reynolds' teacher, Thomas Hudson (1701-1779), who is known to have esteemed Guercino's drawings.

According to Northcote's book *The Life of Reynolds* (1813), at the time Reynolds studied with Hudson in c. 1742-1743, the latter recommended to his gifted pupil that he make careful copies of the drawings of Guercino.[53] In light of this information about Hudson and Reynolds, it is tempting to speculate that a "careful copy" after Guercino from Hudson's own collection might in fact be the work of Reynolds himself.

The evidence for attributing the copy of the exhibited sheet to Reynolds (1723-1792) is only circumstantial, but the Notre Dame - Lulworth Manor case does, at least, find certain parallels with other case studies in which the clues are more conclusive. There are four circumstances here which point toward Sir Joshua as the author of the copy: 1) the fact, as previously mentioned, that the original owner of the copy was Thomas Hudson; 2) the fact that the copyist chose as his subject one of Guercino's "gravure style," pen-and-hatching drawings;[54] 3) the fact that the pen drawing which was imitated came from the collection of Edward Bouverie; and 4) the fact that the imitation is of high quality and quite faithful to the original.

The *type* of drawing which has been imitated by the draftsman of the Lulworth Manor sheet—a pen drawing with clear lines and fine, restrained hatching—is similar to that discussed in a case fully documented by Nicholas Turner,[55] which centers on a very Guercinesque drawing of a *Head of a Monk* formerly in the collection of Thomas Hudson (recently London, Art Market). This sheet is a fine copy of a recently discovered Guercino original (now Eng-

land, Private Collection) with a Casa Gennari-Bouverie provenance. A label on the backing of the ex-Hudson *Monk* sheet carries an early-nineteenth-century inscription describing the work as having been done by Reynolds (!) *while Pupil to M. Hudson* (which, as we have said, was around 1742-43). Turner points out that part of the statement on the label must be incorrect, since Reynolds could only have had access to Casa Gennari-Bouverie drawings in 1752, when he went to Bologna, and "following their [the Casa Gennari drawings] purchase in 1768 by Bouverie." Mahon has suggested that Reynolds is likely to have made his copies in 1769-70, during his visits to make two portraits of Mrs. Bouverie, and not in 1742-43.[56]

An unpublished eighteenth-century pen drawing of a three-quarter-length *Bearded Old Man Gesturing to the Right,* now in San Francisco, Collection of Mrs. Jack Schafer (fig. XVII),[57] has been identified by Mahon and Turner[58] as a copy, probably by Reynolds, of an original, ex-Bouverie Guercino drawing (in the same English private collection as the *Monk*) on a Casa Gennari mount and bearing, on the sheet itself, a characteristic Casa Gennari inscription in ink: *40 P. Dol.*[59] This original by Guercino in England appears to be a detailed costume sketch for a figure of the father of the prodigal son, and it may be related, according to Turner, to a sensitive pen-and-ink drawing in a New York private collection of the *Return of the Prodigal Son* (see Suppl. no. 220, repr.).[60]

Some would say that Guercino's legacy as a draftsman—his undoubted influence on Tiepolo and Piazzetta—was only marginally extended by Reynolds, who as a copyist seems to have limited himself to the more classical pen sketches of Guercino, not venturing to imitate (so it seems from the evidence available now) his bold wash drawings or the alarmingly modern oiled-black-chalk nudes that are especially beloved today. But Reynolds, of course, was much more than a great copyist and painter. He was perhaps the most outspoken advocate of seventeenth-century Bolognese painting of his day. When not lecturing on the beauty of Domenichino and Guercino, he was collecting Bolognese drawings of all types, including Guercino's caricatures, as the marvelous album he once owned, now at Princeton (bequest of Platt; cf. cat. nos. 87-91), amply demonstrates. As a painter, teacher, collector, and academician he did more, it could be argued, than any of his colleagues in England to fuel admiration for the drawings of "the squinter" from Cento.

It is hoped that in some small way this exhibition, the first major loan show of the master's works to be held in the United States and Canada, will contribute, as Reynolds might have wished, to the furthering of Guercino's reputation as the consummate Seicento draftsman.

XVIII

1. From the letter written to Don Ferrante Carlo, 25 October 1617; cf. *Dipinti*, p. 45: "Here [in Bologna] there is a young man from Cento who paints with remarkable *invenzione*. He is a great draftsman and terrific colorist: he is a freak of nature [also cleverly implying, perhaps, a "monster of naturalism"], a true miracle who dumbfounds everyone who sees his works. I'm not saying anything [I don't have words to describe this]: even the top painters are awestruck; you will have to see for yourself when you come back.

2. Malvasia, II, p. 257.

3. Malvasia, II, p. 256. Malvasia also refers to G.B. Cremonini (d. 1610) as an early master of Guercino, though this has been refuted by Mahon (cf. *Dipinti*, p. 9, n. 23).

4. *Dipinti*, p. 10. On the Gennari family (with genealogical tables and complete documentation), see Bagni, 1984 and Bagni, 1986.

5. See cat. no. 1.

6. See cat. no. 1.

7. See *Dipinti*, p. 26.

8. On the Academy and its importance, see Dempsey, 1977 and Dempsey, 1980. See also Stone, 1989, Chapters III and IV.

9. Salerno, no. 27.

10. Guercino's early period was the subject of Mahon's groundbreaking article, "Notes on the Young Guercino: I — Cento and Bologna; II — Cento and Ferrara," *Burl. Mag.* 70 (January-June 1937), pp. 112-22; 177-89. Guercino's early development is also discussed in Mahon, 1947; Mahon, 1967; and in greater detail in *Dipinti* and *Disegni*. Of particular importance for the period prior to 1618 are two monographs on Guercino's frescoes in Cento: Roli, 1968 and Bagni, 1984. In my doctoral dissertation, I provide an exhaustive discussion of the early period with particular attention to Guercino's design concepts and problems of chronology: cf. Stone, 1989, pp. 174-353. See also Salerno, pp. 36-40.

11. Salerno, no. 33.

12. For an account of the preparatory drawings for this picture, see Stone, 1989, pp. 265-67.

13. Salerno, no. 47. On the date of Guercino's trip to Venice, see *Dipinti*, p. 48, n. 16.

14. For discussion of an important oiled-black-chalk sketch for the figure of Marsyas, see under cat. no. 64.

15. Comparative illustrations have been numbered in conjunction with the number of the catalogue entry in which they appear: e.g., fig. 7a is the first figure discussed under cat. no. 7.

16. Salerno, no. 73.

17. Salerno, no. 83. For an important iconographical study of this work, see Wood, 1986.

18. Salerno, no. 92.

19. See *Dipinti*, pp. 107 f.

20. Salerno, no. 94.

21. Salerno, no. 127.

22. But not entirely all. Some works which were made as gifts or which were given in trade for goods or services do not appear in the *Libro dei Conti*. Some of these paintings, however, are listed in the *Felsina Pittrice* by Malvasia, who notes that he gathered certain information from sources made available to him at Casa Gennari, the residence of Guercino's nephews and heirs, Cesare and Benedetto, Jr. Mahon believes that Malvasia was not allowed to see the *Libro dei Conti* but was instead shown a different register, one that simply noted the dates of pictures and their patrons and did not contain explicit financial information. For the relationship between the *Libro* and the list used by Malvasia for his biography of Guercino, see *Dipinti*, pp. 2-9. The original *Libro dei Conti* (MS. B. 331) is preserved in the Biblioteca Comunale dell'Archiginnasio at Bologna. It was first published by Calvi in 1808 within his biography of Guercino (see Bibl.). Calvi's text was reprinted in the 1841 edition of the *Felsina Pittrice*. All references to the *Libro* in the Catalogue are to the 1841 publication. There are some cases in which Calvi's transcription has proven to be defective. For an example, see under cat. nos. 40-42, note 8.

23. For example, see under Suppl. no. 122.

24. First published by Bagni, 1986, fig. 108.

25. I thank Mons. R. Varca, Archivist of Palazzo Colonna, for helping me locate these important papers. I am also grateful to Prof. John Moore of Smith College for facilitating my research in Rome in the summer of 1986. My attempts at an accurate transcription of the four documents, part of a large, mainly uncatalogued *fondo artisti* in the Archive, appear at the end of the introductory text. I thank Fabio Paltrinieri for his assistance in deciphering the sometimes frustrating handwriting. In addition to those letters commented on here, there exist seven others by Guercino in the Colonna Archive. These are short Christmas salutations by Guercino to Cardinal Colonna, who, incidentally, after 6 Feb. 1645 had resigned from his post at Bologna and returned to Rome. The letters are from the following years: 1639-1643, 1646, and 1648.

26. By Bagni, 1986, p. 199 and n. 25, who considered, on the basis of inscriptions, that the picture was commissioned for the [re-]inauguration of the church in 1662. The picture was previously mentioned by Hess in 1934 in his edition of Passeri (cf. Passeri, p. 354, n. 3).

27. Until now it was not known with certainty that Guercino used this familiar iconographical source.

28. Inv. 146906/31. Dimensions: 305 x 197 mm. I thank Sir Denis Mahon for his kindness and generosity in bringing this important sheet to my attention and for sharing his learned observations on the San Barnaba commission and documents with me.

29. The style of the drawing is comparable to that of a red-chalk study formerly with Colnaghi's, London for the *Saint Helen Adoring the True Cross*, an altarpiece of 1644 sent to Venice. For references, see M-T, under nos. 110-111 (the two Windsor drawings catalogued by Mahon and Turner for this commission are also quite relevant). See also Suppl. no. 173, repr. for a drawing for the same work but in a very different style.

30. Salerno, no. 252. 1.73 x 2.37 m.

31. Formerly Christie's, London, 8 July 1975, lot 28; purchased from H. Shickman Gallery, N.Y. Dimensions: 216 x 202 mm. Watermark: a cardinal's hat with the Barberini coat of arms. Connected to the Genoa painting by Denis Mahon (according to the Christie's catalogue), who also notes the existence of another *Cleopatra* of around these years (1650) for Girolamo Panessi (see Salerno, under no. 252). The Panessi painting is lost and its composition is not known, but I believe the connection between this drawing and the Genoa picture is so strong that it is unlikely to be for another project.

32. Inv. no. 1988.38, Bequest of Mrs. John Colgate Jessup. Dimensions: 162 x 206 mm. Inscribed in the lower left recto in pen and brown ink: *guarcino*. Prov.: Marquess of Aberdeen; H.M. Calmann, London; Mrs. John Colgate Jessup, N.Y. For another fine red-chalk drawing connected with the *Aurora* fresco, see. Suppl. no. 104, with bibl.

33. We hasten to point out that the case described above in which Guercino sent a drawing to Cardinal Colonna is not in contradiction with what is being stated here as a *general* reluctance on Guercino's part to send "approval" drawings to his clients. Since in the Colonna commission the project was to be executed by a member of the workshop, it is only reasonable that the patron would want to know in advance what he was paying for and that he would want certain assurances that the end result would be carefully supervised by Guercino himself.

34. As quoted in *Disegni*, p. 28, from the article by V. Ruffo, 1916, p. 105.

35. Inv. 1931.66.39. Dimensions: 203 x 267 mm. Laid down. Major losses on left side and throughout the sheet. Prov.: Peoli, Hewitt. Bibl.: *Great Drawings of All Time*, vol. I: Italian 13th - 19th c., ed. by I. Moskowiz, New York: Shorewood Publishers, 1962, no. 283, color repr.

36. Inv. D. 473. Dimensions: 271 x 423 mm. See *Disegni*, p. 97; Bean, 1969, pl. 35; and Roli, 1972, no. 28. Cf. also Stone, 1989, p. 388 and fig. 166; and M-T, p. 13, who offer a detailed and interesting discussion of the designs for the altarpiece.

37. Inv. 6884. 275 x 196 mm. See *Disegni*, no. 58.

38. See under cat. no. 9.

39. Inv. 2343. Dimensions: 133 x 227 mm. See *Disegni,* no. 59.

40. Inv. H. 16. Dimensions: 156 x 234 mm. See *Disegni,* no. 62.

41. Inv. 1. Dimensions: 126 x 171 mm. See *Disegni,* no. 61.

42. For further sketches for this ensemble, see M-T, no. 13.

43. Inv. 1154. Dimensions: 115 x 165 mm. Inscribed in brown ink in the lower right recto: *Cagniasi.* I thank Michael Semff for his help in securing a photograph of this work and for his kindness in allowing me access to the Stuttgart drawing study in the summer of 1989 where I had the chance to confirm my reattribution of this delightful sheet to Guercino. I would also like to thank Sir Denis Mahon for his endorsement of this new addition to the corpus of *St. William* studies.

44. See Christel Thiem, *Italienische Zeichnungen, 1500-1800,* Staatsgalerie Stuttgart, 1977, no. 58.

45. I have borrowed this term from my former undergraduate teacher, Svetlana Alpers.

46. I cannot resist noting that this sheet was owned by J.P. Zoomer (1641-1724) of Amsterdam, probably the greatest collector-dealer of Rembrandt's prints and drawings of all time.

47. "Rembrandt's Sketches of Historical Subjects," in *Drawings Defined,* with a preface and commentary by Konrad Oberhuber, edited by Walter Strauss and Tracie Felker, New York: Abaris Books, 1987, pp. 241-57.

48. For a full discussion of the provenances of the Windsor drawings and of the printmakers who engraved such an impressive number of them, cf. the Introduction to M-T, part II.

49. On the notorious eighteenth-century faker of Guercino's landscapes and figure drawings, see under cat. no. 66.

50. According to important documents soon to be published by Prisco Bagni.

51. Inv. 1989.222. Harry G. Sperling Fund, 1989. Dimensions: 208 x 94 mm. Inscribed on the verso: *M[ol]to [i]ll[ust]re Sig[no]re mio P[ad]ron Oss[ervantissi]mo* (perhaps in the hand of Guercino's brother Paolo Antonio). Prov.: Casa Gennari; Francesco Forni; Hon. E. Bouverie; Mr. Hervey; Earls of Gainsborough; Smithson & Williams, London, 1989 (entry and color repr. on pamphlet, "Old Master Drawings: Recent Acquisitions"). Dated by Denis Mahon to the 1640s according to sale pamphlet. For another illustration of a Gennari mount in the Catalogue, cf. cat. no. 46.

52. Dimensions: 229 x 172 mm.

53. See Mahon, 1967, under no. 49.

54. For this important aspect of Guercino's draftsmanship, see cat. no. 11.

55. Nicholas Turner, Review of James Byam Shaw, *The Italian Drawings of the Frits Lugt Collection,* 1983, in *Master Drawings* 22, no. 2 (1984), pp. 211-12, and figs. 3-4.

56. Mahon, 1967, under no. 45. However, Mr. Turner has recently mentioned to the present writer (oral communication) that there may be cause to reconsider the chronology of the Casa Gennari-Bouverie provenance.

57. Dimensions: 280 x 187 mm. (sight); purchased in Boston in 1958. I thank Barbara Butts, Curator of Prints and Drawings at the Saint Louis Art Museum, for bringing this drawing to my attention.

58. Letter from Mahon to the present writer (6 Dec. 1988). I thank him for allowing me to restate here his and Mr. Turner's observations on this potential Reynolds.

59. On these inscriptions, see Mahon, 1967, under no. 4. Several of these cryptic codes, which may have been used to organize or sell the sheets, occur on drawings illustrated in this catalogue (for example, cf. cat. no. 46, which, as noted previously, is also on a Gennari mount; and in the Supplement, cf. Suppl. nos. 12, 154, 170).

60. I thank Nicholas Turner for discussing aspects of the Guercino-Reynolds drawings with me and look forward with much anticipation to his forthcoming treatment of this fascinating subject.

———————

Documents from the Archivio Colonna, Rome: Fondo Artisti.

(Doc. B is a receipt of payment by Bartolomeo Gennari; Docs. A, C, and D are letters written by Guercino to Cardinal Girolamo Colonna. Salutations have been omitted.)

Doc. A

7 January 1643

Desideroso di approffitare un mio nipote Giacomo Mucci, nelle Lett.^re et costumi di questo seminario di Bologna, confidato nella singolar benignità di V.E.R. al cui con ogni affetto vivo fideliss.^mo servitore, vengo a supplicarLa che si voglia compiacere di concedere gratia, che detto mio nipote habbia luogo ancor egli nel sopra detto seminario, che lo riputerò p[er] favore singulariss.^mo da porre con altri riceuti dalla sua benignità e cortesia.

Al Sig.^r Comiss.^rio ho mandato il disegno da me fatto per Lei, ciouè il Martirio di San Barnaba Apostolo, nel modo che raconta il Voragine, quando fu con una corda al collo strascinato per getarlo sopra di un fuoco, et ho cercato di farlo copioso di figure perche dovendo la misura del quadro essere assai grande, magiorm.^te resterà pieno il sito del quale andrano colorite le figure, e quando il S. Gennaro farà l'opera, non restarò di darli ogni havertim.^to et haiutto per maggiorm.^te servire V.E.R. alla qual riverentem.^te le bacio la sacra veste, come fa mio fratello.
Bologna li 7 Gennaio 1643
Gio: Fran. Barbieri

Doc. B

27 May 1645

Io sottoscritto ho ricevuto dal Sr Leonardo Landini lire duecento cinquanta di g.^eri quali mi a pagato di commissione dal Em.^o et R.^mo Sig.^r Card.^le Colonna a bon conto di un quadro grande di S. Barnaba che io dipingo p[er] servicio di S. Em.^za: che in fede della verita ho scritto et sottoscritto la pres.^te di mia propria mano
Io Bartolomeo Gennari o scritto e confermo questo di 27 di Maggio 1645

Doc: C

5 July 1645

Il quadro del San Barnaba che p[er] V.E.R. fa il Sr Bartolomeo Gennari mio discepolo, è ridotto in assai buon termine e riautosi che sarà di certe febre terzane che lo fano stare in letto, non mancherà di proseguire detto quadro con la maggior solecitudine che lo sarà possibile.
In tanto confermo a V.E.R. la mia buona volontà che ho di servirLe e non ho mancato sino ad hora, di dar al medesimo Gennari alcuni havertim.^ti cosi finito che haurà l'opra, ritocherò il Santo in quelle parte che occorerà, ancorche da qualche tempo in quà, io costummi di non ritocar quadri, p[er] molti rispetti, non meno che p[er] le mie continue occupationi.
Resti certa L'E.V.R. che io hambisco in ogni occasione ovve giungono le mie poche forze di servire al suo gran merito, e facendoLe humiliss.^ma riverenza le bacio le sacre vesti. Bologna 5 luglio 1645
Gio: Fran. Barbieri

Doc. D

28 October 1645

Hò eseguito il comando datomi da V.E.R. con havere ritocato il quadro del San Barnaba che Le ha fatto il S. Gennari mio discepolo, il quale à cercato di fare q.^to à potuto, con usarui ogni diligenza a lui possibile, p[er]ho, riuscendo l'opera di sua sodisfatione et egli ed io ne sentiremo gusto singolariss.^mo si come in altre occasioni si favoriva con suoi comandam.^ti p[er] il che supplicandoLa hambi due, humilissimam.^te: a V.E.R. baciamo le sacre vesti, come fa mio fratello.
Bologna Li 28 ottobre 1645
Gio: Fran. Barbieri

THE CATALOGUE

Frontispiece: Bolognese 18th Century:
Title Page for Guercino's Drawings;
The Art Museum, Princeton University,
Bequest of Dan Fellows Platt, 49-70

Notes pertaining to use of the Catalogue:

Drawings shown only at certain venues are indicated by the following abbreviations in curly brackets:

{H}   Harvard University Art Museums

{O}   National Gallery of Canada, Ottawa

{C}   Cleveland Museum of Art

Drawings are measured in millimeters, height preceding width.
References to the Supplement (Suppl.) direct the Reader to the inventory of Guercino drawings
in North American collections which has been appended to the book.

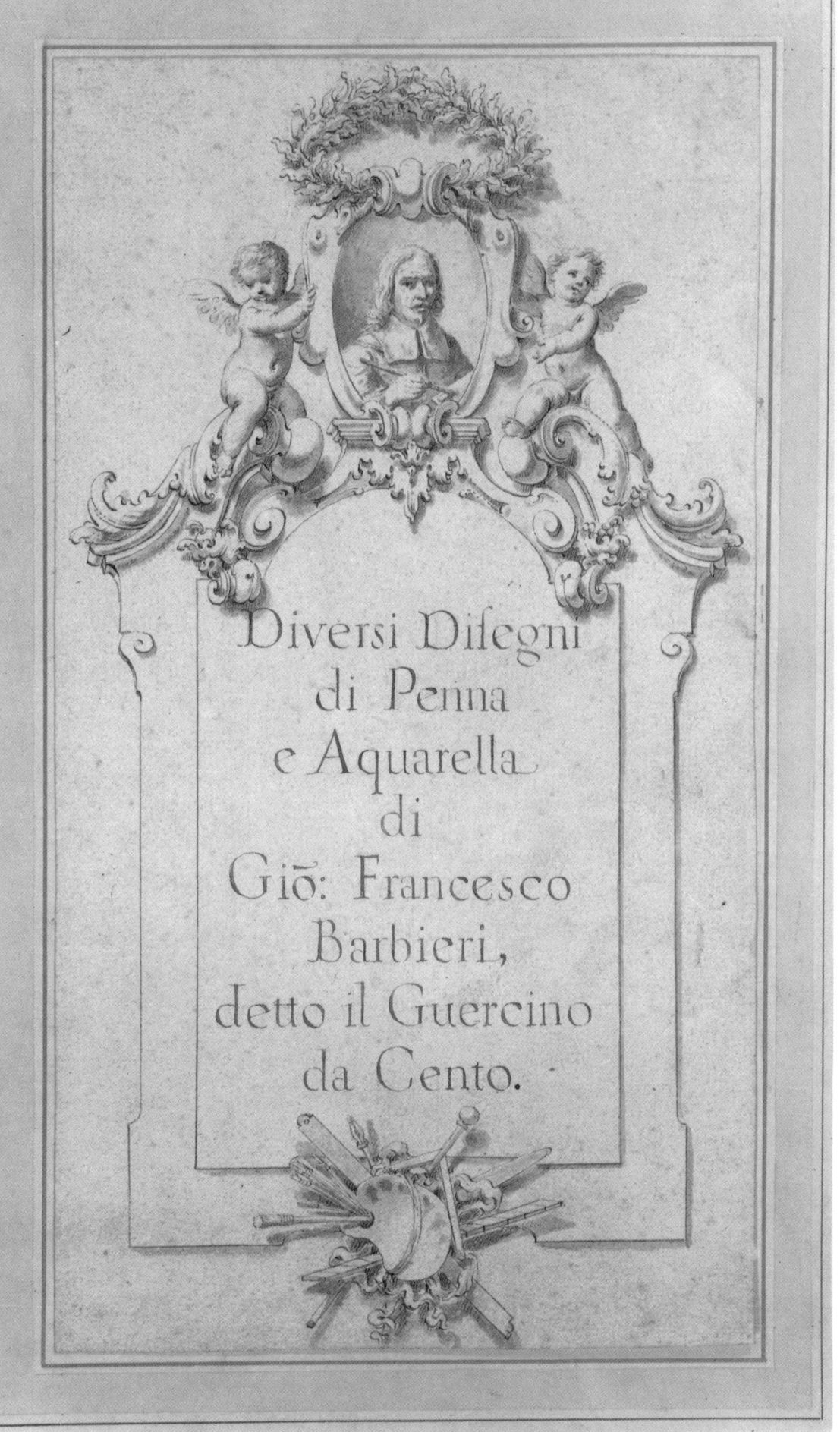

Diversi Difegni
di Penna
e Aquarella
di
Giõ: Francesco
Barbieri,
detto il Guercino
da Cento.

The Madonna and Child with Saint Dominic (?)

Pen and two shades of brown ink, brown wash
242 x 168 mm.
Slight abrasions and stains
PROVENANCE: Dan Fellows Platt (L. Suppl. 750a, lower left verso), purchased from Richeton in London in 1922
BIBLIOGRAPHY: Lynes, p. 91, no. 66; Bean, 1966, no. 34; DeGrazia, 1969, no. 1; Gibbons, no. 275

The Art Museum, Princeton University
Bequest of Dan Fellows Platt, 48-1267

In 1591, Ludovico Carracci's *Holy Family with St. Francis, Two Angels and Donors* (Cento, Pinacoteca) was placed above an altar in the Capuchin church of Cento.[1] One of the most Baroque of all of Ludovico's pictures, the painting gave Cento its first important masterpiece in the naturalistic style created by the Carracci in Bologna.

Like many artists from provincial towns, Guercino was largely self-taught. However, despite the limitations of his background and training, he seems to have realized the importance of Ludovico's achievement and understood how to take advantage of its new style. Though Guercino would later make regular visits to Bologna and become acquainted with a wide range of frescoes, altarpieces, drawings, and prints by the Carracci and members of their Academy, it was the Capuchin altarpiece, as the Cento master many times commented, which had served as his first model and teacher.[2]

The Princeton sheet is one of many interpretations of Ludovico's painting that Guercino made in the first few years of his career, between 1613 and 1617. The long neck and attenuated oval face of the Madonna—with her large eyes and small mouth—and the expressive head of the elderly saint are all classic features of Ludovico's style. The handling of the wash, especially around the Madonna's face, and the fine linear treatment of the *profil perdu* of the Christ Child reflect Guercino's appreciation of Ludovico's drawings.

Guercino's sketch cannot be connected to any known or documented work and the identification of the saint is in doubt.[3] The format of the composition is very similar, however, to that used in several of Guercino's early altarpieces, and it is likely that this sheet was preliminary to a work which was lost or simply never executed.

A pen-and-wash drawing of around 1617 in Vienna, Albertina (inv. 2345)[4] depicts a male saint (St. Dominic ?) with the lilies in his right hand, kneeling before the Madonna and Child. The composition is spatially more sophisticated than that in the Princeton sheet and the contours of forms are decidedly more fluid and rhythmic. However, it is possible that the Vienna sheet is a second attempt, at a slightly later date (perhaps as much as a year), to design the same altarpiece.

A clue to the identity of the saint pictured in the two sheets may be found in a pen-and-wash drawing in the Louvre (inv. 6876) of c. 1619, which represents *St. Dominic Kneeling before the Madonna and Child.*[5] In this work, which is in a horizontal format and, therefore, unlikely to be for an altarpiece, Dominic kisses the hand of the infant Christ, who offers the saint a lily. At the far left, a dog with a lighted torch in its mouth—the symbol of the evangelical mission of the Dominican order—looks on. The Paris drawing is clearly for a later project, but the certain identity of the saint, who crosses his arms on his chest in the same manner as the saint in the Princeton sheet, gives some support to the idea that both the Vienna and Princeton sketches represent St. Dominic, whose tomb, we should note, resides in the church of San Domenico in Bologna.

1. See Freedberg, 1983, color pl. III.

2. Guercino called Ludovico's picture "la mia cara cinna," which in the local dialect meant "my dear wet-nurse." "Cara cinna" is also a clever (and significant) pun on the Italian diminutive of "Carracci." See *Dipinti,* p. 10, n. 26.

3. The saint has been called St. Anthony of Padua by Bean and St. Anthony Abbot by DeGrazia and Gibbons (see Bibl.). DeGrazia connected the drawing to the altarpiece of the *Madonna and Child with SS. Francis, Anthony Abbot, and Bovo* (Renazzo di Cento, Chiesa Parocchiale di San Sebastiano), painted in c. 1615 by Guercino and his collaborator, Lorenzo Gennari (Salerno, no. 9). However, when compared with an important sketch in Berlin that is unequivocally for the 1615 picture (*Disegni,* no. 6. See also Peter Dreyer, *I grandi disegni italiani del Kupferstichkabinett di Berlino* [Milan: Silvana, 1979], no. 46, repr. in color), it is clear that the Princeton sheet is for another subject and must date to a later period.

4. Stix-Spitzmüller, no. 215 (as St. Dominic), repr. See V. Birke, in *Old Master Drawings from the Albertina,* exh. cat., National Gallery of Art, Washington, D.C., 1984, p. 238, no. 60, color repr.

5. Loire, 1990, no. 40, repr.

3

Pen and brown ink, brown wash, over traces of red chalk
255 x 394 mm.
Badly stained and foxed. Numbered in ink in the upper
right corner: *44*

PROVENANCE: P. & D. Colnaghi, London
BIBLIOGRAPHY: Lurie, 1963, figs. 1, 16 (with previous
bibl.); Dwight C. Miller in Detroit, 1965, no. 103, rept.;
Bottari, 1966, no. XXI; *Disegni*, p. 48; Roli, 1972, no. 7;
Bagni, 1984, pl. 119; John E. Schloder, *Baroque Imagery*,
Cleveland Museum of Art, 1984, no. 23; Salerno, under
no. 24-L; Stone, 1989, p. 233, fig. 40; M-T, under no. 1

The Cleveland Museum of Art,
Dudley P. Allen Fund, 25.1188

On the basis of a tiny sketch on the bottom edge of the sheet, Lurie has demonstrated that this drawing relates to one of Guercino's first important commissions at Cento, the decoration of several rooms of the Casa Pannini.[1] Though the subject of the main figures in the Cleveland work is clearly *Venus and Cupid Drawn through the Clouds by a Dove,* a theme which does not appear in the Camera della Venere in Casa Pannini, the thumbnail-size drawing of a female figure corresponds to the ceiling fresco of *Diana in a Chariot,* which formerly decorated a stairwell in the palazzo (transferred to canvas: Venice, Private Collection).[2]

Mahon has suggested that Guercino originally intended to paint *Venus and Cupid in a Chariot* on the ceiling of the Camera della Venere but then decided to paint the pair in a different scene (*Venus Nursing Cupid,* detached fresco, Cento, Pinacoteca)[3] on the chimney breast in the room instead. The vertical format of the chimney ruled out any possibility of adapting the Cleveland drawing to the new site. Moreover, it would have been inappropriate to show on a chimney breast the illusionistic scene proposed in the Cleveland sheet, since the spatial treatment of the original scheme depends on it being observed from below.

The Cleveland *Venus and Cupid* is a breakthrough work for Guercino. An important leap in his development has taken place. Were it not for the secure dates of the Casa Pannini project, 1615 to 1617 (the drawing should probably be placed toward the end of this three-year period), it would have been difficult to establish on the basis of style that this drawing was so early. One can understand why Marangoni[4] maintained that the Cleveland sheet was a preparatory study for the *Aurora* fresco, which Guercino painted for the Ludovisi family in Rome in 1621. The *sotto-in-su* treatment of the figures in Guer-

cino's sketch—the undulating rhythms of the diagonal composition, the flickering modulations of light and shadow produced by the wash—all conspire to achieve a remarkable sensation of movement through clouds and sunlight that anticipates the Ludovisi fresco.

Guercino accentuates Venus's physicality in athletic terms. She is no abstract, metaphysical *idea* but a vital and powerful woman. Her nose looks wind-burned and her lunging posture and bulbous, splayed knees deepen our appreciation of her energy and will. Her very glance seems to command the chariot into motion. It is no exaggeration to say that, with the Cleveland drawing, Guercino has laid one of the foundation stones for the creation of the High Baroque style in Italy.

1. For a complete treatment of this project see Roli, 1968 and Bagni, 1984.

2. Salerno, no. 24-L. I have argued elsewhere (Stone, 1989, p. 234, n. 126) that the fresco seems too weak to have been painted by Guercino himself and that it is more likely to have been executed by his assistant, Lorenzo Gennari, who also painted the accompanying fresco of *Apollo* (Bagni, 1984, pl. 131). It should also be pointed out that Guercino drew another tiny figure along the bottom edge of the sheet, a few centimeters to the left of the sketch for Diana. It has not been possible to identify this figure.

3. Salerno, no. 24-I.

4. Marangoni, 1959, no. 8.

Saint Barbara, a Bishop Saint, and another Male Saint

Pen and brown ink, brown and gray wash, on heavy beige paper
330 x 260 mm.
Small hole lower left corner; crease across the middle of the sheet
Inscription in brown ink in lower right corner, recto: *guarchino*
PROVENANCE: Giuseppe Collection, Paris; purchased from Charles E. Slatkin, N.Y., 1963
BIBLIOGRAPHY: Unpublished

Mrs. Richard L. Selle

Guercino's earliest drawings depend on the example of Ludovico Carracci. In this beautiful sheet, Guercino treats his figures with the kind of attenuation and wavy linear rhythms that Ludovico had made popular during the 1580s and 90s in Bologna.

What is new and wholly original in Guercino's adaptation of Ludovico's style is the virtuoso handling of the wash. The chiaroscuro achieved by the mixture of brown and gray tones does more than model the forms and situate them in space. There is also an emotional resonance from the contrast of light and dark, which, when combined with the almost naïve naturalism of the physiognomies and the unstudied character of the gestures, produces an authenticity of life and energy that would be hard to find in the drawings of any other artist of the early Baroque period.

This drawing cannot be linked with any documented picture, though one can speculate that the odd grouping of saints was meant for an altarpiece, destined perhaps for a chapel or church dedicated to St. Barbara, the patron saint of gunsmiths and armorers, who is shown with her attribute, a cannon, at her feet. The two male saints who accompany her have not been identified, but they also probably relate in some way to the specific requirements of the client. The project (perhaps never executed) may have included the Madonna and Child with putti in the upper zone of the picture: a fragment of one putto (from the knees down) remains at the top edge of the sheet, having survived an unceremonious cropping by a previous owner.

The work can be situated in Guercino's chronology by comparing it with dated sheets like those in Dijon and the Morgan Library for the 1618 altarpiece of *The Madonna del Carmine Presenting the Scapular to Saint Albert the Carmelite in the Presence of St. Francis and another Franciscan* (see cat. no. 4). A very similar treatment of wash and realization of costumes and attitudes appear in a drawing of around 1618-1619 (England, Private Collection) that depicts *SS. Catherine (?), Francis, and Louis of France in the Presence of the Madonna and Child*.[1]

1. Russell, 1973, pl. 27. Cf. also Stone, 1989, p. 247, fig. 95.

7

4

The Madonna del Carmine Presenting the Scapular to Saint Albert the Carmelite in the Presence of Saint Francis and another Franciscan
(Study for the altarpiece, Cento, Pinacoteca, 1618)

Pen and brown ink, brown and gray-brown wash, over traces of black chalk, squared in black chalk
401 x 267 mm.
Some foxing
Inscribed in pen and black ink in an old hand at lower right: *Guerchin 1100;* numbered on the verso in black chalk: *416;* ruled margins in red chalk
PROVENANCE: Sir Peter Lely (L. 2092); Jonathan Richardson Senior (L. 2184); Sir Joseph Hawley (according to the Fairfax Murray Notebooks); [Sir Henry Hawley] sale: Christie's, London, 16 July 1891, part of lot 218; Charles Fairfax Murray; purchased by J. Pierpont Morgan in London, 1910
BIBLIOGRAPHY: Stampfle-Bean, 1967, no. 36; *Disegni,* no. 9; Varriano, 1974, no. 1; Denison-Mules, 1981, no. 42; Stone, 1989, pp. 295 ff., fig. 88

{H}

The Pierpont Morgan Library, New York,   IV, 168a

Previously dated to 1615 on the basis of style,[1] the altarpiece of the *Virgin Presenting the Scapular to St. Albert* (fig. 4a)[2] was actually completed in 1618. Recently discovered documents published by Oscar Mischiati indicate that the painting, originally in the church of Santa Maria Annunziata and now in the Cento Pinacoteca, was paid for in two installments in May and June of 1618.[3] The rather low price for the picture—218 lire—probably reflects a discount based on the intervention of Guercino's assistant, Lorenzo Gennari, in the execution of the two Franciscans on the right side of the canvas. After being called to Bologna in 1617 to paint three pictures for the Ludovisi family,[4] Guercino found that his recent fame had increased his workload.[5] The use of an assistant on the *St. Albert* project may have been a consequence of this fact. It is also possible that the patrons could not afford Guercino's post-Ludovisi prices, and, thus, had to settle for a collaboration of hands.

Even given its poor condition (the colors have darkened considerably) and uneven quality due to Gennari's contributions, the *St. Albert* is one of Guercino's most explicit statements on what an altarpiece should be. Guercino conflates devotional and narrative conventions of religious painting and arrives at a grandiloquent engine of piety. Light and physical energy are supercharged by the coming together of the earthly and heavenly bodies. Empowered by his devotion, St. Albert's hands act like huge magnets, drawing the Virgin and Child toward him as he receives the scapular, the cloth by which the Carmelites will be recognized and saved from purgatory (the rescue of souls is shown in a kind of pictorial inset on the left side of the painting).[6]

4a

4b

9

The expressiveness of hands is a central feature of this work. The brilliant flashes of light that electrify Albert's fingers and hands may derive, as Mahon has suggested, from pictures such as Ludovico Carracci's *Conversion of St. Paul* of c. 1587-1589 in the Bologna Pinacoteca,[7] which Guercino is known to have studied avidly.[8] The motif of the open hands in the *St. Albert*—indeed, the entire concept of a heroic silhouette shaped by billowing drapery—could not be a more eloquent homage to Ludovico. Guercino's image is founded upon Ludovico's depiction of another Carmelite saint in the *Martyrdom of San Pietro Tomà* of c. 1598-1599, originally in the sacristy of San Martino Maggiore and now in the Bologna Pinacoteca.[9] Guercino has changed the pose of Ludovico's figure, increased its physicality, and given it a Baroque space and illumination in which to act.

Because the painting has darkened and contains figures by another hand, it could be argued that Guercino's concepts for this important work are best appreciated in his working drawings. The pen-and-wash sketch in the Musée des Beaux-Arts, Dijon would seem to be the earliest in the group of preparatory studies Guercino made for the altarpiece, since its organization of the scene is quite distant from that in the painting.[10] St. Francis, shown full-size, kneeling and praying to the left of St. Albert, is practically an equal partner in the drama. The pen-and-wash drawing from the Morgan Library exhibited here as cat. no. 4 and another sheet, formerly at Chatsworth (sold Christie's, London, 3 July 1984, lot 19, color repr.) and now in a private collection,[11] are, by contrast, quite close to the structure of the altarpiece itself, although the ex-Chatsworth sheet is in reverse of the final composition. A red-chalk drawing in Dublin, National Gallery of Ireland, which studies the poses of the Madonna and Child, must also have been made towards the end of the design process.[12]

In addition to the drawings mentioned above, there exists a previously unpublished sheet (fig. 4b) in Oslo, National Gallery, inv. B 15236, 166 x 186 mm., lined, formerly in the collection of Count Gelozzi (?) (L. 513, stamp lower right) and Jules Dupan (L. 1440, stamp lower left).[13] The Oslo sketch was probably made early in the series, perhaps just after the Dijon drawing. The brisk linear treatment of the Madonna and Child is similar to the handling of these figures in the Dijon sheet, and the Franciscan gesturing with his index finger is in the same position relative to the overall composition as the figure on the far left of the ex-Chatsworth drawing. The sheet may at one time have been folded or cut to fit into an album, since it would appear to be lacking the bottom half of the composition.

The Morgan Library drawing is one of the most passionate compositions created by Guercino in his early period. It is, perhaps, a more accomplished work of art than the painting itself. The elimination, in the painting, of the dramatic gesture of St. Francis described in the drawing, may ultimately serve to heighten St. Albert's "control" over the composition, but it diminishes, in the opinion of the present writer, the vitality of the overall idea.

1. *Dipinti,* no. 7.

2. Salerno, no. 38.

3. In E. Gilli et al., *L'Ospedale di Cento nei secoli,* Cento: Cassa di Risparmio di Cento, 1975, p. 51. See also Bagni, 1984, p. 223, n. 4.

4. See *Dipinti,* pp. 44-50.

5. See Stone, 1989, pp. 237-42.

6. Stampfle-Bean, 1967, p. 36.

7. Freedberg, 1983, fig. 116. Originally in the church of San Francesco, Bologna.

8. See Malvasia, II, p. 256. Guercino's own treatment of the subject, in a drawing in Turin, Biblioteca Reale, seems to have been inspired by Ludovico's picture (cf. *Disegni,* no. 177).

9. Bologna, 1956, no. 22 (as St. Angelo).

10. Inv. CA 793. See *Dessins du Musée de Dijon,* exh. cat., Cabinet des Dessins, Louvre, Paris, 1976, no. 77, repr. For references to the etching (in reverse) by Bartolozzi and copies of the drawing (including one at Windsor and one in the Fogg Art Museum), cf. M-T, no. 571.

11. *Disegni,* no. 8.

12. *Disegni,* no. 10.

13. Faint inscription (illegible) below the stamp of Dupan.

5
Two Studies of *Hercules Slaying the Hydra*
(Study for the lost fresco, 1618)

Pen and brown ink, brown wash
275 x 193 mm.
Inscribed in ink in an unknown hand at lower left:
Guerchin
PROVENANCE: Unidentified collector's mark; Henri
Delacroix (mark lower right, not in Lugt): his sale, Paris,
Palais Galliera, 31 March 1962, no. 239; purchased from
H.M. Calmann, London in November 1962
BIBLIOGRAPHY: Detroit, 1965, no. 104; Mahon, 1965, p.
385 f., fig. 9; *Disegni,* no. 29; Cazort-Johnston, no. 50

Private Collection

One of the best-known drawings by Guercino in America, this sheet contains two studies for the lost fresco in grisaille of *Hercules
Slaying the Hydra,* painted in 1618, according
to Malvasia, on the façade of Palazzo Tanari
at Bologna.[1] Guercino had treated the subject once before, in one of the illusionistic
niche decorations painted at Casa Provenzale
in Cento in 1614.[2]

To the twentieth-century viewer, the dynamic series of alternatives for the arms and
club of the Hercules on the left creates an effect worthy of Marcel Duchamp. We cannot
know which pose Guercino ultimately used
in his fresco. However, further studies for the
painting noted by Mahon (*Disegni,* pp. 58-59)
reiterate the main, reinforced pose of the Hercules on the left side of the exhibited sheet
and may indicate the solution used in the out-
door mural.

Nicholas Turner has brought to our attention a pen-and-wash drawing (fig. 5a) in the
Kupferstichkabinett of the Kunstsammlung,
Basel (inv. 1978.1015; 255 x 148 mm.;
Bequest of Dr. August Meyer). Unlike the
previously published sketches for the Tanari
fresco, which represent the muscular hero in
the act of his labor, the Basel sheet depicts an
Ercole trionfante. The club is shown at rest,
dangling from the palm of the right hand,
while the confident Hercules stares out
towards the viewer and indicates with his left
hand the defeated nine-headed serpent
pinned down beneath his foot.

1. Malvasia, II, p. 258.
2. Salerno, no. 7-D.

5a

12

Pen and brown ink, brown wash, over traces of black chalk, on laid paper; lower center figure reworked with graphite
320 x 223 mm.
Abraded at right
PROVENANCE: Lionel Lucas (L. Suppl. 1733a, lower right recto); Claude Lucas: sale, Christie's, London, 2 December 1949, no. 78; purchased from H.M. Calmann, London, 1956, through Paul Oppé
BIBLIOGRAPHY: Cazort-Johnston, no. 53 (with previous bibl.); James Hall, *A History of Ideas and Images in Italian Art,* New York, 1983, p. 317, fig. 8.8; Ottawa, 1988 (C. Johnston), no. 10

National Gallery of Canada, Ottawa / Musée des Beaux-Arts du Canada, Ottawa, 6837

The wooden statue of the Madonna and Child, which stood for centuries in the Santa Casa in the Sanctuary of Loreto in the Marches, was one of the most important devotional images of the Renaissance and Baroque periods. In the exhibited sheet, which should be dated to c. 1618, Guercino depicts souls confined to purgatory in the act of seeking their freedom through the intercession of the miraculous Virgin. The two angels at the left have taken up their cause and gesticulate accordingly. Meanwhile, a third figure (without wings) pulls back a curtain, symbolizing entrance to Paradise.

Guercino's altarpiece of 1618, *SS. Bernard of Siena and Francis of Assisi before the Madonna of Loreto* (Cento, Pinacoteca),[1] is the only documented work of the pre-Roman period which treats the subject of the Madonna of Loreto.[2] However, the Ottawa drawing differs substantially in composition and theme from the Cento altarpiece, and it is not likely to be connected with the painting in any way. Guercino's purpose in making the Ottawa sheet is unknown, but the existence of another, equally complete, pen-and-wash compositional sketch of the same subject in the Albertina (fig. 6a)[3] leads one to suspect that a commission of some type was being planned here.

The presence of pentimenti in the Vienna sketch (in the gesturing hand of the angel at left) and their absence in the Ottawa sheet suggests that the exhibited work was a revised version of the composition. The most obvious difference between the two sheets concerns the disposition of the lower right figure of a male youth. In the Albertina drawing, this figure sits rather nonchalantly upon the flames with his legs crossed, his torso shifted slightly to the right, and his head turning upwards and to the left. His counterpart is treated with greater drama and daring in the Ottawa sketch. He is shown reclining at an angle towards the picture plane, supported by his right elbow and gesturing pathetically to the Heavens with his left arm. His head is thrown back so far that the spectator can practically see his entire face. Thus, the contrapposto of attitudes created by the two principal nudes in the Albertina sheet (one figure facing into the picture and one figure looking out) was abandoned in the Ottawa drawing in order to create a more unified composition in which most of the principal figures demonstrate involvement with the scene depicted in the upper half of the sheet. This idea is further strengthened in the Ottawa drawing by the figure crying out with both arms uplifted, who occupies the zone just below the curtain.

The beautiful male nude in the left corner is only slightly changed from one version to the next. In the Albertina sheet he gestures towards the middle of the composition and has his left foot tucked underneath his extended right leg. In the Ottawa drawing, his arm is bent in front of his face and the left leg is not depicted. Such figures were the stock in trade of the Carracci and their followers, who regularly made life studies of nudes in special poses for later incorporation into their compositions. Guercino's previously unconnected black-chalk drawing of a *Seated Nude Boy Seen from Behind* in the National Gallery, Washington (exhibited here as cat. no. 64) is a good example of this practice. With the exception of the right arm (which is not shown), the figure studied from life in the Washington sheet is taken over element by element in the Albertina drawing. One cannot know whether Guercino posed this figure specifically for the purpose of including him in the scene of purgatory or whether the artist simply made an academic study at one point and later applied it to a project where a repoussoir figure seen from behind suggested itself.

1. Salerno, no. 44.

2. Guercino's engraver, Pasqualini, made a print in 1628 of the Madonna of Loreto in a niche surmounted by an angel and two putti. See Bagni, 1988, no. 101. There is no connection between this work and the Ottawa drawing, although Pasqualini's print must derive from a drawing (now lost) by Guercino, one which is not necessarily as late as 1628. Pasqualini often used Guercino drawings and paintings of earlier years as sources for his engravings.

3. Inv. 2349. Stix-Spitzmüller, no. 219. 324 x 209 mm.

6a

15

7

Study for *The Raising of Lazarus*

(Paris, Louvre, c. 1619)

Pen and brown ink, brown wash
200 x 270 mm.
Foxed; lined
PROVENANCE: Sir Peter Lely (L. 2092, lower right
recto); Sir Robert Mond (L. Suppl. 2813a); D.E. Brackley;
sale: Sotheby's, London, 1 December 1966, lot 37; sale:
Sotheby's, London, 28 March 1968, lot 43; purchased in
New York in 1968
BIBLIOGRAPHY: Tancred Borenius and Rudolf
Wittkower, *Catalogue of the Collection of Drawings by the
Old Masters Formed by Sir Robert Mond . . .,* London,
1937, p. 27, no. 103; *Disegni,* no. 45, repr.; Bean, 1979, no.
235, repr.; Salerno, under no. 56; Stone, 1989, p. 338, fig.
113; M-T, under no. 10; Loire, 1990, under no. 1

{O,C}

The Metropolitan Museum of Art, New York,
Purchase, Fosburgh Fund, Inc. Gift and Rogers
Fund, 1968, 68.68

One of Guercino's most carefully structured and dramatic compositions of the early
period, the *Raising of Lazarus,* Paris, Louvre
(fig. 7a),[1] was likely painted around 1619 for
the Papal Legate of Ferrara, Cardinal Jacopo
Serra (1570-1623).[2] Serra, who is known to
have admired Rubens, commissioned from
Guercino several of the master's most ambi-
tious history paintings, including *Samson
Seized by the Philistines* (New York,
Metropolitan Museum of Art)[3] of 1619 and
Jacob Blessing the Sons of Joseph (London,
Mahon Collection) of 1620 (fig. 8a), discussed
in the subsequent entry.

The exhibited sheet testifies to the fact that
Guercino's artistic vocabulary had, in a very
short time, become quite sophisticated. The
mellifluous contrapposto (or symmetry) of
attitudes formed by the figures of Christ and
Lazarus is unique among the early works of
the master.

As with the majority of Guercino's preliminary sketches, which are often quite removed
compositionally from the corresponding
paintings, the Metropolitan drawing does not
predict in any precise way the structure of the
Louvre *Lazarus.* The unusual motif of the un-
binding of Lazarus's hands does, however,
seem to follow from one of Guercino's designs, but not, surprisingly, from one made
for the *Lazarus.* Guercino appears to have
fancied a compositional device he created in
an important drawing at Haarlem, Teylers
Museum, which is a study for the *Samson.*[4]
When the evolution of design in the *Samson*
made it unfeasible to use the binding motif,
Guercino took it over, *mutatis mutandis,* for
the *Lazarus.* Incidentally, this occurrence
makes it all the more likely that the Louvre
painting was made for Cardinal Serra in 1619,
since the two pictures would seem to have
been designed in tandem, though probably
not as pendants, as Longhi speculated.[5]

At Ferrara, Guercino's awareness of composition as an abstract formal language seems
to have been partly inspired by contact with
Serra. It may also have arisen as a consequence of fresh study of Titian's great
paintings in that city.[6]

1. Salerno, no. 56. See also Loire, 1990, no. 1.

2. Malvasia does not mention the work among those
painted for Serra. But Longhi and Mahon have demonstrated that the picture should be included in this group.
See *Dipinti,* no. 35. Cf. also Mahon, 1981b. For an interesting history of Serra's legation and further information
on his role as a patron, see Southorn, 1988.

3. Salerno, no. 58. *The Return of the Prodigal Son*
(Vienna, Kunsthistorisches Museum) is also a Serra commission of 1619. See Salerno, no. 57.

4. *Disegni,* no. 40; Van Tuyll, 1989, no. 24, color repr.
For other sketches related to the *Lazarus,* see *Disegni,*
nos. 44, 46, 47. Cf. also M-T, no. 10.

5. See *Dipinti,* no. 35; and Stone, 1989, pp. 324-25.

6. For a complete analysis of Guercino's Serra pictures
and their place in the artist's development, see Stone,
1989, pp. 316-45.

7a

17

8

Study for *Jacob Blessing the Sons of Joseph*
(London, Mahon Collection, 1620)

Pen and brown ink, gray wash, over traces of black chalk, on ivory laid paper
182 x 245 mm. (max.)
Verso: Study of Saint Christopher in graphite; study of two figures in conversation over money in pen and brown ink
Inscribed, lower left recto, in pen and brown ink: *Gouarchin;* inscribed lower right recto, in pen and brown ink: *85*
PROVENANCE: Bought Dec. 1914 / Puttick & Simpson, stamp (not in Lugt) verso, lower left, in purple; William F. E. Gurley, Chicago, stamp (not in Lugt) recto, lower right, in black; Leonora Hall Gurley Memorial Collection, stamp (L. Suppl. 1230b) verso, lower center, in black
BIBLIOGRAPHY: *Disegni,* no. 54; Posner, 1968, p. 603, fig. 12; Neilson, 1972, no. 28, repr.; Joachim-McCullagh, no. 60, pl. 66; Joachim, Microfiche, 3D8; Salerno, under no. 66

The Art Institute of Chicago,
Leonora Hall Gurley Memorial Collection, 1922.484

Commissioned in 1620 by the Papal Legate of Ferrara, Cardinal Jacopo Serra, Guercino's *Jacob Blessing the Sons of Joseph,* London, Mahon Collection (fig. 8a),[1] depicts a biblical scene (Genesis 48:13-18) of true pathos and humanity. Pictures like the *St. Albert* altarpiece (fig. 4a) of 1618 and the *Raising of Lazarus* (fig. 7a), painted in c. 1619 almost certainly for Serra, celebrate the beauty and expressive power of gesticulating hands and arms. What more perfect subject for this artist than that of *Jacob's Blessing,* in which the nearly blind grandfather is interrupted by a fatherly protest as he crosses his arms to confer the right-handed blessing, usually reserved for the eldest child, upon Joseph's younger son Ephraim.

The composition was studied in three drawings, of which the exhibited sheet would seem to be the earliest, since it shows the scene in reverse of the painting and the other sketches (Paris, Collection of Jacques Petit-Horry and Moscow, Pushkin Museum).[2] The Chicago drawing, one of the most moving,

Rembrandtesque inventions ever made by Guercino, does not explore the possibility of counter-rotation of the central figure, as does the preparatory study in Moscow, which is quite close to the painted version. Instead, the blessing seems to be in actual progress and nothing will stop it: Joseph's small hand is no match for the bulging biceps of his determined father's arm.

Denis Mahon has drawn attention to a possible fourth sketch for the Serra *Jacob's Blessing.* A pen-and-wash drawing of a *Half-Length Figure of an Old Man* in the Cento Pinacoteca (fig. 8b) would, indeed, appear to be a "close-up" study for the figure of Jacob, who is shown in a pose similar to the one Guercino used in the Petit-Horry sheet.[3]

1. Malvasia, II, p. 259. Salerno, no. 66.

2. *Disegni,* nos. 55 and 56, respectively.

3. 130 x 130 mm. See Cento, 1987, p. 114, no. 108, repr. (entry by Prisco Bagni).

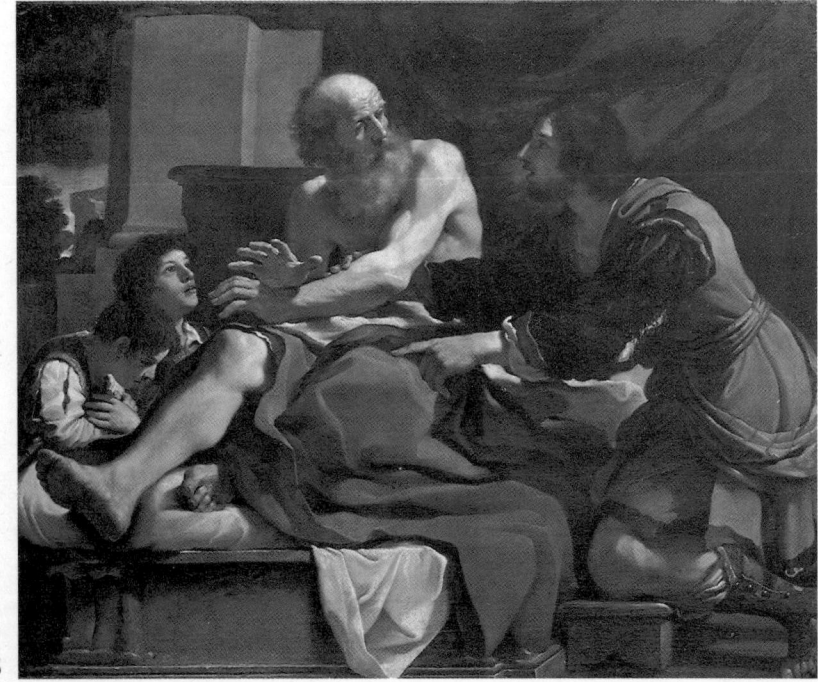

8a   8b

Gonarchin

19

9

Study for *The Investiture of Saint William of Aquitaine*
(Bologna, Pinacoteca Nazionale, 1620)

Pen and brown ink, brown wash, on beige paper
150 x 114 mm.
PROVENANCE: sale: Sotheby's, London, 4 July 1988, lot
60, repr.
BIBLIOGRAPHY: M-T, under no. 14

Dr. Carlo M. Croce

9c

9b: recto

It was probably in early 1620 that Guercino took a two-week leave of absence from Ferrara and Cardinal Serra to travel to Mantua, where he presented Duke Ferdinando Gonzaga with a painting of *Erminia and the Shepherd* (Birmingham, City Museum and Art Gallery)[1] and received a handsome reward.[2] This chance to see the works of Fetti, Rubens, and Caravaggio (the *Death of the Virgin*) in the ducal collections must have been an important opportunity for the artist and could only have convinced him that he was headed in the right direction in his art.

At the end of the painter's return visit to Ferrara, during which he painted two pictures for Serra, *Jacob's Blessing* (fig. 8a), discussed in the previous entry, and *Elijah Fed by Ravens* (London, Mahon Collection),[3] he was honored, as he had been at Mantua, by being made a *Cavaliere* (on 8 December 1620).[4] There are a number of months unaccounted for in the middle of 1620, and these were no

9a

20

doubt spent by the artist in Cento and Bologna in feverish pursuit of a workable design for his first altarpiece for a Bolognese church, the *Investiture of St. William of Aquitaine* (fig. 9a), originally in S. Gregorio and now in the Bologna Pinacoteca.[5] This painting is universally recognized to be one of Guercino's most important works and a landmark in the development of High Baroque style.

From the dozens of drawings made for this famous picture,[6] we learn that Guercino's new concern for compositional structure—exemplified best by the taut, classicizing design of the *Raising of Lazarus* (fig. 7a)—required increasingly more from him intellectually and technically. It can scarcely be imagined that another artist in the Seicento would have made so many studies for a single altarpiece.

Perhaps the largest group of sketches deals with the attitude of St. William and his placement in relation to the bishop, before whom, in the painting, the soldier swears allegiance to Christ and accepts a monastic habit. For example, a double-sided sheet in New York, Metropolitan Museum of Art (fig. 9b: recto), depicts the composition in reverse of the painting and shows William holding a cross rather than receiving the habit.[7] Another sketch, at Dresden,[8] shows the composition in the same basic direction as the painting, but represents the saint standing rather than kneeling, and includes a depiction of the removal of William's spurs.

Only two extant drawings, the exhibited sheet and a more detailed sketch at Windsor,[9] show the saint in the position he was to occupy in the final, that is to say, *retouched* version of the painting. As technical studies carried out on the work before the 1968 exhibition demonstrate, William's left arm originally swung down in an arc and his left hand rested on his hip. Apparently, Guercino (and / o r his patrons) concluded that the

concetto of William's acceptance of monastic life needed to be clearer and so the artist repainted the figure so that he actually reached up to receive the cloth.

The summary treatment of line in the Croce drawing corresponds to the function of the sheet. Guercino was only interested here in resolving the problem he encountered after his work was finished. The Windsor drawing, which includes the second boy and a faint indication of the bishop's hand, displays more hatching and finer treatment of the details of the costume and face; it would logically have been made immediately after the exhibited sketch.

It is worth noting here a vigorous pen-and-wash sketch of a *Trumpeter on a Rearing Horse* in the Louvre (fig. 9c), recently exhibited in Paris,[10] and noted by Mahon and Turner in connection with a study at Windsor of *Two Helmeted Soldiers on Horseback with Archers*.[11] Neither of the works has been convincingly related to a particular commission. In a rare disagreement between the two scholars, Mahon dates the Windsor sheet to the late 1620s and early 1630s and sees affinities in style and subject between it and the Louvre drawing. Turner, on the other hand, believes that the Windsor and Louvre sheets belong to Guercino's earliest period, around 1614, and that they are plausibly connected to the Casa Provenzale frescoes at Cento.[12] As evidence, Turner notes the resemblance between these sheets and a drawing of a *Battle Scene* in the collection of Bowdoin College, Brunswick, Maine (see Suppl. no. 23, repr.), which has been credibly related to the decorations at Cento.

Remarking on their differences in scale and technique, Stéphane Loire rightly doubts the supposed relationship between the Windsor and Louvre sketches of horsemen and dates the Paris work to 1625-1635.[13] I would like to suggest here that the Louvre drawing

may be favorably compared in terms of the use of wash, the treatment of hatching lines, and the rendering of horses with Guercino's sketch in Dresden of a *Soldier and a Monk,* made for the right half of the composition of the *St. William*.[14] The lack of agreement about the Louvre drawing might be resolved if the *Trumpeter* could be interpreted as a "close-up" study for the mounted soldier blowing his trumpet in the middle distance of the S. Gregorio altarpiece, just below William's elbow.

1. Salerno, no. 61.

2. See *Dipinti*, no. 49.

3. Salerno, no. 68.

4. See *Dipinti*, p. 5.

5. Salerno, no. 69. The picture originally occupied a chapel adjacent to Ludovico Carracci's *St. George* altarpiece (*in situ*). See *Dipinti*, no. 43, for references to the numerous commentaries written by Seicento critics, many of whom discuss Guercino's work in relation to Ludovico's.

6. For these drawings and references to still others, see *Disegni*, nos. 57-76 and M-T, nos. 13-14. Cf. also our Introduction.

7. Rogers Fund, 1908; Inv. 08.227.29; 235 x 191 mm.; *Disegni*, no. 63; Bean, 1979, no. 236.

8. *Disegni*, no. 66.

9. *Disegni*, no. 76. See also M-T, no. 14.

10. Inv. 6894, 166 x 142 mm.; Loire, 1990, no. 46, repr. I thank M. Loire for allowing us to reproduce this work.

11. M-T, no. 169.

12. See Roli, 1968.

13. Loire compares the sketch to the preparatory drawings (*Disegni*, nos. 112-114) made for the lost painting of the *Martyrdom of St. James*, which has been dated to c. 1627.

14. *Disegni*, no. 73. See the useful color detail of this section of the canvas in Salerno, p. 149. I tend to agree with Mahon that the Windsor drawing must date to the early 1630s, around the time of Guercino's painting of the *Death of Dido* (Salerno, no. 135).

10
Christ and Saint Thomas
(Study for the *Incredulity of Saint Thomas*, London, The National Gallery, 1621)

Pen and brown ink, brown, gray, and green-blue wash, on cream laid paper
164 x 236 mm.
Lined; damage and small losses due to acid ink corrosion, especially above Thomas's right hand and in areas of his face; soiled
Inscribed in brown ink on the left side of the sheet: *Ill.mo Sig.re* ("Illustrissimo Signore"; in the Seicento, the usual opening salutation in a letter), probably in Guercino's own handwriting (cf. the letter of 9 Dec. 1617 to Enzo Bentivoglio in Bagni, 1984, p. 15); fragments of doodling are still visible above and below Christ's right arm and in the upper right corner (a male profile ?); inscribed at the lower left corner in careful calligraphy with pen and black ink: *Guercino da Cento.* (L. Suppl. 3005 c-d); inscribed on verso in ink: *No. 8*
PROVENANCE: The Collection of the "Reliable Venetian Hand" (L. Suppl. 3005 c-d), Venice (?), second half of the 18th century (?)
BIBLIOGRAPHY: Unpublished

Robert and Bertina Suida Manning

In the introduction to his important catalogue of drawings from the eighteenth-century collection of the "Reliable Venetian Hand" (*Disegni di una collezione veneziana del Settecento,* exh. cat., Fondazione Giorgio Cini, Venice, 1966), Alessandro Bettagno noted that most of the sheets owned by the mysterious Venetian were working sketches rather than "finished," presentation-type drawings. By the end of the Settecento there was a true passion for "disegni di invenzione," graphic work that reveals the artist's creative process through quick, deft pen-strokes and splashes of wash.

The exhibited sheet, whose inscription is in the immediately recognizable calligraphy of the "Reliable Venetian Hand,"[1] is not only a superb example of Guercino's most exuberant drawing style; it is the only known drawing for one of the most important pictures of the pre-Roman period (1613-1621) and one of just a handful of Guercino sheets which have come down to us that contains green-blue wash.[2]

Under the year 1621 (but apparently before May 1621, when Guercino departed for Rome), Malvasia lists two pictures painted by the artist for Bartolomeo Fabri, the man who in 1616 had donated two rooms of his Cento house for the establishment of Guercino's *Accademia del Nudo,* the first drawing academy to be founded in the city.[3] The two paintings are described as: *Un Cristo avanti ad Anna* (Christ before Anna) and *Un S. Tomaso, che tocca la piaga a Cristo* (St. Thomas touching Christ's wound). Based on evidence provided by two dated and inscribed reproductive engravings by Pasqualini,[4] Mahon has demonstrated that the painting referred to by Malvasia as *Christ before Anna* is instead a *Capture of Christ* (Cambridge, Fitzwilliam Museum)[5] and that its pendant, the *Incredulity of St. Thomas* (fig. 10a),[6] is to be identified with the Rubensian picture now in London, National Gallery.[7]

The Manning drawing studies the expressions, postures, and gestures of the main protagonists (there are three other figures in the painting which are not included in the drawing). The resurrected Christ—who seems to be speaking as he leans forward—tugs at Thomas's right arm and draws it towards his wound. Thomas's left hand is raised in astonishment.

No sooner had Guercino worked out this arrangement than he tried to improve it. An alternative position for Thomas's left hand is sketched in: Thomas now holds back his drapery and touches his own chest in a manner not very distant from the solution in the painting. The right hand that touches Christ is shown again (very tentatively), this time pointing higher up on the chest, with the index finger located just above Christ's sternum. In the painting, the doubting saint's torso is turned toward the viewer, alleviating the problem of a foreshortened elbow and creating an uninterrupted passage of drapery along Thomas's right arm, thereby emphasizing the horizontal axis of the picture. Thomas's gesture of astonishment, the raised hand, has been transferred to the old man standing behind Christ.

In the drawing, Christ is even more animated than Thomas. His head and left arm are in motion. In the painting, by contrast, the resurrected figure is grander and more serene. He is shown in a more upright pose and now leans on the standard rather than reaching out to Thomas. The dichotomy between the Saviour who "knows" and the saint who "doubts" is thereby made more intelligible.

A careful analysis of the drawing, however, reveals that Guercino already began to consider the final composition in this preliminary sheet. The line which runs from the top of the drawing, behind Christ's head, 23 through his arm, and ends below Thomas's sleeve in a double line is Guercino's short-hand for the standard. The artist has super-imposed Christ's left hand upon the left upper arm to indicate where Christ will grasp the standard.

Drawings like this one from the period just prior to the artist's departure from Cento to serve Pope Gregory XV in Rome are exceptional demonstrations of the economy, versatility, and animation of line in Guercino's draftsmanship. The construction of the fully three-dimensional drapery folds in Christ's costume—two or three powerful strokes with a pen soaked in ink—is the product of a brilliant technique that only a few masters in history have equalled.

1. Bettagno, 1966, records two examples in which the inscription of the "Reliable Venetian Hand" occurs on a Guercino drawing: 1) Cat. no. 164 (exhibited and repr.), *Seated Child*, Paris, Louvre, inv. no. 7000, inscribed *Gianfrancesco Barbieri da Cento* [the printed text contains an error and reads *Gianfranco*]; 2) Cat. no. 165 (not exhibited), *Study of Male Heads*, Photo: Witt Library, London, inscribed *Gian Francesco Guercino da Cento*. Besides these noted by Bettagno, a red-chalk drawing (100 x 147 mm.) of *A Bearded Old Man and a Male Youth, Both Half Length, Facing Left*, formerly Newling Collection, Birkenhead, sold Sotheby's, London, 8 Dec. 1972, lot 43 (attributed to Guercino, though it is very likely a work of the *bottega*), bears an inscription by the "Reliable Venetian Hand" along the lower right edge: *Gianfrancesco Guercino da Cento*. It may, however, be the very same drawing, *Studio per Teste Maschili*, seen by Bettagno at the Witt Library [in which case, the text for his cat. no. 165, which cannot be checked against the drawing since the latter is not illustrated, is also in error, and should read *Gianfrancesco* instead of *Gian Francesco*].

2. Two drawings from Guercino's early period which contain a similar green-blue wash in the background areas are in Turin, Biblioteca Reale. See *Disegni*, nos. 177-178.

3. Malvasia, II, p. 260. For the citation referring to the Accademia, cf. Malvasia, II, p. 258.

4. See Bagni, 1988, nos. 31, 33.

5. Salerno, no. 73.

6. Inv. no. 3216. Salerno, no. 74.

7. *Dipinti*, nos. 46-47.

10a

Guercino. da Cento.

25

11

The Infant Christ Holding a Bird, and Saint Joseph

Pen and brown ink, brown wash, on laid paper
197 x 251 mm.
Lined, pasted down; considerable foxing; small losses
along lower left edge and in lower right corner
PROVENANCE: Thomas Sadler (according to Pond)
BIBLIOGRAPHY: Robert L. Manning, *The Story of
Christmas,* exh. cat., Finch College Museum of Art, 13
Dec. 1968 - 9 Jan. 1969, no. 59.

Robert and Bertina Suida Manning

This drawing of a charming and intimate subject, which symbolically foretells Christ's resurrection, is quite similar in handling to a drawing at Windsor of the *Holy Family with SS. John the Baptist and Anne.*[1] Mahon and Turner have dated the Windsor sheet to 1621 on the basis of a print in reverse of the original, inscribed *in Roma 1621,* which was made by Guercino's countryman and personal engraver, G.B. Pasqualini, who had traveled with the master to Rome in the middle of May 1621, when the latter was summoned by Pope Gregory XV Ludovisi to serve the papacy.[2]

Pinholes in the margins of the Windsor sheet and black-chalk rubbings on its verso indicate that Pasqualini used the drawing to transfer Guercino's image to the copper plate. In this regard, it is important to note that some of Guercino's drawings are so carefully delineated with a hatching and stippling technique that it could be concluded that the artist made certain sheets in a special style to facilitate their transfer to the print medium. This peculiar phenomenon may be viewed first hand in a drawing of *Saint Luke* of c. 1618-1619, cat. no. 75, which was used by Pasqualini for a print, cat. no. 75A.

While it is true that Guercino sometimes used hatching and stippling in drawings—

Ab Archetypo, quod inter rariora aservat, eruditis oculis officiose proponenda, peritissimus elegantiarum Arbiter, Tho: Sadler Arm, desumptam tabellam hanc eidem dedicat Arth: Pond.

11a

particularly head and costume studies—that were made exclusively for the preparation of paintings (the study of *St. William* at Windsor, discussed earlier, under cat. no. 9, is a case in point), it would be fair to say, nonetheless, that the "gravure style" is applied with a higher degree of precision in drawings which show very finished, complete scenes than in working sketches, where the hatching and stipple are somehow less painstaking or even rough. Complete scenes which use this gravure technique may, indeed, form a separate class or category of drawings that were intended for engraving. Examples recently published by Bagni support this theory.[3]

The Infant Christ Holding a Bird, and St. Joseph was not the subject of a print by Pasqualini, but it might very well have been drawn with the engraver's needs in mind. The net of hatching and stippling around Christ's legs and abdomen is one of the most elaborate demonstrations of this technique in all of Guercino's graphic oeuvre. The suitability of the drawing for reproduction was not lost on the English painter, art dealer, and printseller Arthur Pond (1701-1758). In 1735-1736—three decades before Piranesi, Bartolozzi, and others would make publishing history with a whole volume of etchings devoted to Guercino's drawings,[4] Pond collaborated with the landscape painter Charles Knapton on a volume of *Prints in Imitation of Drawings,* which boasted, among others, sixteen plates after drawings attributed to Guercino, including the Manning sheet, then in the collection of Thomas Sadler.[5] The drawing was etched in reverse by Pond himself (fig. 11a) and features, as was the custom, a fancy Latin inscription dedicated to the owner of the original.

Because of the nature of the exhibited drawing (the fact that it may have been designed for a print), it is difficult to date. On the basis of its monumentalizing approach to the rendering of children, which it shares with several studies at Windsor for the *Aurora* fresco of 1621,[6] the *Burial of St. Petronilla* altarpiece for St. Peter's of 1623,[7] and the *Toilet of Venus* also of 1623,[8] the Manning drawing could be tentatively assigned to Guercino's Roman period, which ended abruptly after the death of the Pope on 8 July 1623.

1. M-T, no. 15.

2. On the date of Pasqualini's trip to Rome, see Bagni, 1988, pp. 8-9, and n. 10.

3. See Bagni, 1988, nos. 41-42 and 78-79. It should not be concluded from what has just been said that Pasqualini could not make an effective print from a drawing executed in the usual manner in red chalk or pen and wash, or that he could not work directly from Guercino's paintings. He did both of these things. On the other hand, some of his best results came when he had a model like Bagni, no. 42, from which to work. Pasqualini, for all his merits, was no Vorsterman (Rubens's engraver), and needed Guercino's help.

4. See cat. no. 22 and fig. 22b, with note.

5. On Pond's career, see the excellent book by Louise Lippincott, *Selling Art in Georgian London. The Rise of Arthur Pond,* New Haven and London: Yale University Press, 1983. For a list of the reproductive prints by Pond and Knapton, see Henry M. Hake, "Pond's and Knapton's Imitations of Drawings," *The Print Collector's Quarterly,* December 1922, pp. 324-49. I offer sincere thanks to Nicholas Turner, who first connected the Manning sheet with the Pond print and who was kind enough to provide me with these references.

6. For example, M-T, no. 18.

7. For example, M-T, no. 24, recto.

8. Especially, M-T, no. 28, but also nos. 27 and 29.

Studies for the *Crucifixion with Saints*
(Church of the Madonna della Ghiara, Reggio Emilia, 1624-1625)

12 Three Studies for a Crucifixion

Pen and brown ink, brown wash
224 x 256 mm.
Slight foxing and paper loss
Inscribed in pencil by Platt on the verso: *B-35 Parsons 1931*
PROVENANCE: Northwick Collection (and thus, probably from Casa Gennari and E. Bouverie); William Bateson (L. Suppl. 2604a, verso); Sotheby's, London, 23-24 April 1929, no. 51; E. Parsons & Sons, London, 1931; Dan Fellows Platt, 1931-38 (L. Suppl. 750a, verso); Mrs. Platt, 1938-50; Museum Purchase, 1950
BIBLIOGRAPHY: Spark, 1949, no. 120; Norfolk, 1950, no. 20; Zafran, 1979, no. 15, repr.; Salerno, under no. 105; M-T, under no. 33

{H}

The Chrysler Museum, Norfolk, Virginia, 50.48.87

13 Christ on the Cross

Pen and iron gall ink, on buff laid paper
258 x 175 mm. (max.)
Laid down; foxed; hole at lower center
Verso: Caricature in profile
Inscribed verso, upper center on mount, in pen and brown ink: *Francesco Barbieri detto il Guercino;* inscribed verso (possibly in Guercino's own hand), lower portion of drawing, in pen and iron gall ink, partially illegible: *Ricordo p: comprare un cenzo di unzio di / loro mare che cia sopra il . . . [?] / Così le p: lavorare in un rame picolo / in un panno della madonna dal / . . . R.A. Padre don Marcho da / Venezia profesore di detto agin / in Santa Maria della Va . . . à Ferrara*
(Based on the notes of a paleographer, Dr. Petrucci [museum file], and the recommendations of Laura Giles, I offer a slightly different transcription: *Ricordo p[er] comprare un terzo di unzia di pura / oltramare che sia bello e [. . .] sottile p[er] [dipingere ??] in un rame piccolo / in un panno della Madonna dal molto R[everendo] padre don Marcho / da Venezia [provveditore ??] di detto [..] in Santa Maria al Va [..] à Ferrara)*
PROVENANCE: Dr. Benno Geiger, Vienna; Charles Deering, Chicago
BIBLIOGRAPHY: Planiscig-Voss, p. 13, no. 35, repr.; Neilson, 1972, no. 31, repr.; Joachim-McCullagh, pp. 53-54, no. 61, pl. 70; Joachim, Microfiche, 3D9; Salerno, under no. 105; M-T, under no. 33

{H,O}

The Art Institute of Chicago,
Charles Deering Collection, 1927.7754

Like the *Investiture of St. William of Aquitaine* of 1620 (see cat. no. 9), the *Crucifixion, with the Virgin, Mary Magdalen, St. John the Evangelist, and St. Prosper, Bishop of Reggio,* painted in 1624-1625 for the church of the Madonna della Ghiara, Reggio Emilia (fig. 12a),[1] required extensive compositional and figural elaboration. This large altarpiece (*in situ*) was to be Guercino's most important commission in the immediate post-Roman period, and the artist seems to have been intent on demonstrating to his Emilian public the new monumentality and plasticity of form he had developed in the *Burial of St. Petronilla,* made for St. Peter's in 1623 (see Intro.).

To judge from a remarkable series of drawings, Guercino was apparently striving for a painting that would integrate grand gestures, impassioned facial expressions, and expansive draperies into a unified, legible design. Important sheets in the Brera, Milan,[2] in the Teylers Museum, Haarlem,[3] and in the Gabinetto Nazionale delle Stampe, Rome,[4] record Guercino's consideration of several alternatives for the placement of the cross and the overall disposition of the figures. In the Haarlem and Rome studies, the cross is depicted from an angle and placed to one side, whereas, in the Milan drawing, Guercino considers both frontal and oblique views on the same page: in three separate studies of Christ on the cross and in a kind of schematic "inset" of the altarpiece in which the frontal and oblique views of the cross (without Christ) are shown side by side. In addition to these three drawings, a fourth, mentioned by Mahon[5] (formerly Paris, Donnadieu-Usslaub collections, presently untraced), is known through copies in the Hermitage, Leningrad (inv. 14536), and the collection of Joseph F. McCrindle, New York.[6] The ex-Donnadieu drawing would seem to predict more than any of the other known sketches the limited spatial depth and the frontality of the com-

12a

position as it was finally rendered in the painting. By keeping the figures close to the picture plane, Guercino was able to achieve remarkable *rilievo* (relief, or sculptural three-dimensionality), a quality for which seventeenth-century critics like Scannelli praised him.[7]

Cat. nos. 12 and 13 belong to a large group of more detailed studies in which Guercino worked out various possibilities for specific areas of the composition and experimented with different gestures and attitudes for his actors.[8] On the Norfolk sheet are three separate figure studies. On the left is a kneeling St. John the Evangelist (or possibly the Magdalen) hugging the cross from the

12

13

right side with his legs turned slightly into the composition. In the painting, by contrast, St. John is placed on the opposite side and is shown with the bare soles of his feet pushing in a diagonal direction toward the spectator, creating a dramatic visual "bridge" between audience and pictorial space, much as Caravaggio had done in the *Madonna di Loreto* (Rome, S. Agostino) and as Guercino had himself so effectively accomplished in the *St. Petronilla* by placing the body of the saint *in scorcio*. In the center and on the right are two ideas for the grief-stricken Virgin (Zafran calls the female on the right the Magdalen; however, the veil over her head is consistent with the Virgin's costume in the related drawings and in the painting). Though there is no indication of the placement of the cross in relation to these full-length, standing females, considering their disposition, we might suppose that the Virgin with her head inclined was intended to stand to the left of the cross and that the Virgin who glances upwards (at Christ) with her arms extended in a baroque gesture of distress, was meant to occupy the right half of the composition, where ultimately St. Prosper would be placed. Neither of these poses was used; however, the vibrant contrasts of light and dark produced by Guercino's bold use of wash anticipate the dramatic chiaroscuro in the altarpiece. Guercino went on to produce a complex type of design in which the Virgin, Magdalen, and St. John are all placed on the left side of the cross and are linked to each other and to the crucified Christ through a series of carefully arranged gestures and glances. Such unity could not be reached by studying the figures in isolation from one another, although Guercino's invention of a particular pose in a separate figure study often led him to reconsider his earlier general compositional schemes.

The Chicago drawing focuses on the figure of Christ in a pose strikingly similar to that eventually used in the painting. Note, however, the almost spectral alternative image of Christ's head (hanging straight down) portrayed in thinner pen lines. The choices represented here are not unlike those given for the Virgin in the Norfolk sheet: the upward glance is the more dramatic, open, externalized pose; the downward glance is somewhat more serene, closed, and internal. In the case of Christ, it is also the difference between two moments in the story, his suffering on the cross and his death.

1. Salerno, no. 105. New documents relating to the commission are published in Artioli-Monducci, pp. 93-96, and Documents XLIV-LVI, LVIII-LXI, LXIV-LXVI.

2. Inv. 9, cf. Emiliani, 1959, no. 69, repr.

3. Inv. H.3, cf. *Disegni*, no. 94, repr.

4. Inv. F.N. 120, formerly 22615, cf. *Disegni*, no. 95, repr.

5. *Disegni*, p. 102.

6. Bean, 1969, p. 430, pl. 36.

7. Cf. Scannelli, 1657, p. 361. See also *Dipinti*, p. 66; Stone, 1989, p. 312.

8. For these related drawings, see *Disegni*, nos. 92-93, 96-100; and M-T, nos. 30-33.

14
Seated Woman, Reading a Book, with Two Putti Holding Hourglasses (Allegory of *Memoria*)

Pen and iron gall ink
199 x 310 mm.
Foxed, stained; partially pasted to old mount
Inscribed in pencil on verso of mount in Platt's hand:
Rogers State[s?] as in Sir Joshuas coll.
PROVENANCE: Colnaghi (1859, from notation); Dan Fellows Platt (L. Suppl. 750a, lower right verso)
BIBLIOGRAPHY: Lynes, p. 90, no. 63; DeGrazia, 1969, no. 7, repr.; Varriano, 1974, no. 36; Gibbons, no. 265; M-T, under no. 162

The Art Museum, Princeton University
Bequest of Dan Fellows Platt, 48-722

Datable to c. 1624-1625, this sheet is the earlier of two studies for an allegory of *Memoria*. The second drawing, a pen-and-wash sketch in the Victoria and Albert Museum, London, which removes one putto and adds a figure of Time,[1] is recorded in a print reversing the composition by G.B. Pasqualini (fig. 14a)[2] dedicated to Duke Federico Savelli, military commander to Urban VIII.[3] In the London sheet, Guercino has given indications of an irregular field for his image, a horizontal oval intersected by a vertical rectangle, which is not taken over by the engraving. The putto flies beyond the border at the top of the drawing and the clouds at the lower right glide freely past a heavily inscribed portion of the oval. This subtle exercise in Baroque illusionism is a repetition in miniature of Guercino's brilliant manipulation of space in the quadratura framework of the Casino Ludovisi *Aurora* of 1621, particularly in the area of *Night*.[4]

Companion allegories of *INTELLECTVS* and *VOLVNTAS*—likewise treated with *di sotto in su* type foreshortening, engraved by Pasqualini,[5] and dedicated to Savelli—are also prepared in drawings with specially shaped fields. The sheets are preserved, respectively, at Windsor[6] and in the Albertina.[7]

Mahon and Turner speculate that the designs may have been preparatory for a lost or unexecuted ceiling decoration, possibly at the Casa Provenzale at Cento,[8] where Guercino had worked in c. 1614.[9]

1. Inv. no. Dyce 306 (232 x 282 mm.); Ward-Jackson, p. 57, no. 718, repr.; Bagni, 1988, no. 86, repr.

2. Bertelà, no. 834, repr.; Bagni, 1988, no. 85, repr.

3. M-T, p. 83, note that this establishes a *terminus post quem* for the engraving, since Urban was not elected pope until August 1623.

4. See Salerno, p. 163, color repr.

5. Respectively, Bagni, 1988, nos. 81 and 83, repr.

6. M-T, no. 162.

7. Bagni, no. 84. For other material related to the series, see M-T, no. 162.

8. For a drawing related to this project, see Suppl. no. 23, repr.

9. A pen-and-wash copy, 244 x 383 mm., of the exhibited sheet with significant changes (e.g., the hourglass held up by the putto at left no longer overlaps the throne) was sold at Sotheby's, London, on 20 April 1967, lot 46, repr. It is also reproduced in a sale catalogue entitled *Master Drawings* (no date, but probably 1967 or 1968) from the Charles E. Slatkin Galleries, New York, as pl. 8 (*Clio Muse of History*). The sheet bears the mark of Sir Joshua Reynolds (L. 2364) and was engraved (and noted as being in the Reynolds collection) by W.W. Ryland in 1763 (Charles Rogers, *A Collection of Prints, in Imitation of Drawings . . .* , London, 1778, II, p. 116, repr.). The drawing also bears the mark of Thomas Banks (L. Suppl. 416a), who probably owned the work prior to Reynolds. The sheet later came into the possession of Lord Overstone and C.L. Loyd (Wantage, Berkshire, Lockinge House), the latter being the seller of record in the Sotheby's catalogue. The error in Platt's inscription on the verso of the exhibited sketch, confusing his drawing and its provenance with the one reproduced in Rogers, is understandable, since Platt undoubtedly did not know of the Reynolds-Loyd copy from which Ryland states he made his reproduction.

14a

Pen and brown ink, brown wash, on brownish paper
198 x 302 mm.
Foxed; lined
Inscribed in ink on the verso of old mount, in an
unknown hand: *Daudet / Ce 18 fevrier 1788 / Ce dessin
provient de la vente de M. Chariot huissier Commissaire
priseur qui c'est* [s'est?] *faite vers la fin janvier de la dite
annee et qui m'a coute — 251.1.*[5]
PROVENANCE: Nogaret: sale, Paris, 2 June 1780, no. 68;
Chariot: sale, Paris, 28 January 1788, no. 87; Daudet; Dan
Fellows Platt (L. Suppl. 750a, purchased at Parsons,
London, 1923)
BIBLIOGRAPHY: Lynes, p. 95, no. 76; Bean, 1966, no. 36;
DeGrazia, 1969, no. 9; Roli, 1972, no. 40; Varriano, 1974,
no. 4; Gibbons, no. 273; Cazort-Johnston, no. 55

The Art Museum, Princeton University
Bequest of Dan Fellows Platt, 48-744

No painting of this subject from the period
following Guercino's return to Cento (in the
second half of 1623) has come to light. *The
Capture of Christ* in the Fitzwilliam Museum,
Cambridge of 1621,[1] the companion to the
Incredulity of St. Thomas discussed in cat. no.
10, is too early to be connected in any practical way with the turbulent drawing at Princeton, although it surely provided the point of
departure for Guercino's concept for the
work. As Mahon has suggested,[2] the style of
the sheet places it in the late 1620s. It may
belong to a moment just prior to that of Guercino's drawings for the *Assassination of Amnon,* a documented work of 1628.[3]

The existence of three other drawings of
comparable style depicting the *Arrest of
Christ* (two autograph and one a weak sketch
or copy at Windsor by a member of Guercino's School that may be based on a lost
original)[4] would seem to indicate that Guercino was preparing a painting of this subject.
Several compositional solutions are offered by
the exhibited work, the Windsor *bottega*
piece, a marvelous drawing in a vertical format in Rome, Gabinetto Nazionale delle
Stampe (fig. 15a),[5] and a less-violent sketch
with only three figures in a private collection
(fig. 15b).[6] Despite this variety, the physiognomic types and the costumes remain quite
consistent in all four works.

1. Salerno, no. 73.

2. See Bean, 1966, under no. 36.

3. See M-T, nos. 52-53, with references to other drawings.

4. For the School drawing, which is described but not illustrated, see M-T, no. 454. I thank Nicholas Turner for
providing me with a photocopy of this interesting work,
which is quite close to the ex-Harewood sheet mentioned
below, although it contains four figures.

5. F.C. 129578; 345 x 233 mm. See Marangoni, 1959, no.
11., repr.

6. Formerly in the Harewood collection. 222 x 267 mm.
Sold, Christie's, London, 6 July 1965, lot 116; and again 8
July 1975, lot 130; and yet again 9 December 1986, lot 47.
Both the ex-Harewood sheet and the Rome drawing are
mentioned in Cazort-Johnston, p. 94.

15a

15b

36

16
Saint Peter as Pope and Saint Jerome
verso: *Saint Jerome*

(Study for the *Assumption of the Virgin with SS. Peter and Jerome*,
Giroldo Chapel, Cathedral of Reggio Emilia, 1626)

Pen and black and brown ink, brown wash of three tones,
squared in black chalk (recto); pen and brown ink (verso)
199 x 251 mm.
Inscribed by Bernasconi (verso)
PROVENANCE: Giuseppe Vallardi (L. 1223, lower left
recto); Captain Carlo Prayer (L. 2044, lower right recto);
Collection of Juan and Felix Bernasconi; sale: Christie's,
London, 1 April 1987, lot 64
BIBLIOGRAPHY: Mario di Giampaolo, *Dal Disegno
all'opera compiuta*, exh. cat., Torigiano, Museo del Vino,
29 October - 12 November 1987, repr. (recto only) on p.
54, under cat. no. 18; Salerno, under no. 113

Private Collection

16a

Documents published by Artioli and Monducci in 1982 demonstrate that when Guercino returned to Reggio Emilia from Cento to deliver the Ghiara *Crucifixion* (see cat. nos. 12-13), he signed a contract—on 9 May 1625—to paint an altarpiece for the chapel of Giroldo Fiordibelli in the local Cathedral.[1] Both the subject and the placement of figures in the painting were carefully specified in the documents, and Guercino complied with the stipulations to the letter. The picture, *The Assumption of the Virgin with Saint Peter as Pope and Saint Jerome* (fig. 16a),[2] was completed in Cento and delivered in person by Guercino in May of 1626 as the artist made his way to Piacenza to carry out a large fresco project in the cupola of Piacenza Cathedral (see cat. nos. 19-21).

Besides the exhibited sheet, which is a detailed study for the lower half of the composition, two other drawings have been connected with the project: 1) a pen-and-wash study of the Madonna with an angel and putti (Lucas sale, Christie's, London, 9 Dec. 1949, the second drawing of lot 78),[3] now in an American private collection, and 2) a detailed pen-and-wash study (fig. 16b) for the head and torso of St. Jerome, shown in a pose similar to that used in the painting (260 x 170 mm.; Paris, Collection Alain Moatti).[4] The verso of the exhibited sheet looks more cursory and tentative than the Moatti drawing, which is quite finished and concerned with effects of light and shadow. However, the angle of the head in the former is much closer to the design used in the painting, and the position of the exposed left leg corresponds almost exactly.

The disposition of St. Jerome occupied Guercino in another double-sided, pen-and-ink drawing (fig. 16c), formerly on the London art market (Christie's, 6 July 1982, lot 40; 242 x 163 mm.; apparently two sheets glued back-to-back; prov.: Richard Cosway, London [L. 628, stamp lower right recto]). In this sheet, Guercino shows the saint kneeling in a position similar to that depicted on the recto of the exhibited drawing, but with the right hand on the knee rather than on the drapery near the chest and with the left hand touching the heart rather than pointing down. The drawing on the other side of this sheet can be discerned in the photograph of the recto: here St. Jerome is shown from the side and has his hands clasped in a praying position.

The solemn figure of St. Peter in the exhibited sheet would seem to have pleased Guercino, for he made only small adjustments to it. In the painting the saint's head is placed more frontally and his right hand performs a benediction.

Since this is not a historical scene but a devotional picture, Guercino was not compelled to have the saints interact. The narrative impulses that are so dear to Guercino are present all the same, however. Representation of St. Peter in the act of blessing the spectator and depiction of St. Jerome in the process of adoring the Virgin and writing a letter provided Guercino with the possibility of creating a more vital image.

1. See Artioli-Monducci, p. 99 f.

2. Salerno, no. 113.

3. See Salerno, under no. 113.

4. M. di Giampaolo, *op. cit.*, no. 18., repr. on cover. I would like to thank M. Moatti for allowing me to reproduce his drawing.

16: verso

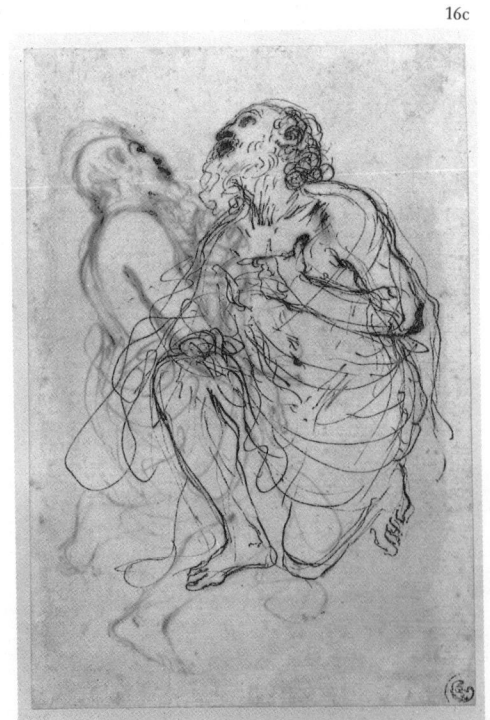

16b

16c

38

39

Christ Among the Doctors

(Studies for the painting by Antonio Bonfanti, Ferrara,
Chiesa di San Francesco, c. 1625-1627)

17 Christ Among the Doctors
Pen and brown ink, brown wash
269 x 427 mm.
Inscribed lower right recto in black ink: *112*
PROVENANCE: Baron D. Vivant-Denon (L. 779, lower
left recto); sale: A.N. Pérignon, Paris, 1-19 April 1826, lot
443; Baron de Malaussena, Indre (L. 1887, lower right
recto); Marie Marignane, Paris (L. 1848, lower left and
lower right recto); Hubert Marignane, Paris; unidentified
collector (mark, lower right recto); Jacques Petit-Horry,
Paris (mark, lower left recto)
BIBLIOGRAPHY: *Monuments des Arts,* Paris, 1829, II, pl.
211 (etching in reverse by Vivant-Denon); G.A. Caviggioli,
*Catalogue de l'exposition de dessins italiens du XVe au
XVIIIe siècle de la collection H. de Marignane,* Monte
Carlo, Palais des Congrès, May-June 1966, no. 81; Bean,
1967, p. 304, pl. 50; Riccòmini, 1969, p. 38, no. 21a;
Varriano, 1973, pp. 11-15, fig. 3; Gibbons, under no. 334;
Goldner, 1988, no. 16

{H}

The J. Paul Getty Museum, 84.GG.23

18 Christ Among the Doctors (?)
Pen and brown ink, brown wash
264 x 389 mm.
Extensive iron gall ink corrosion
PROVENANCE: P. Brandt
BIBLIOGRAPHY: W. Vitzthum, *A Selection of Italian
Drawings from North American Collections,* Norman
Mackenzie Art Gallery, Regina, Saskatchewan, and
Montreal Museum of Fine Arts, Quebec, 1970, no. 34; Roli,
1972, no. 39, repr.; Varriano, 1973, p. 15, n. 5 (as
unrelated to the project); Feinblatt, 1976, no. 94, repr.

Los Angeles County Museum of Art,
Los Angeles County Funds, 64.24

Since his earliest days in Cento, where he
founded a drawing academy in the Casa Fabri
in 1616,[1] Guercino was active as a teacher
and the director of a productive workshop.
He sometimes employed his students and associates on large projects, particularly when
the fee was below normal. This seems to
have been the case with the *St. Albert* altar,
for which Lorenzo Gennari contributed two
Franciscans based on designs supplied by
Guercino (see cat. no. 4). After returning
from Rome in 1623, Guercino reestablished
his Cento workshop, which quickly became
one of the busiest in Italy, placing ever
greater demands on the artist's time. The two
sheets exhibited here provide an occasion to
examine the kind of collaboration between
designer and executant that must have been
fairly frequent, though difficult for scholars to
substantiate, in the post-Roman period.

Documentation on the matter is scarce,[2]
but it seems certain that an associate of Guercino's named Antonio Bonfanti, called "il Tor-
ricella," was given a commission by Cardinal
Bonifacio Bevilacqua (perhaps on Guercino's
recommendation) to paint two large pictures
for the church of San Francesco at Ferrara, a
Christ Among the Doctors (fig. 17a)[3] and a *Presentation of Christ at the Temple*.[4] Since the
Cardinal died in 1627, it has been suggested
that the commission was probably completed,
or at least well-advanced, by that date.[5]

A group of sheets—all now in America—
sheds considerable light on the preparation
for one of the pair of paintings ordered by
Bevilacqua. A drawing at Princeton (fig.
17c),[6] first published by Riccòmini and identified by him as a preliminary sketch by
Bonfanti for the *Christ Among the Doctors,*
depends, as the author states, on a pen-and-
wash sheet by Guercino now in the J. Paul
Getty Museum (cat. no. 17; formerly Paris,
Jacques Petit-Horry).[7] In addition, Varriano
has noted an interesting double-sided sketch

(pen / pen and wash) of *Christ Among the
Doctors* in the Mount Holyoke College Art
Museum, South Hadley, Massachusetts (figs.
17b: recto and verso), which he has published in an article examining the project.[8] A
fourth sheet—a very dramatic but somewhat
damaged drawing by Guercino in the Los Angeles County Museum of Art (cat. no. 18)—
has been put forward by Denis Mahon as a
possible study for the Ferrara commission.[9]

The earliest in the sequence of the studies,
as Varriano has convincingly shown, is the
recto of the Mt. Holyoke sheet. Guercino
here conceives of a centralized composition,
with Christ's legs and torso shifted to the right
while his head is twisted toward the left as he
argues his case, punctuating it with an often-
used rhetorical gesture expressing the
enumeration of a point (the index finger of
one hand touching the thumb of the other indicates "item number 1"). The style of the
sheet may be compared with a study at Windsor (M-T, no. 48) for a lost painting of *David
and Abigail*, which is datable to c. 1625-
1627.[10] One could also very effectively jux-
tapose the recto at Mt. Holyoke with the
verso (*St. Jerome*) of the exhibited sheet (cat.
no. 16) discussed in the previous entry, which
is for a fully documented altarpiece of 1626.

The Mt. Holyoke verso is a different type
of drawing from the recto and must be understood as such.[11] It is a more detailed compositional sketch that fusses with architecture
and costumes, and consequently elicits from
Guercino a (slightly) different approach in
handling from the recto, where he was more
concerned with generating the primary figural
poses and contrasting attitudes than with
clothing and scenery. The composition is
now more frieze-like, with Christ initiating a
left-to-right axis by his placement at the far
left of the scene and his glance and gesture
directed toward the right.

The figures are smaller in the beautifully

17b: recto

17b: verso

17a

17c

17

18

43

preserved Getty drawing (cat. no. 17) and have an elegance and precision of movement they lack in the rougher, less-balanced composition depicted in the Mt. Holyoke verso. Guercino returns to the idea shown on the Mt. Holyoke recto of having Christ act as a pivot between the two groups of doctors, but maintains the idea explored on that sheet's verso of situating Christ on the left side. These motifs, and many other aspects of the Getty and Mt. Holyoke sheets, are explored in Bonfanti's drawing and in his painting, both of which reinstate the proud parents, Mary and Joseph, seen on the extreme right of the Mt. Holyoke verso (they are lacking in the Getty sheet). We should mention that the painting has a certain Veronesian—or at least Venetian—quality that comes about from Bonfanti's decision, already adumbrated in his sketch, to forego the complex architectural background and to open up the space to a landscape that echoes the contours of the figural design in the foreground. Though obviously quite dependent on Guercino for his ideas, Bonfanti was able to come up with a painting that contains something of his own artistic personality, which may have been formed in Venice or Verona, or, as Riccòmini has suggested, in Mantua in the wake of Domenico Fetti (who also worked in Venice).

The Los Angeles sketch exhibited here (cat. no. 18) can be reasonably integrated into this series of preparatory studies, even if—as is so often the case with Guercino—it is not followed in the painting. In two of the other studies (the Mt. Holyoke recto and the Getty drawing) there is a standing man moving to the left behind a seated figure (or figures) reading or holding a book. The Los Angeles study seems to take up the idea once again. This focused compositional sketch may have been made to give Bonfanti some assistance in characterizing the disgruntled Temple

44 fathers.[12]

1. See cat. no. 10.

2. See Riccòmini, 1969, p. 38. The primary document is a manuscript written at the beginning of the eighteenth century by Brisighella.

3. Riccòmini, 1969, no. 50, fig. 20.

4. Riccòmini, 1969, no. 49, fig. 19.

5. Riccòmini, 1969, p. 38.

6. Inv. 48-730, Bequest of Dan Fellows Platt. Pen, brown ink, brown wash on gray-brown paper. 313 x 424 mm. Prov.: Dan Fellows Platt (L. Suppl. 750a, lower left verso), bought in London in 1922. Bibl.: Lynes, p. 94, no. 75; Riccòmini, 1969, no. 52, fig. 21b; Varriano, 1973, p. 12, fig. 2; Gibbons, no. 334.

7. He cites Denis Mahon's opinion on the connection.

8. Inv. no. P.RIV.1.1954, Museum Purchase, Nancy Everett Dwight Fund, 1954. 261 x 394 mm. Prov.: Count Nils Barck (L. 1959, stamp on verso); Mr. Herbert Bier, London. Bibl.: Varriano, 1973, p. 14, figs. 4-5; Varriano, 1974, no. 6.

9. Mahon's communication was reported by Vitzthum, 1970, p. 44 (see Bibl.), on the occasion of a Canadian exhibition of the sheet. In the present writer's opinion, Varriano, 1973, p. 15, n. 5, has too hastily rejected Mahon's suggestion relating the drawing to the project (see below).

10. The assignment of 1625-1627 is based on a dated print by Pasqualini of *King David Giving Uriah a Letter* (1627), which is believed to represent a lost pendant to the *David and Abigail*. For the details of this complicated commission, which is understood only through copies and the Pasqualini print, see M-T, no. 48, and Salerno, nos. 116-117.

11. Varriano, who assigns the Mt. Holyoke recto to c. 1620 without providing comparative evidence, notes that the design on this side of the sheet has been badly cropped, especially along the top edge. He further points out that the verso fits easily within the boundaries of the sheet, and, thus, hypothesizes that it came after the reduction of the paper. Based on style, he dates the verso to c. 1625-1627. The amount of time elapsing between the two sides could have been a matter of minutes or months, but not years, since the studies are demonstrably of the same stylistic moment. I would maintain that the only serious pruning of the original sheet was done on the top edge and a little along the right side of the recto. On the verso, the right arm of Christ along the left margin could literally have been given more elbow room before the trim. It is quite possible that an inch or so could be missing from the top of the composition on this side, since in the Getty sheet (cat. no. 17), which is a recapitulation of this very composition, the height of the architectural space is nearly double that shown here. Thus, although I endorse Varriano's argument placing the verso after the recto in the sequence, I do not believe that the cropping occurred between the execution of the two studies; this was more likely to have taken place long afterward. The different appearance of the verso, observed by Varriano, can partially be explained by its technique and condition. It is a wash drawing, which ink corrosion has made to look flatter than it would have originally. It is not of a later date than the recto, but, as I explain, it does represent a different kind of study, which might make it appear to be later.

12. Bonfanti is known to have executed other works de-

signed by Guercino. See Riccòmini, 1969, pp. 37-39, and M-T, nos. 75-76, and 183 (where the two exhibited works and the Mt. Holyoke and Bonfanti studies are mentioned *en passant*).

Studies for the Fresco Decorations in the Cupola of Piacenza Cathedral (1626-1627)

19 The Prophet Hosea and an Angel
Red chalk, on buff paper
298 x 217 mm.
Very slight stain above the angel's hand; some damage along right margin
PROVENANCE: Unidentified collection (stamp: coat of arms in a circle, in black, lower right recto); Captain Carlo Prayer (L. 2044, lower left recto, in red); Aldega-Gordon, N.Y.
BIBLIOGRAPHY: Reproduced in D. Stephen Pepper, "Guercino's Drawings at Windsor Castle" (Review of M-T), *The Journal of Art* 2, no. 5 (February 1990), p. 29

Collection of Lisa Donneson and Henry Weisburg

20 The Rest on the Flight into Egypt
Pen and brown ink, brown wash, squared in black chalk, on antique laid paper
236 x 376 mm.
Inscribed at lower right in an old hand, in pen and brown ink: *5*
PROVENANCE: Thomas Dimsdale; Count Brownlow; Dan Fellows Platt; Mr. and Mrs. John Davis Hatch, Jr.
BIBLIOGRAPHY: *Disegni*, p. 110; Lurie, 1970, p. 97 f., repr. (as for an unidentified painting); Robinson, 1973, no. 12, repr.; Bagni, 1983, no. 51, repr.; M-T, pp. 23-41

{H,O}

National Gallery of Art, Washington, D.C., Ailsa Mellon Bruce Fund, 1979.14.1

21 The Presentation at the Temple
Pen and brown ink, brown wash, on antique laid paper
265 x 387 mm.
Inscribed in brown ink, lower right: *Rembrandt*
PROVENANCE: Dan Fellows Platt (L. Suppl. 750a)
BIBLIOGRAPHY: Vassar College Art Gallery, *Selections from the Permanent Collection*, Poughkeepsie, 1967, p. 19, repr.; *Disegni*, p. 111; Bagni, 1983, no. 47, repr.

Vassar College Art Gallery, Poughkeepsie, New York, Purchase, 41.4

The three works shown here as cat. nos. 19-21 belong to a large group of drawings made by Guercino in preparation for the fresco decoration of the cupola of the Cathedral of Piacenza. Guercino received this important commission immediately following the death of the Lombard painter Pierfrancesco Mazzucchelli, called il Morazzone (1573-1626), who had completed only two (*Isaiah and David*) of the eight compartments of the octagonal cupola when he died.[1] Guercino kept to Morazzone's scheme, which placed a single prophet with attendant putti or angels in each triangular *vela* of the cupola. In addition, Guercino painted decorations on the eight large lunettes below the cupola. On the four lunettes without windows he painted scenes from the Nativity of Christ (*The Annunciation to the Shepherds, The Adoration of the Shepherds, The Presentation at the Temple, and The Rest on the Flight into Egypt*). Alternating with the four Nativity scenes are four pairs of *Sibyls,* each pair divided by a central window. Below the lunettes, Guercino painted a narrow frieze of putti. According to documents published by Bagni, the entire work was completed between May of 1626 and November of 1627.

Prior to the Piacenza cupola, Guercino had not used true fresco technique in his large mural decorations (Casa Provenzale, Casa Pannini, the Casino Ludovisi, etc.).[2] Works like the *Aurora* (1621) were done *fresco secco,* allowing the artist to paint on top of dry plaster at his own speed and to make corrections as he saw fit. True, *buon fresco* painting, such as that employed at Piacenza, places the artist in a race against time as he attempts to paint on the fresh plaster before it dries. Because of the chemical bonding which takes place, true fresco is much more durable than *fresco secco.* However, it requires greater skill and considerable advance planning. The great height

of the Piacenza cupola, moreover, meant that Guercino had to foreshorten his figures drastically in order to make them appear to float overhead in a three-dimensional space. Consequently, the artist had to make numerous studies. He could not devise his scheme and calculate the foreshortened areas as he painted.

In response to the special conditions at Piacenza, Guercino developed a remarkable drawing technique in red chalk and created a sophisticated drapery style with a rich topography all its own. In dozens of special drapery studies for this project, which were kept together by Guercino's heirs and are now in the Fachsenfeld Collection (Stuttgart, Graphische Sammlung),[3] the folds are worked out in meticulous detail and the surfaces are caressed by a cool, refreshing light that predicts the brilliant colors painted on the cupola itself. Although none of these studies is to be found in an American collection, the draperies in the Morgan Library *Holy Family* (cat. no. 23) are very similar in style to those made at Piacenza. This stunning sheet—one of the most beautiful made by this master—must have been made soon after Guercino returned to Cento in late 1627.

The red-chalk drawing exhibited here as cat. no. 19 has been connected by Turner to the compartment representing the *Prophet Hosea and an Angel* (fig. 19a).[4] Although the painted Hosea faces in the opposite direction of the figure in the drawing and sits in a more frontal position, the shape of the head and beard of the latter is, indeed, close to that of the prophet in the fresco. What is particularly apparent in the drawing is Guercino's concern with foreshortening: the great height of the leg and knee and the somewhat awkward rendering of the arm are calculated to appear "correctly" when seen from below. In the painting, Guercino substituted a putto holding up a piece of parchment for the angel, who

19

46

20

20a

21a

19a

21

19b

19c

in the drawing seems to be taking dictation.

This is the only known drawing for the figure of Hosea, but other—later—sheets, which correspond more closely to the composition of the final work, must have been made. The drapery in the drawing is rather summary; it is not at all like the highly finished and faceted "jewels" of cloth that are represented in the red-chalk Fachsenfeld sheets, which Guercino followed quite faithfully in the fresco. While most of the red-chalk drawings for Piacenza seem to come late in the design process, after the execution of general compositional sketches in pen and ink, drawings like the *Hosea* demonstrate that red chalk was also used at relatively early stages.

It is worth noting here the existence in Naples of yet another red-chalk drawing, which has never been connected to the frescoes at Piacenza. This sheet, in the Museo di Capodimonte (fig. 19b),[5] is a study for the prophet *Jeremiah*,[6] for which Guercino made several drawings, each one showing the figure in a different position.[7] The connection with *Jeremiah* is based on specific details, such as the face and turban. More significant, however, is the fact that both drawing and painting share the *concetto* of the prophet reaching out with his left arm to hold up a banderole.[8] This motif appears only in the fresco of *Jeremiah* and, with variations, in three of the drawings made for it.[9]

This new assignment of the Naples sheet to the Piacenza project now sheds light on the correct identification of a red-chalk drawing of *Two Putti Seated on Clouds, Opening a Book* in Florence, Uffizi (fig. 19c).[10] Johnston[11] placed the sheet around the time of the drawing of *Four Putti* at Windsor,[12] which has been connected to the altarpiece of *St. Gregory the Great with SS. Ignatius Loyola and Francis Xavier*, 1625-1626, in the Mahon Collection.[13] However, the Uffizi drawing

must be one or two years later, since it is a reiteration of the most exacting kind of the poses and activities of the two putti indicated summarily in the lower right corner of the Naples drawing.

Cat. nos. 20 and 21 are preliminary studies for two of the four lunette paintings, the *Rest on the Flight into Egypt* (fig. 20a)[14] and the *Presentation at the Temple* (fig. 21a),[15] respectively, which Guercino painted below the prophets.[16] The lunette scenes are in a more lyrical vein than the Prophet cycle, as one can see very clearly in the *Rest on the Flight* fresco and in the beautiful sketch now in the National Gallery, Washington (cat. no. 20). In the fresco itself, however, Guercino chose to limit the discursiveness and charm of the scene described in the drawing, where Joseph's face is hidden from view as he fusses with unpacking. The Vassar sketch (cat. no. 21), which is a remarkably monumental and dramatic compositional study that Guercino followed closely in the fresco, was once attributed to Rembrandt, according to an inscription at the lower right edge of the sheet. The powerful wash and linear flourishes of the pen are exceptional. Nicholas Turner has suggested that a pen-and-ink drawing in a Swiss private collection (fig. 21b) might be an autograph "close-up" study for the head and upper torso of the high priest in the *Presentation*.[17] The rather aggressive hatching and hard contours used in this sheet are not unlike those found in a fine sketch in Rome, Gabinetto Nazionale delle Stampe, for the head and beard of *Jeremiah*.[18]

As our discussion in this section has shown, Guercino's design methods and the function of his drawings became more diverse and complex at Piacenza. Only a large fresco project can force a painter to rely so heavily on his drawings. We should also note that Guercino did not employ a cartoon

21b

to transfer his ideas onto the cupola but relied on his own judgment and a wide range of compositional sketches and finished chalk drawings.

1. The visual and archival documents relating to this project, some of which were previously discussed by Mahon, *Disegni*, and Thiem, 1979, have been gathered together by Bagni, 1983. See also Salerno, no. 114; and M-T, cat. nos. 38-45.

2. See *Disegni*, p. 111; Bagni, 1983, pp. 46-47.

3. See Thiem, 1979.

4. Bagni, 1983, no. 20; Salerno, no. 114-B. Turner, 1984, p. 642, has suggested that a damaged black-chalk drawing of *Two Putti* in the Los Angeles County Museum of Art (inv. 54.12.6), 168 x 162 mm. (see Suppl. no. 3, repr.) may be a preliminary study for the two putti holding a tablet in the *Hosea* fresco. Neither putto in the drawing corresponds in pose with his painted counterpart, and there is no sign of a tablet in the drawing. The head of a third putto (or an alternative for the putto on the left) is sketched in very lightly between the main figures, making the insertion of a tablet less probable. It is likely that this sheet is connected with the Piacenza project in a general way, but it is not necessarily for the *Hosea* compartment.

5. Inv. no. 234. 305 x 225 mm. Inscribed lower right recto in pen: *Genari*. Identified by the museum as *St. Matthew and the Angel*; cf. Rosanna Muzii, *I grandi disegni italiani nella collezione del Museo di Capodimonte a Napoli*, Milan: Silvana, 1987, fig. 46.

6. Bagni, 1983, no. 29; Salerno, no. 114-F.

7. Bagni, 1983, nos. 30-34.

8. We should point out a faint sketch of a small putto in the upper right, who would seem to be assisting in holding up the banderole. This idea was used in the final version, though the putto was placed lower down in the composition, adjacent to Jeremiah's knee.

9. Bagni, 1983, nos. 30-32.

10. Inv. 20190 F; 218 x 180 mm. See Marangoni, 1959, no. 44, repr.

11. Johnston, 1973, no. 84.

12. M-T, cat. no. 35.

13. Salerno, no. 112.

14. Bagni, 1983, no. 50; Salerno, no. 114-L.

15. Bagni, 1983, no. 46; Salerno, no. 114-I.

16. Besides the nine drawings connected with the *Rest on the Flight* and the three drawings for the *Presentation* mentioned by Bagni, 1983, nos. 51-59, 47-49, respectively, see now also M-T, p. 24.

17. 215 x 191 mm. See Turner, 1986, p. 842, fig. 70. For a detail study in red chalk for the head of St. Anne in the *Presentation* (Switzerland, Private Collection), see Turner, 1984, p. 642 and fig. 44. A retouched offset of this sheet exists at Windsor (inv. 3141; cf. M-T, no. 608).

18. Bagni, 1983, no. 31.

Pen and brown ink, brown wash
271 x 346 mm.
PROVENANCE: Jean-Denis Lempereur (L. 1740);
Lempereur sale: Paris, 24 May and following days, 1773,
no. 173; Sir James Knowles: his sale, Christie's, London,
27 May 1908, no. 145 or 146; purchased in London in 1908
BIBLIOGRAPHY: Bean, 1979, no. 241

{O,C}

The Metropolitan Museum of Art, New York
Rogers Fund, 1908, 08.227.30

This drawing has never been satisfactorily explained. Bean dated it on the basis of style to the 1620s, without going so far as to place it during or after Guercino's trip to Rome between 1621 and 1623. There can be no doubt that this sheet, which has such stable, frieze-like compositional motives and such relaxed treatment of line in the costumes and gestures, must date toward the end of the decade. I would like to propose here that this work was a rejected study for the Piacenza cupola, which was decorated

with frescoes by Guercino between May of 1626 and November of 1627 (see the previous entry).

Two of the four lunette scenes deal with the Shepherds: the *Annunciation to the Shepherds* and the *Adoration of the Shepherds*. It would have been quite understandable for there to have been a scene of the *Adoration of the Magi,* but ultimately the other two available spaces received frescoes of the *Presentation at the Temple* and the *Rest on the Flight into Egypt*.

One hypothetical explanation for the existence of the Metropolitan drawing is that Guercino, at an early stage in the planning of his great work, decided to include the *Adoration of the Magi* in the cycle, but sometime later, perhaps at his patrons' request, changed his mind. It is extremely valuable to compare the composition and handling in the Vassar drawing of the *Presentation* (cat. no. 21) with the New York sheet. The scale of the figures, the density of the grouping, and the use of wash are all quite similar. The composition of the fresco of the *Adoration of the Shepherds* (fig. 22a) is itself quite close to the type of organizational concepts followed by Guercino in the Metropolitan sketch, and a drawing in a Belgian private collection for the *Rest on the Flight into Egypt*,[1] which I know only from photographs, takes an identical approach to the treatment of the Madonna's face and veil.

An impressive drawing of the *Adoration of the Magi* (now lost) that once belonged to the eighteenth-century Venetian painter Giovanni Battista Tiepolo is recorded in a large reproductive etching by the Florentine printmaker Francesco Bartolozzi (fig. 22b),[2] which appeared in the volume of etchings in imitation of Guercino's drawings published in Rome by Piranesi in 1764.[3] This sheet, which might very well be reproduced without reversal of its composition,[4] repeats

22a

53

many of the facial types and compositional motives created in the New York sketch. It could be argued with some conviction that the lost drawing was another and more developed study for the same picture planned in the Metropolitan sheet, which, so far as we know, was never executed. Whether or not these drawings were originally intended for a fresco at Piacenza cannot be proven based on the evidence at hand. At the very least, though, our argument has resulted in placing these sheets rather comfortably in the *period* of the Piacenza project, around 1627.[5]

1. Bagni, 1983, no. 56 (badly cropped). See also R.-A. d'Hulst, *Dessins du XV au XVIIIème Siècle dans les collections privées de Belgique*, exh. cat., Société Générale de Banque et L'A.S.B.L. Les Amis du Dessin, 27 Oct.-21 Dec. 1983, no. 70, repr. Pen and brown wash. Provenance: Sir Thomas Lawrence (L. 2445); Earl Spencer (L. 1530); Hulin de Loo, his sale: Palais des Beaux-Arts, Brussels, 29 October 1947; Leo van Puyvelde.

2. Fogg Art Museum, Harvard University, Cambridge, Mass., inv. R11,685. Gift of Belinda L. Randall from the Collection of John Witt Randall. 320 x 451 mm. (plate). Reinforced in a few places with ink. Le Blanc, no. 22; Tuer, no. 2044; Calabi, no. 2121.

3. *Raccolta di alcuni disegni del Barberi* [sic] *da Cento detto Il Guercino, Incisi in rame, e presentati al singolar merito del Sig. Tommaso Jenkins Pittore, ed Accademico di S. Luca, in atto di rispetto, e d'amicizia dall'Architetto, e suo Coaccademico Gio. Battista Piranesi*, Rome, 1764. Like many of Guercino's drawings in Venetian collections, particularly those in the possession of Count Antonio Maria Zanetti, the Tiepolo sheet passed into the hands of Baron Dominique Vivant-Denon. It was published in a lithograph, in the same sense as the etching by Bartolozzi, by Dagneau in: Pierre-Amaury Pineux-Duval, *Monuments des Arts du dessin . . . recueillis par le Baron Vivant Denon*, Paris, 1829, II, pl. 205.

4. A sheet representing a *Scene of Sacrifice with Six Figures*, Toronto, Private Collection (see Suppl. no. 234, repr.), was etched in the same sense by Bartolozzi, and so were other Guercino drawings. See M-T, p. 167, fig. 32.

5. A sheet in the recognizable hand of the eighteenth-century faker of Guercino's figure drawings, who relied heavily on prints rather than the originals themselves for his forgeries, depicts only the Madonna and Child with the kneeling King from the left half of Bartolozzi's etching. Joseph has been eliminated from the upper left corner and the background has been changed. According to a photograph at the Witt Library, the drawing (roughly 292 x 204 mm.) was formerly in the collection of William Bates (see cat. no. 75), and was sold by Parsons, London as no. 39 (no date, but probably in the later 1920s), and sold again in 1933 as no. 12 by the R.E.A. Wilson Gallery, London. A good photograph shown to me by Mr. Jack Baer of Hazlitt, Gooden & Fox would indicate that the sheet was sold through them after 1933. See also cat. no. 66.

Ex Collectione Ioannis Baptistæ Tiepolo
Celebris Pictoris Veneti

22b

Colored chalks (black, red, blue, brown, ocher),
blue-gray wash
358 x 268 mm.
Watermark: Three hills surmounted by a tree within a
shield (cf. Heawood 3951)
Inscribed in pen and brown ink at upper left: *ZAMC*
PROVENANCE: Antonio Maria Zanetti; Baron Dominique
Vivant-Denon (L. 779, lower left recto); Robert Staynor
Holford (L. 2243, verso); Charles Fairfax Murray; J.
Pierpont Morgan
BIBLIOGRAPHY: Stampfle-Bean, 1967, no. 48 (with prev.
bibl.); *Disegni*, no. 188; Roli, 1972, no. 35; Varriano, 1974,
no. 17; Denison-Mules, 1981, no. 43

The Pierpont Morgan Library, New York, I,99

Arguably one of the finest old master drawings in America, this sheet is unique in Guercino's oeuvre. While the artist often used red chalk or black chalk, and in certain cases a combination of the two, no other drawings in this luminous, extraordinary pastel technique are known by him.

Highly finished drawings of this type often served as *presentation* drawings. In contrast to the majority of works in the first section of the exhibition, they were not used in the planning of a commission. Such sheets were works of art in their own right and were given away by the draftsman as gifts to friends, fellow artists, or patrons. Michelangelo's drawings for Tommaso de' Cavalieri and Vittoria Colonna are among the most celebrated examples of this practice by sixteenth-century artists, and they surely raised the status of drawing as an art form as a consequence of their association with that master.[1]

Even as late as the seventeenth century, however, it was not uncommon to find critics who regarded drawings as the "mechanical," laborious side of art and who would not think of esteeming a drawing as much as a painting. Guercino—his whole life a testament to the intellectual, aesthetic, and creative possibilities of the graphic medium—was one of the first painters of his age to make drawings as finished, independent pieces. It is really not surprising that he should have been one of the first artists in history to be as famous for his drawings as for his paintings.

The Morgan sheet anticipates the great chalk drawings of the Settecento by Piazzetta, Boucher, and Watteau, who lived in the age of great drawing connoisseurs like the Venetian Antonio Maria Zanetti, who owned the exhibited work. The learned and passionate French collector, P.-J. Mariette, praised it in his notes after viewing the etching in reverse of the composition by Bartolozzi (Calabi, no. 2111), published in Piranesi's *Raccolta* of 1764.[2] Mariette also records the great enthusiasm ("un grand éloge") for the original sheet expressed by an English collector, Henry Constantine Jennings, who must have seen it in Venice.[3]

The style of the drawing, which is especially noteworthy for the sublime organization of the draperies and the monumentality of the composition, depends on Guercino's recent experiences as a *frescante* at Piacenza. The sheet may, thus, be situated in the period immediately following the completion of the cupola frescoes in 1627. For further commentary, with particular reference to Guercino's new attitude towards drapery, see cat. nos. 19-21.

1. See Michael Hirst, *Michelangelo and his Drawings*, New Haven and London: Yale University Press, 1988, Chapter X, "The Making of Presents."

2. For the Piranesi publication, see the previous entry. A pen drawing by the eighteenth-century faker, in the same sense as the Bartolozzi print (in reverse of the Morgan sheet) and undoubtedly derived from it, was sold (as Guercino) by Klipstein & Kornfeld, Bern, 12 June 1974, no. 80, pl. 13 (376 x 278 mm.).

3. See *Disegni*, p. 177.

57

Studies for *The Martyrdom of Saints John and Paul, with the Madonna and Child Above* (Toulouse, Musée des Augustins, 1627-1632) and *The Visitation* (Rouen, Musée des Beaux-Arts, 1627-1632)

24 The Martyrdom of Saints John and Paul (recto and verso)

Pen and brown ink, brown wash
251 x 301 mm.
Slight foxing
PROVENANCE: Sir Charles Greville (L. 549, lower left verso); Earls of Warwick (L. 2600, lower right recto); unidentified collector's mark in pen and black ink at lower right recto: *J* (probably L. 1404); Charles Fairfax Murray; purchased by J. Pierpont Morgan in London, 1910
BIBLIOGRAPHY: Stampfle-Bean, 1967, no. 40; *Disegni*, no. 128; Varriano, 1974, no. 12; Artioli-Monducci, pl. 50 (recto); Salerno, under no. 139

The Pierpont Morgan Library, New York I, 101h

25 The Visitation

Pen and brown ink, brown wash
248 x 191 mm.
Repaired loss of upper right corner
PROVENANCE: Sir Charles Greville (L. 549, lower left verso); Earls of Warwick (L. 2600, lower right recto); Charles Fairfax Murray; purchased by J. Pierpont Morgan in London, 1910
BIBLIOGRAPHY: Stampfle-Bean, 1967, no. 39; *Disegni*, no. 133; Varriano, 1974, no. 10; Artioli-Monducci, pl. 48; Salerno, under no. 140; M-T, p. 39

The Pierpont Morgan Library, New York, I, 101f

26 The Visitation (recto and verso)

Pen and brown ink, light gray-brown wash (recto); pen and brown ink (verso)
200 x 223
Foxed, stained, vertical crease at left, tipped to old mount
PROVENANCE: E. Parsons & Sons, London; Dan Fellows Platt (L. Suppl. 750a, lower left verso), purchased from Parsons in 1920
BIBLIOGRAPHY: Lynes, p. 93, no. 71; Bean, 1966, no. 39; *Disegni*, no. 132; DeGrazia, 1969, no. 12; Varriano, 1974, no. 9; Gibbons, no. 274; Artioli-Monducci, pl. 47 (recto); Salerno, under no. 140; M-T, p. 39

The Art Museum, Princeton University
Bequest of Dan Fellows Platt, 48-745

Soon after supplying the Giroldo Chapel of the Cathedral of Reggio Emilia with an altarpiece representing the *Assumption of the Virgin with SS. Peter and Jerome* (see cat. no. 16 and fig. 16a), Guercino was apparently under consideration for the commission of the chapel's laterals. Documents published by Artioli and Monducci demonstrate that discussions about the project were underway already in the summer of 1626, while the master himself was at Piacenza, beginning the fresco decorations for the cupola of the Cathedral (see cat. nos. 19-21).[1] As Mahon and Turner explain in their exhaustive study of the Reggio works (M-T, nos. 62-68), it was not until about a year later (30 June 1627) that Guercino signed a contract to paint the *Visitation,* Rouen, Musée des Beaux-Arts (fig. 25a),[2] for the left (west) wall and the *Martyrdom of SS. John and Paul, with the Madonna and Child Above,* Toulouse, Musée des Augustins (fig. 24a),[3] for the right (east) wall of the chapel.[4] Due to his involvement with a number of other projects, including the 1627 altarpiece of the *Martyrdom of Saint James the Greater* for the church of SS. Pietro e Prospero at Reggio (untraced),[5] it seems that Guercino did not have time to begin work on the commission until long after the two-year deadline specified in the contract had passed. It is unlikely that Guercino's sketches for the project were executed much before 1630. The paintings themselves were not delivered until May or June 1632.[6]

Studies for the lower portion of the *Martyrdom of SS. John and Paul,* such as the powerful, double-sided sheet in the Morgan Library exhibited here (cat. no. 24), emphasize the violence of the subject, which deals with the beheading of two brothers, both Roman officers, under the rule of Julian the Apostate. Besides a beautifully preserved pen-and-wash study in the Mahon Collection[7] and a double-sided drawing in the Witt Col-

lection which is stylistically cognate to the exhibited work,[8] there exists a gruesome but spectacular pen-and-wash study in the Rijksmuseum, Amsterdam, which must rank among the most horrifying illustrations of decapitation in European art before Goya.[9]

By comparison with the drawings, the painting is quiet and restrained. Human suffering is alleviated by the divine presence of the Madonna and Child, who seem not the least bit troubled by the scene before them, so strong is their sense of redemption through sacrifice and faith.

It should not go unnoticed that Guercino's executioner as represented in the painting is derived from Correggio's proto-Baroque *Martyrdom of SS. Placidus and Flavia* of c. 1525 (now Parma, Gallery), one of the first lateral paintings of the Italian Renaissance. It was painted, along with its lateral partner depicting the *Deposition,* for the Del Bono Chapel in San Giovanni Evangelista at Parma, where Guercino is known to have travelled, between 13 and 18 May 1624,[10] just before undertaking to paint the *Crucifixion* for the church of the Madonna della Ghiara at Reggio (see cat. nos. 12-13).[11] The influence of Correggio's illusionistic ceiling frescoes (in San Giovanni Evangelista and the Cathedral of Parma) may be discerned in Guercino's Piacenza cupola decorations of 1626-1627.[12] The Cento master's recollection of the Del Bono Chapel is unusually specific (citations of this type are rare in Guercino's oeuvre) and is surely meant to be recognized. The quotation was no doubt triggered by the coincidence of Guercino's having to execute a lateral depicting a similar martyrial scene.[13]

Several preparatory drawings are known for the upper half of the *Martyrdom* commission, which depicts the Madonna and Child seated in the clouds. In addition to a remarkably "geometric" pen drawing with areas of parallel hatching at Windsor (M-T, no. 62), a

24a

25a

59

24: recto

24: verso

61

24b

24c

25b

25c

looser, less austere pen drawing (fig. 24b) in the collection of Kate de Rothschild and Yvonne Tan Bunzl, London (formerly K. Meissner, Zurich),[14] and a double-sided, red-chalk drapery study for the Madonna's gown in the Fachsenfeld Collection,[15] there is a drawing of the *Madonna and Child* in the Rijksmuseum, Amsterdam (fig. 24c), not mentioned in the Guercino literature, which should be associated with the project.[16] This exquisite sheet, which provides three ideas for the position of the Madonna's head, is done in exactly the same style as the Windsor drawing. The main, reinforced study of the Madonna shows her head inclined to the left side, looking down. Her face is shown in a three-quarter view, with her right cheek turned into the picture. The first alternative study renders her head in an upright and frontal position, tilted slightly to the right, and staring out toward the spectator—just as it appears in the painting. This alternative design outlines the eyes, nose, and mouth of the Madonna such that her physiognomy is virtually identical to that of the Madonna pictured in the Windsor sheet, who also addresses the viewer, but with her head inclined forty-five degrees to the left. The second alternative is no more than a schematic oval, which tips the Madonna's head toward the right, close to the Christ Child, who sits on his mother's left knee extending his left arm across her chest, as in the final version. The basic motif of this third configuration is similar to that featured in the ex-Meissner drawing, and it is studied again in an unpublished sheet with a Casa Gennari provenance owned by the Stanford University Museum of Art (Suppl. no. 12, repr.). Because of the position and gesture of the Christ Child, the Stanford drawing, which is very close in style to the Amsterdam and Windsor sheets, warrants serious consideration as an extreme "close-up" study for the figures in the upper half of the *Martyrdom*.[17]

Although the composition of the Windsor drawing is furthest from the final design, it is the only one of the connected drawings that shows the important motif employed in the altarpiece of the Madonna touching the foot of the Christ Child. Guercino must have analyzed his drawings—dissected, rotated, and reconstituted them in his mind—with virtuoso speed and precision. Once again, we must point out how rarely we find a compositional study, or even a "close-up," which matches the final idea used in a painting.

Numerous studies exist for the *Visitation,* which Guercino painted in a decidedly more lyrical mode as a counterpoint both to the violence in the *Martyrdom* on the opposite wall as well as to the hieratic, "official" quality of the *Assunta* on the altar (fig. 16a). The Rouen painting reiterates and redefines a new and quite serious shift in Guercino's artistic development that began to gain momentum after Piacenza (1627). This tendency towards a graceful and elegant style with clear colors and idealized poses emerges for the first time as a complete aesthetic in 1630 with the *Virgin Appearing to the Risen Christ* now in Cento Pinacoteca.[18] Guido Reni's seemingly effortless *grazia* and shimmering colors are utilized by Guercino to ennoble his subjects. In the *Visitation,* Guercino's elaborately constructed draperies, which zig and zag upwards, give the figures a certain lightness or musicality, which eloquently sets the tone for the joyous event in which the elderly St. Elizabeth takes the hand of the post-Annunciation Virgin and places it on her stomach so that Mary may feel the miracle of the child—St. John the Baptist—growing inside her.

The Morgan Library sheet (cat. no. 25) and the recto of the Princeton drawing (cat. no. 26) experiment with the direction in which the narrative will unfold and study the relationship between the two women and the placement of their husbands, Joseph and

Zacharias, around them. The idea of showing Mary dismounting from the donkey was also explored on the recto of a double-sided pen-and-wash sketch in the Fodor Collection in the Historisch Museum, Amsterdam.[19] A rapid pen-and-wash sketch formerly in the Johann Török collection and now in the Morgan Library (fig. 25b) is perhaps the closest of the general compositional sketches to the final painting.[20]

Four drawings at Windsor (M-T, nos. 64-65, 67-68), the verso of the Fodor sketch mentioned above, and the verso of the Princeton sheet exhibited here (cat. no. 26) investigate the Virgin and Elizabeth alone with varying degrees of precision with respect to their faces and costumes. The Princeton verso is heartening in its tenderness, but Guercino could not bring himself to paint it lifesize in a chapel decoration. Of the related drawings, only two at Windsor—the first in red chalk (M-T, no. 64) and the second in pen and wash (M-T, no. 68)—show the motif of the touching of the womb. The chalk drawing shows Elizabeth touching Mary, whereas the pen drawing shows a scene almost identical to that used in the final version.[21]

A pen drawing in the collection of Yvonne Tan Bunzl, London (fig. 25c) of a *Man and Woman, Half-Length,* in the same style, technique, and format as a study of the *Virgin and St. Elizabeth* at Windsor (M-T, no. 67), may, in fact, be a "close-up" study for the heads of Zacharias and Elizabeth. What is not clear is whether the sheet is compositional in nature or merely juxtaposes the two figures on the same sheet to save paper.[22]

1. Artioli-Monducci, Documents LXX and LXXI.

2. Salerno, no. 140. Cf. also Artioli-Monducci, pl. 37, color.

3. Salerno, no. 139.

4. The full text of the contract is given in Artioli-Mon-

26: recto

ducci, Document LXXIII. The price agreed on—400 ducats—is 200 ducats short of Guercino's normal price for works of this size and number of figures. For a discussion of this unusual breach of practice, see M-T, pp. 37-38.

5. See Salerno, no. 118. The work is recorded in a print by Pasqualini.

6. For problems of chronology relating to this commission, see M-T, under nos. 62-68.

7. *Disegni*, no. 129. See also Mahon-Ekserdjian, no. 23, ill. in color on cover.

8. *Disegni*, no. 130.

9. *Disegni*, no. 127. For other studies for the martyrdom, see *Disegni*, pp. 127-28; M-T, no. 63; Artioli-Monducci, pl. 60.

10. Artioli-Monducci, Document XLIX.

11. In a letter of 2 May 1624, written by Guercino from Cento to G.B. Silva, Counselor of the Comune of Reggio Emilia, the artist agrees to come to Reggio to negotiate the Ghiara contract and expresses his desire to visit nearby Parma as part of his trip "per mio gusto, non essendolo mai più stato . . ." (for my [Guercino's] own delight, not having been there again [for some time]). Artioli-Monducci, Document XLVI. See also Stone, 1989, p. 413, n. 22.

12. See Stone, 1989, p. 414. On Correggio's impact on later Italian art, see especially, DeGrazia, 1984.

13. Posner, 1968, p. 604, n. 11, has also noticed this connection but seems to suggest that the executioner's pose comes to Guercino via Niccolò dell'Abate's variation on Correggio's theme (in a painting of the *Martyrdom of SS. Peter and Paul* now in Dresden) rather than directly from Correggio himself. The documentation concerning Guercino's trip to Parma makes the derivation from the Del Bono lateral more likely, I think.

14. The drawing measures 192 x 135 mm. See "Calendar" section of *Burl. Mag.* 132, no. 1047 (June 1990), p. 455, fig. 80. Loss in lower right corner. The work was exhibited in *Old Master Drawings* from the Collection of Kurt Meissner, Stanford University Museum of Art, 1969-1970, as no. 33 (repr. on p. 52 of the catalogue). See also M-T, p. 38.

15. *Disegni*, no. 131.

16. Inv. A2125. Pen and brown ink, 161 x 205 mm. See L.C.J. Frerichs, *Keuze van Tekeningen Bewaard in het Rijksmuseum,* Rijksmuseum, Amsterdam, 1963, no. 53, with provenance, repr. (as c. 1625). See also Frerichs, 1973, p. 27, no. 74, who somewhat hesitantly relates this sheet, as well as the "close-up" study at Stanford (see below), to the *Martyrdom*. Neither drawing is mentioned by Salerno or M-T.

17. Since the Supplement went to press, my reservations concerning the identification of the Stanford sheet have somewhat diminished, and I would state now that its possible connection to the Giroldo Chapel commission is at least arguable, if not convincing. In light of the considerable similarities in style and technique between the Stanford drawing and the Amsterdam study (also apparently noted by Frerichs), the tentative tone of my argument in the Supplement should be modified.

18. Salerno, no. 127. For a full discussion of the classicizing characteristics of this work and its importance in Guercino's development, see Stone, 1989, pp. 424-33.

19. Ben Koevoets, *Oude Tekeningen in het bezit van de Gemeentemusea van Amsterdam waaronder de Collectie Fodor, I: Italië, 15e - 18e eeuw,* Amsterdam, 1976, no. 24, recto and verso, repr. See also *Disegni*, p. 130.

20. Inv. 1956.21, Gift of Hall Park McCullough. Pen and brown ink, gray-brown wash. 233 x 166 mm. Watermark around the Virgin's head (circle with crowned eagle?). Inscribed lower left recto in graphite: *33.* Inscribed upper right verso: *B* (in red chalk or pencil). See A. Stix and H. Leporini, *Die Handzeichnungen der Sammlung Török,* Vienna, 1927, no. 55, pl XI. Cf. also Stampfle-Bean, 1967, under no. 39; and *Disegni*, p. 130. The drawing was sold from the Török collection at the American Art Association, New York, 3-8 November 1928, no. 5 (as the *Banishment of Hagar* [sic]), pl. XI.

21. For other drawings related to the composition, including a fine red-chalk study for the costume of the Madonna (London, British Museum), see M-T, nos. 62-68. A photograph (no. 366442 [?]) in the archive of Thomas Agnew & Sons, London, of an untraced pen-and-ink drawing of the *Virgin and St. Elizabeth* in a composition similar to that displayed on the verso of the Fodor sheet, but showing the figures three-quarter length, may document a copy of a lost drawing (possibly by Guercino) relating to the Reggio *Visitation*.

22. 159 x 249 mm. The connection of the Tan Bunzl drawing to the *Visitation* was first made by Nicholas Turner (cf. *Old Master Drawings,* exh. cat. of drawings in the collection of Yvonne Tan Bunzl, London, 1987, cat. no. 34, repr.). It was previously with Christie's, London, sale: 12 Dec. 1985, lot 255.

26: verso

27

Saints John the Baptist and John the Evangelist
(Study for the *Madonna and Child with SS. Lucy, Francis, John the Evangelist and John the Baptist,* formerly Pesaro, S. Giovanni Battista, 1631-1632)

Red chalk
275 x 275 mm.
Inscribed lower right recto: *Guercino*
PROVENANCE: Casa Gennari; Henry Oppenheimer (cf. L. Suppl. 1351); Baron P. Hatvany; sale: Christie's, London, 27 Nov. 1973, lot 345; sale: Thomas Agnew & Sons Ltd., London, *Master Drawings and Prints,* 16 March - 15 April 1976, p. 13, no. 29, repr.
BIBLIOGRAPHY: Mahon, 1967, under no. 22; Bisogni, 1975, fig. 6; Mahon-Ekserdjian, under no. 24; Salerno, under no. 141; M-T, under nos. 624-625

Los Angeles County Museum of Art
Graphic Arts Council Fund, M.78.25

27a

Listed in the master's account book, the *Libro dei Conti,* are two payments—6 May 1631 and 18 July 1632—for an altarpiece commissioned by Giovanni Mosca and destined for the Franciscan church of S. Giovanni Battista at Pesaro. As Fabio Bisogni has recounted in his fully documented study of the project,[1] the altarpiece, which depicts the *Madonna and Child with SS. Lucy, Francis, John the Evangelist and John the Baptist,* was badly damaged by inept restorers in the eighteenth century, and was eventually cut in two and sold. A fragment of the picture representing *St. Lucy* (Private Collection)[2] is all that remains of what must have been a very fine painting.

The Los Angeles sheet (cat. no. 27), which studies two figures for the lower zone of the painting, contains passages of red-chalk drawing technique of unparalleled beauty and luminosity. The condition of the drawing is equally remarkable, especially when one considers that the sheet was "squeezed" for a counter-proof (or "offset") to record its composition, probably in the early eighteenth century by Guercino's heirs, the Gennari.[3] The offset and 233 others like it after Guercino drawings are preserved in the Queen's collection at the Royal Library at Windsor.[4] Virtually all of them have been coarsely retouched.

Cat. no. 27, which has an almost Raphaelesque quality that anticipates late Seicento classicism, can be related to several other studies for the project, including a quick pen sketch in the Mahon Collection depicting the seated St. John the Evangelist (on the left, looking straight up) and a standing or kneeling St. Francis (on the right) holding a crucifix and looking down.[5] A sensitive red-chalk study of the *Baptist* alone (fig. 27a) in the Nationalmuseum, Stockholm, which shows the saint gesturing with his right hand instead of his left (as in the exhibited sheet),

also clearly belongs to the group of designs for the dismembered painting.[6] A red-chalk drawing in a similar style representing the kneeling *St. Lucy* exists in the Teylers Museum at Haarlem.[7]

1. Bisogni, 1975, pp. 338 ff.

2. Salerno, no. 141.

3. M-T, no. 625. Another offset, after an untraced original, depicts a similar composition of the two saints, cf. M-T, no. 624.

4. For a complete account, see M-T, pp. 177-78, and nos. 598-836.

5. See Mahon, 1967, no. 22; Mahon-Ekserdjian, no. 24. See M-T, under no. 624 for two other studies related to the project, in Frankfurt and Haarlem.

6. Inv. 1113/1863. 278 x 104 mm. The connection is mentioned by M-T, under no. 624.

7. See *Disegni,* no. 135. The drawing was recently shown in New York (cf. Van Tuyll, 1989, no. 29, with bibl.).

Saint Francis Receiving the Stigmata

(Study for the altarpiece, Piacenza, Chiesa dei Cappuccini, 1632-1634)

Pen and brown ink, on oatmeal paper
274 x 184 mm.
Laid down
PROVENANCE: U. Price (L. 2048, script, upper left on verso of mount, in pen and brown ink); bought at his sale by R.S.B. (unidentified inscription, not in Lugt, upper left on verso of mount in red chalk); Dr. Wm. Ogle, London (stamp, not in Lugt, lower right on verso of mount, in purple); William F.E. Gurley, Chicago (stamp, not in Lugt, lower right recto in black); Leonora Hall Gurley Memorial Collection (L. Suppl. 1230b, verso, center on mount, in black)
BIBLIOGRAPHY: *Disegni*, no. 136; Neilson, 1972, no. 32; Joachim-McCullagh, no. 62, pl. 69; Joachim, Microfiche, 3D10; Salerno, under no. 147; M-T, under no. 72

{H,O}

The Art Institute of Chicago,
Leonora Hall Gurley Memorial Collection, 1922.492

28a

Of the three paintings representing *St. Francis Receiving the Stigmata* ordered from Guercino in 1632-1633, only two are extant, and both are quite damaged. The first of these to be completed is still in its original location in the church of the Sacre Stimmate at Ferrara (Salerno, no. 142) and was paid for in July and August of 1632 (*Libro dei Conti,* p. 310 f.). The second, which displays a very similar composition, but with the saint's arms raised overhead instead of pointing downward, resides in the Chiesa dei Cappuccini at Piacenza (fig. 28a).[1] This picture was ordered on 20 March 1632 and paid for two years later, on 23 March 1634 (*Libro dei Conti,* p. 312). A third rendering of this popular subject, completely untraced, was made for a church in San Giovanni in Persiceto, a small town near Cento (payments on 31 March and 2 October 1633; *Libro dei Conti,* p. 311).

Mahon has connected the exhibited work to the Piacenza commission. The Chicago sheet, whose rapid pen lines eloquently communicate the ecstasy of the saint, shows obvious affinities with the painting. But it is also possible that the San Giovanni commission enjoyed a similar treatment of the subject. Mahon and Turner have addressed this issue by dividing all the known drawings for St. Francis whose style can justifiably be related to the period of c. 1632-34 into three groups based on composition and the attitude of the saint. Those which deviate most from the two known paintings and the drawings that evidently match them (like the Chicago work) are considered potential studies for the lost *St. Francis,* whose composition is not known. The authors identify a pen-and-wash sheet in the Witt Collection (inv. 1369) as a possible design for the third picture.[2]

This process-of-elimination methodology, which in most cases is very useful, is less so here. One must immediately confront a problem like the pen-and-wash drawing in the Mahon Collection, London,[3] which depicts two separate studies of St. Francis side by side, the first showing him approximately as in the Chicago drawing and Piacenza painting with his arms up, and the second representing him falling to his knees with his arms spread apart at waist level, as in the Ferrara painting. Which painting is being designed here? Perhaps both are.

If the Piacenza painting was not well advanced when the Ferrarese made their request for a similar work, Guercino may have experimented with the designs of the two pictures simultaneously. An artist as busy as Guercino did not jettison ideas that went unused on a particular commission; he saved them for future projects.[4] The San Giovanni *St. Francis* may not have been "designed" as such. It may have originated as a rough, unexecuted sketch for Piacenza or Ferrara. The artist could very well have made fresh drawings for the third project, but we can not verify this based on the available evidence.

It should not go unmentioned that Guercino's Chicago *St. Francis* shows two alternative positions for the saint's head. The thumb of the left hand is also reconsidered. This sheet is among the most successful of Guercino's quick sketches of this period. For its intensity of feeling and velocity of movement, it should be compared to the Seattle *Ecstasy of St. Teresa* (cat. no. 31).

1. Salerno, no. 147.

2. A pen-and-wash drawing at Windsor (M-T, no. 72) has been related to the Ferrara picture. Another pen-and-wash sketch, in the Louvre (inv. 6881), which was recently exhibited in Paris, also appears to be for the Ferrara *Francis* (see Loire, 1990, no. 41, repr.).

3. Mahon, 1967, no. 23; Mahon-Ekserdjian, no. 25.

4. For example, the binding motif rejected for the *Samson* of 1619 and cleverly inserted in the *Lazarus;* cf. cat. no. 7.

71

Pen and brown ink
200 x 265 mm.
PROVENANCE: Thomas Banks (L. Suppl. 416a); Mathias Komor, New York; Mrs. Tiffany Blake
BIBLIOGRAPHY: Unpublished. Mentioned in Salerno, under no. 261; M-T, under no. 657

Honolulu Academy of Arts, 13.427
Gift of Mrs. Tiffany Blake, 1954

A favorite among Baroque artists, the sexually-charged story shown in the exhibited sheet from Honolulu (cat. no. 29) derives from Genesis 39:7-20. As one scholar has described the passage:

> Potiphar, captain of Pharaoh's guard, bought Joseph, son of Jacob [see cat. no. 8], from the Ishmaelites and made him steward of his household. Potiphar's wife "cast her eyes over him and said, 'Come and lie with me.'" He refused her though she continued to press him. One day when they were alone together she clutched his robes, pleading with him to make love to her. At this, Joseph fled so precipitately that he left his cloak in her hands. When Potiphar came home she avenged her humiliation by accusing Joseph of trying to violate her, using the cloak as evidence. Joseph was promptly thrown into prison.[1]

The style of the Honolulu drawing is consistent with that employed in the many studies for the Giroldo Chapel laterals, which were executed in c. 1630-1631 (see cat. nos. 24-26 and Suppl. no. 12). The line-and-dot technique used in the Wife's face and the strong, open pen lines of Joseph's costume correspond closely to a pen study at Windsor for the *Visitation* (M-T, no. 65). A drawing in the Mahon Collection of *St. Elizabeth, Queen of Hungary,* which is a study for an altarpiece commissioned in 1630 that is now in the Potocki Chapel in Cracow Cathedral (Salerno, no. 129), also helps situate the Honolulu sheet in Guercino's chronology.[2]

A coarsely retouched red-chalk offset at Windsor (M-T, no. 657, not repr.) depicting two half-length figures seems to reflect another design for the same project studied in the exhibited work.[3] I shall describe the Windsor sheet in reverse in order to convey some idea of what the structure of the original would have looked like.[4] Potiphar's Wife is shown on the right side of the horizontal composition lunging toward Joseph, who is situated on the left. She wears the same low-cut blouse as in the exhibited drawing, but her right arm is placed somewhat differently: she reaches straight across (not on a diagonal) to the fleeing Joseph, who in this version looks back toward her with fear in his face (rather than modesty or chastity) and raises his left arm and elbow well above his shoulders.

Thomas Willette has brought to our attention a photograph of a very Guercinesque painting in a private collection representing *Joseph and Potiphar's Wife* (fig. 29a).[5] The picture, which was illustrated in a catalogue of an antiquarian exhibition held at Florence in 1969,[6] has been convincingly related by Willette to the drawing in Honolulu.[7] The only major changes in the final version are: 1) the new placement for the Wife's right arm and hand, which now gestures toward the upper left corner instead of grasping Joseph's right forearm in the lower portion of the picture, and 2) the more upright position of the Wife, who instead of lewdly reclining and exposing herself voluptuously on the bed as she seduces Joseph, now seems more dignified and less erotic. The tug-of-war over Joseph's garment is more symbolic than actual in the painted representation.

While the ex-Florence painting cannot be by the master himself, it may represent a copy or variant executed in Guercino's workshop after a lost original that was based on the Honolulu drawing and the design shown in the offset. It is also possible that there was no "original," and that Guercino gave his drawings to one of his collaborators for independent development and execution. We have documented this type of procedure in the *Christ Among the Doctors* commission of c. 1625-1627, which was designed by Guercino and executed by Antonio Bonfanti (see cat. nos. 17-18).

Nothing in the style of the ex-Florence

73

29a

29b

canvas, which shares ideas developed in two drawings datable to c. 1630-1631, argues against it too being assigned to the early 1630s. The Honolulu sheet and the composition reflected in the Windsor offset are very likely connected to a painting project of around this time—perhaps even the ex-Florence painting itself—and cannot, contrary to what has been recently suggested,[8] be preparatory for the *Joseph and Potiphar's Wife* in the National Gallery of Art, Washington, D.C. (fig. 29b),[9] one of a pair of paintings ordered by a patron from Reggio Emilia in 1649. In the Washington *Joseph,* Guercino takes the opportunity to depict a female nude and supplies Joseph with an aesthetically "correct" response to the seduction. The total effect is quite distinct from the more descriptive treatment he gave the same characters in the Honolulu drawing in c. 1630-1631.

The pendant to the 1649 *Joseph,* a picture of *Amnon and Tamar* also in the National Gallery (fig. 29c),[10] provides the basis for sorting out a great deal of confusion about a painting with two half-length figures in the Galleria Estense at Modena, whose identity is unsettled. As I will demonstrate momentarily, the proper identification of the subject matter of the Modena picture has some bearing on the historical status of the Honolulu drawing, the Windsor offset, and the ex-Florence painting.

In the highly classicizing work now in the National Gallery (fig. 29c), Guercino represents, as Malvasia writes, "Amnone, quando discaccia la violata Tamar" [Amnon, who expels the raped Tamar].[11] The biblical story is culled from the second book of Samuel, chapters 13-19, in which David's son Absalom had a sister named Tamar, who was raped by her half-brother Amnon, another son of David.

> Then [after raping his half-sister, supposedly because he loved her] Amnon hated her exceedingly: so that the hatred wherewith he hated her was greater than the love wherewith he had loved her. And Amnon said unto her, Arise, be gone.
>
> And she said unto him, There is no cause: this evil in sending me away is greater than

the other that thou didst unto me. But he would not hearken unto her.

> Then he called his servant that ministered unto him, and said, Put now this woman out from me, and bolt the door after her.
>
> *And she had a garment of divers colours upon her:* for with such robes were the king's daughters that were virgins apparelled. Then his servant brought her out, and bolted the door after her.[12]

In Guercino's 1649 *Amnon and Tamar,* which to our eyes may seem to lack the theatrics built into the passage itself, Amnon is shown in sharp, austere profile and stands aggressively, his elbow aimed toward his victim and his fist clenched .in anger. Tamar's departure towards the right side of the canvas is interrupted by a parting glance (perhaps expressing, as stated in the text, her desire to remain) and an admonishment of Amnon, at whom she points a blaming finger. Her clothes are of "divers colours," ironically alluding to her loss of virginity. (Notice that the immoral Wife of Potiphar wears no clothes and does not maintain the classic *pudica* gesture covering her breasts as does her

74

29c

29d

tragic counterpart, Tamar.) In a beautiful red-chalk study for the *Amnon and Tamar* recently acquired by the National Gallery (Suppl. 166, repr.), Guercino shows the figures in reverse and treats several elements differently. The most important of these is the addition of a long expanse of Tamar's drapery, which is pinned down quite firmly by Amnon with his left hand. Nothing could better express the love-hate duality in Amnon's confused mind, which the biblical text dwells on. He seems to cast her out and reel her in simultaneously. Guercino understandably rejected this second "drapery-pulling" idea, since—visually—the repetition of the motif rhymed too obviously with the *Joseph and Potiphar's Wife,* and there was always the possibility, however remote, that ambiguity might arise as to who was pulling whom.

The 1649 commission is instructive since it establishes Guercino's basic understanding of these scenes of sin, chastity, and hate. Having reviewed the pictures and texts, I would now like to examine the painting at

Modena (fig. 29d),[13] whose subject, as previously mentioned, has proven difficult to decipher.

With the advantage of hindsight provided by Guercino's 1649 pendants, one is forced to come to the conclusion that the Modena painting represents the hateful Amnon in the act of ungraciously escorting his half-sister, clad to the hilt in "divers colours," to the door, the direction of which he has rather blatantly indicated with his right hand. It is difficult to tell, but Amnon (remember the Washington drawing!) may be holding in his left hand a piece of Tamar's clothing. The strict profile of Amnon's head and the position of his outflung elbow, her movement out of the picture and glance backward—all foreshadow the motives, albeit prettified for more delicate, classical tastes, in the National Gallery's *Amnon and Tamar.* Tamar's hands in the Modena painting, by contrast, seem to call for hesitation and reconsideration ("There is no cause . . .") rather than reproof, but she appears to be on her way out, all the same.

Based on two reliable documents, Denis

Mahon has recently identified the Modena picture as a *Joseph and Potiphar's Wife.*[14] Under the year 1631, Malvasia cites a Guercino commission as follows: "Fece un Gioseffo sforzato dalla moglie di Putifarre al Sig. Gioseffo Fallia Piacentino, & questo si trova nella Galleria del Serenissimo di Modena" [he made a Joseph, who is forced by Potiphar's Wife . . ., which is now in the Gallery of the Duke of Modena].[15] In Guercino's account book, under 25 August 1631, we find a confirmation of the same: "Dal Ser.mo Sig Duca di Modena si è ricevuto per il quadro di Giuseppe e la moglie di Putifare due mezze figure—scudi 130."[16] These are the only references in Malvasia and the *Libro dei Conti* to a painting of this type destined for the Duke of Modena during this time period that are relevant to the debate. The documents seem especially promising, given that there is currently in the Galleria Estense only one picture by Guercino (fig. 29d) that could conceivably be tied to them.

No one can contest the evidence supplied in the two documents—Guercino certainly did make a *Joseph* for the Duke in 1631—but do they apply to the painting now in the Modena Gallery? Beginning in the late seventeenth century, the collection inventories list an "Ammone e Tamar" in the Camera dei Sogni at Sassuolo (the Duke of Modena's suburban palace).[17] The title is repeated by Niccolò Panelli in his unpublished *Descrizione* of 1722.[18] Only Baruffaldi, at the beginning of the eighteenth century, makes a reference to the painting (the same painting?) as a "Joseph and Potiphar's Wife" ("un Gioseffo tentato dalla moglie di Putifar, in atto di chieder soccorso a chi lo rimira" [a painting of Joseph, tempted by Potiphar's Wife, in the act of requesting relief from her, who casts her eyes on him]).[19]

How can Malvasia's and Baruffaldi's descriptions, which clearly deal with a traditional representation of the *Joseph* theme, apply to the picture in the Galleria Estense, which equally clearly belongs to the *Amnon and Tamar* tradition as carried out some years later in the National Gallery painting and drawing?

Now that the Honolulu drawing and the lost sheet recorded in the Windsor offset have been reassigned on the basis of style to 1630-1631 (not 1649), and, consequently, now that the ex-Florence painting, which derives its composition directly or indirectly from them, has been brought to light and properly situated in the same general time period, there exists an alternative explanation for what has appeared to be a contradiction in the documents. It could be hypothesized (but by no means stated as a fact) that the Honolulu drawing, the lost drawing recorded by the Windsor offset, and the ex-Florence painting (fig. 29a) might reflect the general composition of the documented but untraced picture of *Joseph and Potiphar's Wife,* made for the Duke of Modena in the second half of 1631 ("un Gioseffo sforzato," as Malvasia called it).

76

At some point the picture probably disappeared, was sold, or was given away as a gift; though Baruffaldi—if he is referring to the lost picture—might actually have seen it, either in the original or in a deceptively good copy made as a substitute that he mistook for an original.[20]

The fact that Guercino's account book does not begin until 4 January 1629 might provide an explanation for the lack of any references in it to an *Amnon and Tamar* for Modena. If the canvas presently at Modena (fig. 29d) were to have been made, say, in late 1628 (I believe it could be this early), then the picture would, of course, fail to appear in the *Libro dei Conti*. Malvasia, who does not list all of Guercino's works, may not have been familiar with the picture or may simply have declined to make mention of it. The style of the painting could, in fact, be described as developing an idea explored some four years earlier (compare the costumes) in the *Semiramis* of 1624 in the Museum of Fine Arts, Boston.[21]

The Honolulu drawing and the related ex-Florence picture have led to some important discoveries and have provided a new context in which to understand Guercino's spirited interpretations of these two fundamental biblical stories. Perhaps further archival research in Modena will yield a confirmation of what has been hypothesized here.[22]

1. James Hall, *Dictionary of Subjects and Symbols in Art,* rev. ed., New York: Harper & Row, 1979, p. 176.

2. See Mahon, 1967, no. 18; and Mahon-Ekserdjian, no. 20.

3. I thank Thomas Willette for sharing with me his photocopy of the Windsor sheet. On the history of the offsets at Windsor, see cat. no. 27. M-T, under no. 657, have also related the design shown in the offset to the drawing in Honolulu, but believe both to be of c. 1649. See below.

4. The original sheet, which may have been by the master himself, is untraced.

5. I would like to thank Thomas Willette for his generosity in sharing his discovery with me and allowing me to publish it in this context.

6. *Sesta Biennale mostra mercato internazionale dell'antiquariato,* Florence, 1969, repr. on p. 423. The seller is listed as an art dealer named Vittorio Frascione. The picture and catalogue are cited in A. Pigler, *Barockthemen,* Budapest, rev. ed., 1974, I, p. 82. The dimensions and medium are given as 121 x 161 cm., oil on canvas.

7. Oral communication.

8. See Salerno, no. 261-262, and M-T, no. 657.

9. Inv. 1986.17.2, Patrons' Permanent Fund. 1.243 x 1.587 m. Salerno, no. 261. For details on the commission, see Suppl. no. 166.

10. Inv. 1986.17.1, Patrons' Permanent Fund. 1.239 x 1.587 m. Salerno, no. 262. For details on the commission, see Suppl. no. 166.

11. Malvasia, II, p. 267.

12. II Samuel 13: 15-18.

13. Salerno, no. 133.

14. See Salerno, under no. 133.

15. Malvasia, II, p. 262.

16. *Libro dei Conti,* p. 309.

17. Inventory of 1692-1694, published by M. Pirondini, *Ducale Palazzo di Sassuolo,* Modena, 1982, p. 94. See also Southorn, 1988, pp. 146-47.

18. See Salerno, under no. 133.

19. Baruffaldi, II, p. 453. As cited in Salerno, under no. 133.

20. If he is mistakenly describing as a *Joseph and Potiphar's Wife* the picture currently at Modena (fig. 29d), then there is no eyewitness documentation for there having been an actual *Joseph and Potiphar's Wife* by Guercino in the collection—just Malvasia's note and Guercino's record in the account book. I do not see how an intelligent letterato like Baruffaldi could describe the *Amnon and Tamar* now at Modena as "un Gioseffo *tentato* dalla moglie." There is no seduction going on in this picture. Until proven otherwise, I see no reason not to maintain that all the documents mean what they say. There may be no real contradictions in the palace records and the other sources; there may simply have been two different pictures which were never described together in the same inventory or document. This circumstance has given rise to the conclusion that in each case the *same* picture—by different titles—is being mentioned.

21. Salerno, no. 102. For a related drawing at Princeton, see Suppl. no. 53.

22. Van Tuyll, 1989, p. 61, no. 28, repr., has suggested that a pen drawing in the Teylers Museum, Haarlem (H. 79) might be related to the *Amnon and Tamar* (his identification of the subject) in the Galleria Estense at Modena. The drawing, dated by Van Tuyll to c. 1631, has every appearance of being a *primo pensiero* for the Modena project. Indeed, the gestures and costumes in the sketch are analogous to those in the painting, though they are less detailed and do not supply additional clues for resolving the iconography of the undocumented canvas (though the sketch certainly reinforces one aspect: Amnon's intense anger). I would broaden Van Tuyll's dating of the sheet (which he links to Denis Mahon's assignment of the picture to c. 1631) to c. 1625-30, based on its demonstrable affinities with a pen drawing at Windsor of *Abigail and Two Attendants* of 1625-1627 (M-T, no. 48).

30

An Angel Sheathing the Flaming Sword, with
Saints Roch and Sebastian in a Landscape
(Study for the Nonantola altarpiece, 1632-1634)

Pen and brown ink, small areas of brown wash, on laid paper
218 x 152 mm.
Loss in lower left corner, made up
Inscribed lower left corner in graphite: *8*; inscription by James Byam Shaw on back of mount noting a copy of this drawing in the collection of Captain G.F. Weld-Blundell at Ince Blundell Hall, Lancashire [now in the collection of Col. Joseph Weld, Lulworth Manor, Dorset]
PROVENANCE: Casa Gennari; Francesco Forni; Hon. Edward Bouverie, M.P. (d. 1810); by descent to his nephew, Mr. Hervey; the Earls of Gainsborough; Gainsborough sale: Christie's, London, 27 July 1922, probably from lot 81 (68 drawings); Sir Robert Witt (inv. no. 1340; photo, Witt Library); Colnaghi, London; Private Collection, New York; purchased in 1988
BIBLIOGRAPHY: Unpublished, but noted in M-T, under nos. 75-76

On extended loan as a promised gift from
Mr. John D. Reilly,
The Snite Museum of Art, University of Notre Dame,
L88.60.1

30a

This important drawing—one of many sheets originally belonging to the Gennari (Guercino's heirs)[1] that were purchased in the eighteenth century by Edward Bouverie—has recently been connected to an altarpiece completed by Guercino in 1634.[2] Payments received and noted in Guercino's *Libro dei Conti* on 27 January 1632 and 11 August 1634 refer to a picture of the *Madonna and Child with SS. Roch and Sebastian* for the town of Nonantola.[3] From other documents, we learn that the painting was set up in an oratory built at Nonantola in 1630 in hopes of protecting the city against further destruction by the plague. (There were terrible outbreaks all over North Italy around this time.)

Before the first payment was actually made, Guercino must have had an understanding with his patrons that the upper section of the picture should depict the angel sheathing a flaming sword—a popular representation of the termination of pestilence—since both the exhibited sheet and a more developed pen-and-wash compositional study in a private collection[4] show this figure instead of the Madonna, who is specified in the initial payment.

The altarpiece is lost, but a feeble copy (fig. 30a)[5] was put up in its place when the original was sold at Bologna in 1796. The substitute altarpiece, which was apparently removed from the original site in 1963 when the oratory was closed, has been traced by Dr. Fausto Gozzi of Cento, who located it in the church of San Michele at Nonantola. If the copy is an accurate reflection of Guercino's painting (the inclusion of the head of St. Francis on the right is surely the invention of the copyist), the final design is reversed from that explored in the known compositional sketches. Two further pen drawings, both at Windsor, re-examine the pose and expression of St. Sebastian in three separate studies.[6] Each shows him facing towards the

right, and, therefore, situates him on the left side of the composition, just as he is placed in the painting, but in reverse of his position in the two general studies. The Windsor drawings logically came after Guercino was forced to create a new design that would properly integrate the Madonna and Child into the scene.

For an account of the copy of the exhibited sheet in the Weld Collection, Lulworth Manor, Dorset, and its possible authorship by Sir Joshua Reynolds, see the Introduction.

1. On this distinguished provenance, with full documentation, see above all Mahon, "Casa Gennari," 1968. Cf. also the Introduction to M-T.

2. M-T, under nos. 75-76 (as formerly in the collection of Sir Robert Witt, whereabouts unknown). The following is in part a summary of their long and informative account of the commission and related studies. I thank Mr. Stephen Spiro, Chief Curator of the Snite Museum, and Mary Frisk, Assistant Curator, for bringing the exhibited sheet to my attention.

3. The first payment does not mention that there should be a Christ Child included in the painting.

4. M-T, p. 45, fig. 15.

5. Salerno, no. 148. A painting of *St. Sebastian* in the Museo de Arte de Ponce, Puerto Rico, published by Salerno (no. 357) as a possible, although unexamined, original of Guercino's late period, takes up various elements of Guercino's Sebastian in the Nonantola altar. This observation should not lead to the conclusion, however, that the Ponce picture is a product of the *bottega*, for Guercino often returned to earlier designs for inspiration. An undated etching of *St. Sebastian* (240 x 170 mm.; Rome, Gab. delle Stampe, F.C. 30947) by the too-little-known Neapolitan miniaturist, Teresa del Pò (1646-1713) has been published by Simonetta Prosperi Valenti Rodinò (*Incisori napoletani del '600*, exh. cat., Villa Farnesina, 19 March - 24 May 1981, Rome: Multigrafica, 1981, p. 194, no. 192, repr.), who remarks that the image is Bolognese in character. The etching, which carries only the inscription of the etcher herself (*Teresa del Pò Accad.ca Romana scul.*), who joined the Academy of St. Luke in Rome in 1678, is a very faithful reproduction, in reverse, of the composition of the Ponce *Sebastian*.

6. M-T, nos. 75-76.

31

The Ecstasy of Saint Teresa

(Study for *Christ Appearing to Saint Teresa*, Aix-en-Provence, Musée Granet, 1634)

Pen and brown ink, brown wash, on laid paper
244 x 235 mm.
Small loss upper right corner (made up)
WATERMARK: Circle, 50 mm. in diameter (located in the area of Teresa's neck), with two rows of scallops or waves and below it another object (illegible)
PROVENANCE: Purchased by Lee from Schaeffer Galleries, N.Y., 2 May 1951
BIBLIOGRAPHY: Mandowsky, 1980, p. 19, no. 17, repr.; (as attributed to Guercino, but with comment that experts assign the sheet to "Venetian, 18th century")

Seattle Art Museum
Gift of Dr. and Mrs. Sherman E. Lee, 51.115

31a

This extremely dynamic and powerful drawing is completely unknown in the Guercino literature. It is a great pleasure to be able to present this small masterpiece here, for the first time in its historical and artistic context.

Guercino's Account Book records two payments in 1634 from an agent acting on behalf of Bartolomeo Lumaga (Barthélémy Lumague)—an Italian living in Lyons—for a painting of Saint Teresa.[1] According to Malvasia, the picture was ordered for the Church of the Discalced Carmelites in Lyons and was to depict Christ showing St. Teresa the glory of Paradise.[2]

As one can see in a seventeenth-century engraving by Gilles Rousselet (fig. 31a), which reproduces the uncleaned and possibly damaged altarpiece now in the Musée Granet in Aix-en-Provence,[3] Guercino's Lyons picture represents the risen Christ standing before St. Teresa, who is shown kneeling in her Carmelite habit. Christ gestures upwards to indicate the dove of the Holy Spirit, God the Father, an angel, and several putti. Just behind Teresa, on the right, is a standing angel who looks out at the spectator and makes a blessing gesture.

Guercino was in Rome in 1622 when his patron, Pope Gregory XV Ludovisi, canonized St. Teresa. No doubt the artist was familiar with her life and works. The Spanish saint's writings had an extremely important role to play in the Counter-Reformation. Her description of her mystical/physical union with Christ, in which an angel penetrated her heart with a flaming arrow—known to us best through Bernini's Cornaro Chapel—was represented in prints and paintings before her sainthood was bestowed. One of the earliest altarpieces to deal with Teresa's transverberation was made by the Venetian painter Palma Giovane (whom Guercino met in Venice in 1618) for the Roman church of S. Pancrazio (fig. 31b).[4] Palma's painting, which is signed

and dated 1615, shows St. Teresa kneeling near an altar. Swooning, she is supported by one angel while another prepares to thrust an arrow into her heart. A miraculous shaft of light connects Teresa to a heroic Christ, who occupies the upper left portion of the painting where he is surrounded by putti and clouds. With his left hand he indicates a wound on the right side of his chest and with his right arm he gestures heavenward.

Guercino's painting only alludes to the ideas manifested in Palma's work. Though Christ's wounds are clearly visible, they are not singled out; moreover, Teresa's "wounding" is only referenced obliquely by the presence of the handsome angel who stands behind her. A group of preparatory drawings at Windsor, the British Museum, Haarlem, and Angers, and another sheet formerly on the London art market (Colnaghi, exh., June-July, 1971) only confirm Guercino's seeming disinterest in representing the most famous event in Teresa's life.[5] None of these sheets, including a dramatic study for the altarpiece at Windsor Castle (fig. 31c),[6] would lead to the conclusion that Guercino wished to emulate Palma's painting (or similar images)—though the Angers drawing does, in fact, depict Christ pointing to his wound.

The Seattle drawing exhibited here is precisely the link with the iconographical tradition that one would expect to find in Guercino's preparations for a painting that was destined to be the most influential Italian Baroque work of art in Lyons during the Seicento.[7] It was standard practice for Guercino to make highly dramatic, focussed studies of the central figures that would occupy the lower half of an altarpiece. We have seen this design method at work in the 1630-1632 studies for the Giroldo Chapel *Martyrdom of SS. John and Paul* (cat. no. 24, recto and verso), which offer no sign that the upper half of the painting will contain the Madonna and Child. Thus, one can easily imagine that Teresa's gesture and glance upwards would have been connected in the final version with an image of the risen Christ in the top half of the picture. It should be recalled that Lumaga paid a total of 400 ducats, which in Guercino's pricing system would signify four full-length figures, or the equivalent. The three figures in the drawing—by contract—would not have been sufficient.

There can be no doubt whatever that the Seattle drawing belongs to the group of studies made in connection with the Lyons project. The handling of the wash and the style of the draperies are identical with those found in the other examples; moreover, the unusual visage of Teresa, with its bulbous eyes and broad forehead, can be virtually superimposed on the Windsor drawing illustrated here. What is less clear, perhaps, is the activity of the second angel. Typically, this figure would be supporting a fainting Teresa (as in Palma) or opening her outer garment to make an easy path to her heart for the arrow wielded by the other angel. In this case, though, it is possible that the assistant is placing a heart-shaped badge on her habit as a symbol of her love of Christ, while at the same time marking the spot where her body will be "martyred" by the fiery shaft.

As is so often the case in Guercino's oeuvre, the dynamic and baroque compositions worked out in the preliminary sketches are abandoned at the painting stage for a more elegant and less *graphic* characterization of the subject. This trend begins very early in his career but becomes more marked in the period after 1630, when the influence of the graceful Guido Reni comes to take a more dominant position in the development of his style. However, it is important to note that even if Guercino completely changed his scheme for the Lyons altarpiece, the basic concept of the Seattle sketch—two angels

supporting a saint with raised arms—was resuscitated in 1647 for the altarpiece of *St. Philip Neri* in Santa Maria in Galliera, Bologna (see cat. no. 52).

1. *Libro dei Conti*, pp. 312-13; the payments were made by Lodovico Mastri on 5 January and 18 August 1634.

2. Malvasia, p. 263. Malvasia gives Lumaga's name as Giovanni, but as M-T, p. 47, point out, though it is possible that the commission came from Giovanni, the chapel in Lyons was founded by Bartolomeo. This fact is confirmed by the inscription on Gilles Rousselet's engraving (fig. 31a) after the picture. Both the painting and the print display the Lumaga coat-of-arms, which includes three snails ("lumaca" means snail or slug in Italian). Loire, 1988, p. 310, notes that Bartolomeo was a member of an important Lyonnais banking family originally from Les Grisons and that he is known to have been engaged on the decoration of the chapel already in 1627. Mahon, "Le Guerchin et la France," p. 14, in Loire, 1990, has suggested that Lumaga may have acted in c. 1629 as banker/agent to Marie de' Medici for her ill-fated purchase of Guido Reni's *Rape of Helen* (Louvre), which wound up in the appreciative hands of La Vrillière, Secretary of State to Louis XIII, perhaps as late as 1642. Lumaga may have owned the painting for a number of years prior to its sale and it may have been the banker who advised the Secretary to consider purchasing some paintings by the Cento master. For a drawing connected to a Guercino picture made specifically for La Vrillière, see cat. no. 50.

3. Salerno, no. 152. The painting remained in the chapel at Lyons until the Revolution.

4. See Lavin, 1980, pp. 112 f., figs. 269-70. I thank Irving Lavin for confirming the identity of the subject of the Seattle drawing. My discussion of the iconography is indebted to his exhaustive study.

5. For these seven compositional sketches (three of which are at Windsor) and references to other studies connected with the altarpiece, see M-T, nos. 78-82. In addition to these studies, two "close-up" sketches in pen and ink for the figure of St. Teresa (shown from the waist up, facing left) have recently come to light. The first of these belongs to the Musée d'Art et d'Archéologie at Besançon, inv. D 1920 (122 x 108 mm.), and will be published shortly by Stéphane Loire, whom I would like to thank for providing me with a photocopy of the drawing. The second, a more finished drawing with extensive hatching, depicts Teresa in a very similar pose, but with her body turned slightly more towards the viewer. This sheet is in the collection of the Palazzo Rosso at Genoa (inv. no. 1736; 195 x 156 mm.) and has been recently identified and published (as fig. 32, with a mistaken caption placing the work at the Louvre Guercino exhibition) by Nicholas Turner (uncredited) in his review of Loire, 1990 (cf. *Burl. Mag.* [October 1990], pp. 652-4).

6. Inv. 2696; 295 x 210 mm.; M-T, no. 78, pl. 82.

7. Loire, 1990, p. 310.

31b

31c

Studies for the *Martyrdom of Saint Bartholomew*

(San Martino, Siena, 1635-1636)

32 The Martyrdom of St. Bartholomew
Pen and brown ink, brown wash
203 x 254 mm.
Slight stains, foxing and damage along edges; tipped to
old mount
PROVENANCE: William Bateson (L. Suppl. 2604a, recto);
E. Parsons & Sons, London; Dan Fellows Platt (L. Suppl.
2066b and 750a, verso), purchased from Parsons in 1929
BIBLIOGRAPHY: Lynes, p. 96, no. 79; Bean, 1966, no. 40,
repr.; Stampfle-Bean, 1967, under no. 41; DeGrazia, 1969,
no. 14, repr.; Roli, 1972, no. 54, repr.; Varriano, 1974, no.
13; Gibbons, no. 272; Martin, 1977, p. 36, fig. 15;
Joachim-McCullagh, under no. 63; Salerno, under no. 158;
Van Tuyll, 1989, under no. 30

{H,O}

The Art Museum, Princeton University,
Bequest of Dan Fellows Platt,   48-734

33 The Martyrdom of St. Bartholomew
Pen and iron gall ink, brown wash, on ivory laid paper
296 x 204 mm.
Tipped in
PROVENANCE: Collection of Mr. and Mrs. Norman H.
Pritchard
BIBLIOGRAPHY: Joachim-McCullagh, no. 63, pl. 68;
Joachim, Microfiche, 3D11; Tedeschi, no. 8, repr. color;
Salerno, under no. 158; Van Tuyll, 1989, under no. 30

The Art Institute of Chicago,
Gift of Mr. and Mrs. Norman H. Pritchard,   1960.832

34 The Martyrdom of St. Bartholomew
Pen and brown ink, brown wash, on antique laid paper
247 x 334 mm.
Lined
PROVENANCE: Capt. H.S. Reitlinger; purchased at
Sotheby's, London, 9 Dec. 1953, lot 53 by Agnew's for
Vincent Korda; by descent to the present owner
BIBLIOGRAPHY: Unpublished, but noted in the
following: Stampfle-Bean, 1967, under cat. no. 41 (as in
the collection of Stephen Korda, London);
Joachim-McCullagh, under no. 63; Van Tuyll, 1989, under
no. 30 (who mentions that the work was illustrated in an
advertisement in *Burl. Mag.* 117 [1975], p. xxxvi)

Collection of Michael and Margaret Korda

35 The Martyrdom of St. Bartholomew
Red chalk, on very thin off-white paper
377 x 284 mm.
Minor restorations along right edge; horizontal line in red
chalk across middle
Inscribed on verso in graphite, lower right: *174576,*
upper left: *34,* and in brown ink: *P*
WATERMARK: shield with crown and illegible device
surmounted by a cardinal's hat similar to Heawood 793
PROVENANCE: Sotheby's, 21 Nov. 1974, lot no. 49
BIBLIOGRAPHY: S. Cook in Oberhuber, 1977, no. 18,
repr. (as c. 1619 for a *Raising of Lazarus,* according to
Mahon); H. Van Miegroet and A. Moir in Moir, 1986, no.
23, repr. (for a *St. Bartholomew,* but much earlier than
1636)

Private Collection

The four drawings shown here as cat. nos.
32-35 offer an unusually complete overview
of Guercino's design process and the function
of his drawings.

The project elaborated in these extraordinary sheets is documented by the *Libro dei
Conti* in three entries for receipts of payment
(200 ducats each on 16 Jan. 1635, 1 Sept.
1636, and 4 Dec. 1636) for an altarpiece to be
made "for Siena" with six figures representing
the martyrdom of St. Bartholomew.[1] Guercino's biographer, Malvasia, reports that the
painting (made in Bologna) was sent to the
church of San Martino in Siena and that it was
so admired that the artist was given an extra
200 ducats and 14 *braccia* of Sienese woolen
cloth as a gift.[2] At the behest of Archbishop
Colonna, a copy was made by Giacinto Campana and supposedly retouched by the
master himself. The copy (fig. 32a) was sent
to the Colonna palace in Rome. From there it
was later dispatched to the church of San Barnaba at Marino Laziale, where the painting remains today.[3] Malvasia predicted that the
Colonna copy would one day serve as the
"original," since only a few decades after the
Siena altarpiece was painted it began to de-
teriorate.   Indeed, the San Martino canvas,

which is still in the church, can be described
as a virtual ruin.

The Princeton drawing (cat. no. 32) is one
of four known general compositional studies
for the painting and is in many ways the
closest to the final scheme. The other studies, at the Morgan Library,[4] the British
Museum,[5] and the Witt Collection, Courtauld
Institute,[6] show an impressive variety of
poses for the flayed saint and his tormentors.
The Morgan Library sheet (fig. 32b) is the
most complete of all the drawings, and yet it
is the furthest from the structure of the painting. Not a single feature of the drawing is
taken over in the final version: the architecture is on the opposite side, the saint's arms
are tied up above his head on some type of
rack, and his legs are spread far apart in a
less-than-dignified manner. In the dynamic
Princeton drawing, which is a tour-de-force of
Guercino's unique combination of open pen
lines and bold patches of wash, there are
many ideas that are repeated in the altarpiece
itself, especially the general attitudes of the
two executioners, who cut and tear the apostle's flesh. It must be noted, however, that
even in this sheet there are important devia-
tions from the painting. Bartholomew's right
arm is tied up above his head, not at his side,
as in the final version.

Guercino's design process does not seem
to move in a strictly linear progression from
the most general to the most specific type of
study. Rather, as we have seen in the drawings for the Ghiara *Crucifixion* (cat. nos. 12
and 13), the artist often worked from "the inside out" by focusing on particular figures or
figural relationships in "close-up" studies.
These sketches had the potential of inspiring
the artist to revise his general compositional
schemes.

The Chicago and Korda drawings (cat.
nos. 33 and 34, respectively) are superb examples of this practice. Guercino knew from

the outset that his composition had to include six full-size figures, but this practical matter did not deter him from exploring the psychological aspects of the scene in sketches that do not suggest easy, and certainly not automatic integration into any one of the general schemes established by the four designs mentioned above. In both of the "close-ups," the saint is shown with a single executioner, though in all the known compositional sketches, there are always two of them, one on each side of Bartholomew. The richer use of wash and the greater attention paid to costume and facial expression in these sketches would seem to serve Guercino as much as an intellectual and experiential exercise aimed at preparing himself mentally and spiritually to paint as for any practical purpose. At the same time, it is possible that Guercino felt that these big projects were per-

fect opportunities for generating ideas for future altarpieces and devotional pictures. One suspects that his students and assistants would use these "research" sheets as the point of departure for their own commissions (some of which were given to them by their teacher), and that the master himself occasionally returned to his drawing collection for inspiration. We have already suggested an affinity between the Seattle *St. Teresa* drawing (cat. no. 31) and the *Vision of St. Philip Neri* altarpiece (fig. 52a), an affinity which may not be coincidental or merely typological in kind.

Guercino availed himself of a third type of drawing and a different medium as he worked on this altarpiece. A sensitive red-chalk study of the saint and one executioner (cat. no. 35) in a private collection, has been identified as a drawing by Guercino of a St.

Bartholomew scene.[7] It has never been connected to the San Martino altarpiece, although it is entirely consonant with the other studies for the project. Chalk drawings often were made after the live model to help the artist bring the actuality of appearance and the subtleties of anatomical structure to his painting. In this case, however, the features and anatomy are somewhat generalized, enough perhaps that it may be appropriate to suggest that the study was done from memory, albeit in imitation of the type of life studies that Guercino habitually made (e.g., cat. nos. 63-65).[8]

Analysis of these dramatic products of artistic brainstorming reveals that Guercino was concerned with resolving one overarching problem in his treatment of the subject—finding the proper integration of an extreme act of violence and human suffering with a representation of Christian faith and salvation. It is important to note that the final version of the composition depicts Bartholomew in a pose which shows the least amount of struggle and consequently engenders the greatest amount of contrast between the innocence of the saint and the brutality of those sent to flay him alive.

1. *Libro dei Conti*, pp. 313-15.

2. Malvasia, p. 263.

3. See Salerno, no. 158.

4. Inv. I,101e. See Stampfle-Bean, 1967, no. 41.

5. Inv. 1989-6-17-278 (cf. Smithson & Williams, *Old Master Drawings: Recent Acquisitions*, London, 1989, unpag., color repr.). Pen and brown ink, brown wash. 249 x 236 mm. On Casa Gennari mount (see L. Suppl. 2858c).

6. Inv. no. 1337. Pen and brown ink, and wash. 234 x 256 mm. Photo, Hertziana Library, Rome, no. 369605. Cf. Blunt, 1956, p. 75.

7. See the Bibl. for cat. no. 35.

8. Another study for an individual figure—this one in pen and brown ink and brown wash—is in the Teylers Museum, Haarlem (H. 48) and depicts the large angel in the clouds, who gestures upwards. It is followed rather faithfully by the painting, although in the latter the right arm is bent at a considerably sharper angle, so that the whole forearm is on the vertical axis. See Van Tuyll, 1989, no. 30, repr.

32a

32b

32

34

Pen and brown ink, gray and brown wash
193 x 235 mm.
Foxed; creased along upper edge; tipped to old mount
PROVENANCE: Dan Fellows Platt (L. Suppl. 750a, lower left verso), bought at Parsons in 1920
BIBLIOGRAPHY: Lynes, p. 112, no. 129; DeGrazia, 1969, no. 31; Varriano, 1974, no. 38; Gibbons, no. 267; M-T, under no. 228

The Art Museum, Princeton University
Bequest of Dan Fellows Platt, 48-726

The astronomer (or astrologer) shown in this wonderfully vibrant, extroverted drawing of the 1630s seems to beckon the spectator to appreciate the mysteries of the universe. Unconnected to a painting, the sheet was probably done for the artist's own amusement.

Guercino explored several themes of this type in his drawings and paintings.[1] He was also apparently interested in scenes of alchemy and witchcraft. A pen-and-wash drawing of a *Magic Scene,* formerly in the collection of Vivant-Denon and now in Houston, Museum of Fine Arts (fig. 36a),[2] is one of the most extraordinary and elaborate of such works. For a bizarre drawing of a *Witch, bust length, Two Bats, and a Demon in Flight,* now in the Art Gallery of Ontario, Toronto, see Suppl. no. 169 (repr.).

1. See M-T, under no. 228. Cf. also cat. no. 62.

2. Inv. 70.21, Museum Purchase with Funds provided by Laurence H. Favrot Bequest. 276 x 311 mm. Inscribed in ink, lower right recto: *Guerzin da Cento;* inscribed in ink upper right recto: *S* [...]. Prov.: Unidentified collector (mark, coat of arms, lower right recto); Baron D. Vivant-Denon (L. 779, lower left recto); Jules Dupan (L. 1440, lower right recto). Reproduced in reverse (lithograph by Mlle. Bouteiller) in *Monuments des Arts,* 1829, pl. 214. I thank Rodney Nevitt of Harvard University for his help in cataloguing this sheet.

36a

Pen and iron gall ink, brown wash
138 x 156 mm.
Some stains; paper torn and eaten away in darkest areas;
some restoration; tipped to old mount
WATERMARK: Two insects (?) in oval with filigree border
PROVENANCE: Dan Fellows Platt (L. Suppl. 750a and
2066b, lower left verso), bought at Parsons in 1920
BIBLIOGRAPHY: Lynes, p. 122, no. 164; DeGrazia, 1969,
no. 2; Gibbons, no. 258

The Art Museum, Princeton University
Bequest of Dan Fellows Platt, 48-711

This lively pen-and-wash drawing from the Platt Collection may have been made as a preliminary sketch for an evangelist. Although no painting exists which can be connected to the composition, the sheet probably dates to c. 1630.[1] Such swirling pen lines and deep pools of wash may also be found in several of the studies for the Giroldo Chapel *Martyrdom of SS. John and Paul, with the Madonna and Child Above,* which were most likely executed in 1630-1632 (see under cat. no. 24). Of these sheets, that in the Mahon Collection (*Disegni,* no. 129) is perhaps the closest in style and figural design to the exhibited work.

1. Dated to c. 1617 by DeGrazia and Gibbons, the sheet has been properly reassigned to the end of Guercino's transitional period by Nicholas Turner, Review of Gibbons, *The Art Bulletin,* 62, no. 3, 1980, pp. 488-89.

38

Sisyphus
(Study for the lost painting, 1636)

Pen and brown ink, brown wash
295 x 210 mm.
PROVENANCE: Casa Gennari; F. Forni; E. Bouverie; Mr. Hervey; Earls of Gainsborough (according to Oberhuber); Dan Fellows Platt (no mark); Schaeffer Galleries, New York
BIBLIOGRAPHY: Konrad Oberhuber and Sabine Kehl-Baierle, *Meisterzeichnungen aus New York: Vier emigrierte Altösterreicher als Sammler,* exh. cat., Vienna, Graphische Sammlung Albertina, 29 Nov. 1988 - 29 Jan. 1989, Vienna, 1988, p. 66, no. 37, repr.; M-T, under no. 84, fig. 17

Robert and Bertina Suida Manning

38a

GUERCINO {Gianfrancesco Barbieri} 1590-1666

Punished in Hades for his crimes, Sisyphus, a greedy king of Corinth, was condemned forever to push an enormous stone up to the top of a mountain. Each time, when he had almost reached the peak, the stone would fall all the way back to the bottom again.

This thought-provoking theme, which today serves as an existentialist allegory of futility, was the subject of a full-length painting commissioned from Guercino in 1636 by Conte Girolamo Ranuzzi of Bologna (100 ducats payment on 28 October 1636; *Libro dei Conti,* p. 315). The picture is lost, but a number of preparatory studies have been identified and related to the work, including the exhibited sheet, which is surely the most dramatic and captivating of the entire group.[1]

To judge from the five studies noted by Mahon and Turner, Guercino could not make up his mind whether he wanted to show the king pushing the rock (as in the exhibited sheet), carrying it (as in a pen-and-wash drawing at Windsor, and two others),[2] or posing with it above his head like Atlas (as in fig. 38a, a sketch with a Casa Gennari provenance sold at Christie's, London, 23 Nov. 1971, lot 72, not repr.; 234 x 194 mm.).

Guercino also struggled to cast the right type of figure for the role. An unpublished, double-sided study in black chalk in the Teylers Museum, Haarlem (inv. H. 29) characterizes Sisyphus (on the recto) as a young man with long locks. On the verso, he is more of a Hercules type with a Carraccesque physique.

A poor illustration of a fascinating but untraced pen-and-wash drawing that was exhibited in New York as a *Sisyphus* by Guercino (Herbert E. Feist Gallery, *Master Drawings,* 11 Oct. - 30 Nov. 1980, no. 16; 381 x 273 mm.) may record yet another study (or, more likely, a copy of another study) for the picture. A nude figure with a broad, billow-ing cape is shown in reverse of the Manning drawing and is depicted in a composition with a strong diagonal axis. Sisyphus pushes the rock up to the left with both arms fully extended but looks down over his left shoulder toward the bottom right corner. His abdomen is shown frontally and is shaped in a manner somewhat like that depicted in the ex-Christie's drawing (fig. 38a). The up-down contrapposto featured in this image is not echoed in any of the autograph studies for the project.[3]

Visitors to the exhibition should note with care the remarkably fine condition of the Manning *Sisyphus.* The variety of tone and transparency in the wash, which almost magically creates a believable, three-dimensional form for the rock, makes this one of Guercino's greatest accomplishments in the medium.

1. The connection of the ex-Platt drawing to the other studies and to the citation in the account book was first made by M-T, under no. 84.

2. Besides the study at Windsor (M-T, no. 84) which depicts the figure moving to the left with a long rock slung over his back and looking straight down, there is a drawing, formerly in the collection of Robert Laurent of Indiana, which shows Sisyphus carrying the rock on his shoulders and above his head, with both his hands in front of the load (an improbable, if not ridiculous way to carry a rock). This sheet, in which the figure moves toward the right, is illustrated in Colnaghi, London, *Old Master Drawings,* June 1970, no. 21, pl. vii (incorrectly captioned as no. 18, pl. vii). A third study, with an interesting letter by Guercino on the verso, is preserved in the Witt Collection, Courtauld Institute of Art, London (inv. no. 1366). The Witt drawing shows the king lumbering to the right and struggling to carry a large stone, which he holds like a box in front of his chest.

3. It is impossible to come to any conclusions whatsoever on the question of the sheet's authorship, since the illustration by which it is known to me is so unclear. Nicholas Turner, to whom I have shown this recent discovery, has mentioned in conversation that, even if the drawing is not by Guercino, it might represent the composition of the final version of the project, which, alas, is completely unknown.

93

Pen and iron gall ink, brown wash
160 x 207 mm.
Slight stains; losses from acid ink; repaired on verso
WATERMARK: Bird on triple mound in circle
PROVENANCE: Casa Gennari; F. Forni; E. Bouverie (L. 325, lower left recto); Mr. Hervey; Earls of Gainsborough; Dan Fellows Platt (L. Suppl. 750a, lower left verso), bought at Parsons in 1922
BIBLIOGRAPHY: Lynes, p. 95, no. 78; Bean, 1966, no. 38; DeGrazia, 1969, no. 11; Gibbons, no. 308

The Art Museum, Princeton University
Bequest of Dan Fellows Platt, 49-40

The documented date of the *Sisyphus* painting and related drawings (see the previous entry), provides the basis for assigning the fine study at Princeton of *Joseph with the Flowering Staff* (cat. no. 39) to roughly the same time period, c. 1636. Like the Manning *Sisyphus* (cat. no. 38), Guercino's *Joseph* creates dramatic contrasts of light and shadow with bold areas of brown wash laid down with extraordinary control and economy. The pen lines have a special *vibrato* and arbitrariness, not often encountered prior to the 1630s, which break up the light and surfaces (compare, for example, a drawing in a similar technique, cat. no. 16, in which the lines are much firmer and contain the forms).

We have followed the suggestion of Luigi Salerno and Sir Denis Mahon (Salerno, p. 429) that the exhibited sheet is the likely source of a painting of the same subject in the Galleria Doria Pamphilj, Rome (fig. 39a),[1] which they ascribe to a member of Guercino's workshop, possibly Bartolomeo Gennari (1594-1661),[2] elder brother of Ercole Gennari (1597-1658), who in 1628 married Guercino's sister, Lucia Barbieri (mother of the painters Cesare and Benedetto, Jr., Guercino's assistants and heirs).[3]

For a similar but fully documented case in which Guercino supplied Bartolomeo with a preparatory drawing, see the Introduction.

1. Inv. 115. 73 x 97 cm.

2. This is Denis Mahon's opinion (oral communication), with which I fully concur.

3. On the Gennari family and Guercino's workshop in general, see the important study by Bagni, 1986, *passim*.

39a

Studies for *Esther before Abasuerus*

(Ann Arbor, The University of Michigan Museum of Art, 1637-1639)

40 Esther before Ahasuerus

Pen and brown ink, brown wash
216 x 259 mm.
Laid down
PROVENANCE: Casa Gennari; F. Forni; E. Bouverie (L. 325, lower right recto); Mr. Hervey; Sir Thomas Fowell Buxton, Bt.; his sale: Sotheby's, London, 23 March 1978, lot 157, repr.; Dr. Alfred Bader, Milwaukee
BIBLIOGRAPHY: Salerno, under no. 180; M-T, under no. 356; Shelley Perlove, "Guercino's *Esther before Ahasuerus* and Cardinal Lorenzo Magalotti, Bishop of Ferrara," *Artibus et Historiae* 19 (1989), pp. 133-47, fig. 9

The University of Michigan Museum of Art, 1978/2.41

41 Esther before Ahasuerus

Pen and brown ink
180 x 235 mm.
PROVENANCE: Jan Pietersz. Zoomer, Amsterdam (L.1511); Mrs. Ralph Booth, Detroit; Curtis O. Baer
BIBLIOGRAPHY: Agnes Mongan, *Drawings from the Collection of Curtis O. Baer,* exh. cat., Fogg Art Museum, Harvard University, Cambridge, 1958, no. 5, repr.; Herbert C. Barrows, "Observations on Guercino's *Esther Before Ahasuerus,*" *Bulletin of the University of Michigan Museum of Art* 5 (1970-71), pp. 27-38, fig. 3; Eric M. Zafran, *Master Drawings from Titian to Picasso: The Curtis O. Baer Collection,* exh. cat., High Museum of Art, Atlanta, 1985, no. 12, repr.; M-T, under no. 356; Perlove, 1989, p. 140, fig. 7

Private Collection

42 Study for Ahasuerus

Pen and brown ink, brown wash
235 x 178 mm.
Inscribed in ink lower left recto: *Guercino;* the mount inscribed in black ink on the verso, lower left: *No. 311*
PROVENANCE: Christie's, London, 11 April 1978, lot 49, repr. on pl. 21; Spencer A. Samuels & Company, Ltd., N.Y. (*Master Drawings,* New York, 1981, no. 9, repr.)
BIBLIOGRAPHY: Unpublished. Mentioned in: Zafran, 1985, p. 34 (incorrectly cited as Christie's, London, 23 Nov. 1971, no. 106); M-T, under no. 356; Perlove, 1989, p. 146, n. 21

The Arkansas Arts Center Foundation Collection, The Fred W. Allsopp Memorial Acquisition Fund, 1984, 84.27.2

Commissioned by Cardinal Lorenzo Magalotti, Bishop of Ferrara, shortly before his death in 1637 and completed in 1639,[1] Guercino's painting of *Esther before Ahasuerus,* Ann Arbor, University of Michigan Museum of Art (fig. 40a),[2] passed quickly into the collection of Pope Urban VIII Barberini, to whom the Cardinal was related (his sister married Urban's brother).[3] The picture, which is particularly noteworthy for its fine costumes, is a reminder that Guercino's artistic presence in Rome did not greatly diminish after he left the Eternal City in 1623.[4]

In this work, the painter chose to illustrate a turning point in the story recounted in the Old Testament Book of Esther, when the Jewish Queen faints as she risks her life entering the court of her husband, the Persian King Ahasuerus, without an official summons. The heroine's collapse depicted by Guercino is not only brought on by her fear of the law (the King's offering of the golden scepter will pardon her); it is also due to her anguish at having to make public her Jewish faith, which up until now she has kept a secret. Esther's mission is to alert her husband to the machinations of the evil minister, Haman, whose plot to destroy the Jews is unknown to the King.[5]

Like many of the works we have discussed, Guercino's *Esther* was the result of an intricate design process that relied on various types of preparatory drawings, each having a slightly different function, and each inflecting style and technique to some degree in accordance with that function.[6] The three sketches gathered here from Michigan (cat. no. 40), a private collection (cat. no. 41), and Arkansas (cat. no. 42) provide an opportunity to observe the artist as he develops narrative structure, figural relationships, and costumes for a history painting. (For other cases in the exhibition where it has been possible to assemble more than one study for a given pro-

ject, see cat. nos. 11-12, 17-18, 19-21, 24-26, and especially 32-35.)

The most complete compositional study known for the painting, a pen sketch at Windsor ascribed to Guercino by Mahon and Turner (fig. 40b),[7] depicts the King reaching out to the fainting Queen, putting the scepter in her hand, and grabbing her right wrist with his left hand as if to catch her. As in the painting, Esther is supported by two maids, but here she swoons away from her husband, whereas in the painting she leans towards him and closes off the composition. There is an intense exchange of glances in this sheet between the maid shown in profile and the King. The motif is treated more generally in the final version; the woman looks more in the direction of the viewer than at the King. The Michigan drawing (cat. no. 40), which was probably intended as a partial compositional sketch (it does not appear to have been trimmed on the right side), documents the stage at which Guercino adjusted the maid's attitude and moved Esther closer to the King, who reaches out to her with both arms, just as in the Windsor sheet, but perhaps more gently.

It is worth pointing out the differences in technique between the Windsor and Michigan drawings. In the former, Guercino uses many fine and very long pen strokes and shades the figures with his familiar line-and-dot style. This method serves to clarify the overall situation of forms and brings out certain details in the costumes and hair. In the Michigan sheet, Guercino uses brush and wash almost exclusively, creating a very painterly effect that helps him to block out the forms quickly and to prepare for the eventual placement of lights and darks on the canvas.

The positions of the figures in a drawing formerly in the Curtis O. Baer Collection (cat. no. 41) are reversed relative to the painting and the previously mentioned studies, but

40

Guercino

42

41

this is not what is unusual or remarkable about the sheet. Far more important is the fact that it depicts only two of the four characters and that it employs a graphic style distinct from that used in either the Windsor or Michigan sketches.[8] As he sometimes does when working on a narrative picture, Guercino temporarily puts aside general compositional issues and makes a "conversation" drawing, a sheet which studies the psychological relationships between characters.[9] Here Guercino focuses on the drama unfolding between the King and Queen. The swirling calligraphy racing across the Baer drawing in big loops suggests a more positive and uplifting subject than the brooding contrasts of light and shadow in the Michigan drawing. This change in approach is wholly appropriate, since Guercino is representing a later moment in the narrative when the Queen is given the opportunity to tell her story. We hasten to point out that, although compositionally unrelated to the final work, this drawing appears to be responsible for the invention of Ahasuerus's gesture of compassion, the touching of his heart. Guercino adopted it in the painting after rejecting the idea explored in the Windsor and Michigan sketches of having the King take hold of Esther's wrist. It is a subtle detail, but in our interpretation, the change allowed Guercino to conflate two moments in the narrative, where before he had only one: 1) the Queen's physical collapse and 2) the King's receptiveness to Esther's cause. Technically, based on the narrative moment we are shown in the painting, Ahasuerus does not yet know her cause. But Guercino knew that he could rely on his audience to be wholly familiar with the story, and it is likely that they would have recognized in the King's gesture an allusion to the conversation episode that lies just ahead. Guercino's is a completely traditional narrative device that would otherwise not warrant

much comment. What we are stressing here is the role played by his drawings in arriving at such a solution. In this sense, the artist is exceptional among seventeenth-century Italian draftsmen.

The sequence of studies for the ex-Barberini painting also includes a rapid pen sketch in Christ Church, Oxford, of the swooning Esther and one of her female attendants (the one on the far right side of the painting)[10] and two "close-up" studies of Ahasuerus, in which Guercino further explores the physiognomy, posture, expression, and, especially, the costume of the King. Perhaps the earlier of the two is a sheet formerly on the London art market (fig. 40c), which shows Ahasuerus facing left, as in cat. no. 41, but without his hand on his chest (we warned the reader that the process was intricate!).[11] The second study, now in the Arkansas Arts Center at Little Rock (cat. no. 42), was followed carefully by the artist when he made his painting, and must have come towards the end of the series.

One should recognize how much the character of line in the Arkansas "close-up" study (the broad, parallel strokes in the drapery and turban, for example) differs from the handling in the "conversation" sketch shown in cat. no. 41 and the brush-and-wash compositional sketch in Michigan (cat. no. 40). The variety of techniques and functions in Guercino's design process is truly impressive and no doubt made a huge contribution to his success as a painter and storyteller.

1. See M-T, under no. 356. For Magalotti, see also Perlove, 1989.

2. Inv. no. 1963/2.45. Salerno, no. 180.

3. Perlove, 1989, p. 138. Numerous documents concerning the commission have been published. For these, besides Perlove, 1989, see Barrows, "Observations" and M-T, under no. 356.

4. Guercino received a fairly steady stream of commissions for altarpieces for Roman churches. To cite two ex-

amples that are still in situ: the Holy Trinity of 1638 in SM della Vittoria (Salerno, no. 176) and St. Philip Neri of 1644 in the Chiesa Nuova (Salerno, no. 211).

5. For an interesting interpretation of the painting as a tendentious reflection of Magalotti's political and religious posture vis-à-vis the Jewish community in Ferrara's ghetto (he apparently wanted to convert them all to Catholicism), see Perlove, 1989. Perlove's suggestion that Guercino's Esther is a portrait of a Sienese convert from Judaism named Lucretia Seghizzi who was active in Ferrara in c. 1625 cannot be correct, since the physiognomy of the Queen is idealized and is otherwise thoroughly interchangeable with any number of Guercino's Old Testament female protagonists of the 1630s or 1640s. Moreover, the identification is not based on a comparison with a documented portrait of Seghizzi.

6. This inflection of style and/or technique in accordance with function or subject may be called "modality."

7. M-T, no. 356. 210 x 294 mm.

8. Since, in this period, Guercino customarily charged 100 ducats per full-length figure and the account book states that a member of Magalotti's family paid 300 ducats for the work (on 12 July 1639), it is likely that Guercino knew in advance that he would have to paint the equivalent of three full-length figures or, as he demonstrates already in the Windsor sketch, four three-quarter-length figures, as in the final version. The drawing exhibited here as cat. no. 41, were it to be misinterpreted as a general compositional sketch, would mean that Guercino decided to paint only two figures instead of four and that he did not mind having to return 150 ducats to the client. (As M-T, under no. 356, have pointed out, the Libro dei Conti as published by Calvi [p. 319] incorrectly states the sum as 200 ducats, whereas the original manuscript itself [MS B. 331, fol. 17 recto, Biblioteca Comunale dell'Archiginnasio, Bologna] gives the figure as 300 ducats.)

9. For more about this type of drawing and its role in Guercino's design process, see the Introduction.

10. See James Byam Shaw, Drawings by Old Masters at Christ Church, Oxford, 2 vols., Oxford, 1976, no. 997, pl. 603.

11. Christie's, London, 23 Nov. 1971, lot 106. 226 x 184 mm. Prov.: Casa Gennari; F. Forni; E. Bouverie; Mr. Hervey; the Earls of Gainsborough. Bibl.: unpublished, but mentioned in Zafran, 1985 (incorrectly cited as Christie's, London, 11 April 1978, lot 49); M-T, under no. 356; and Perlove, 1989, p. 146, n. 21.

40a

40b

40c

101

The Temptation of Saint Francis

Black chalk, pen and brown ink, brown wash
242 x 197 mm.
Small losses and repairs
WATERMARK: encircled bird
PROVENANCE: G. Vallardi (L. 1223, lower left recto);
Captain Carlo Prayer (L. 2044, lower right recto); sale:
Christie's, London, 1 April 1987, lot 62, repr.
BIBLIOGRAPHY: Unpublished

Dr. Hilary Koprowski

Probably an independent work and, in any case, not connected with a documented painting or engraving, this extraordinary sheet should be dated to the late 1630s or early 1640s. The drawing represents a rarely depicted scene in the life of Saint Francis of Assisi, who is more typically shown receiving the stigmata (see cat. no. 28), having an ecstatic vision just before receiving the wounds (as in cat. no. 44), being consoled by a music-making angel, or praying and meditating in the wilderness. The terrifying image of the devil, who appears to the saint in human form, has a curious, specter of a fox-like face preceding it (overlapping the devil's left arm).[1] This hallucinatory aspect of the devil's appearance makes the saint's clutching of the book and rosary beads and his appeal to Christ for strength (he reaches out to the crucifix on the right) especially poignant.[2]

1. I do not believe this is a pentimento or alternative study.

2. As mentioned, representations of this scene are rare, even during the Counter-Reformation. For several precedents, see *L'immagine di San Francesco nella Controriforma,* exh. cat., 9 Dec. - 13 Feb. 1983, Calcografia Nazionale, Rome, especially p. 87, no. 61, repr. (a drawing by Jacopo Ligozzi in Siena, Pinacoteca Nazionale, inv. 92).

Pen and brown ink, extensive brown wash
242 x 198 mm.
Laid down
Minor damage and repairs in heaviest areas of wash
Verso: a letter, probably in Guercino's hand
PROVENANCE: Casa Gennari; F. Forni; E. Bouverie (L.
325, lower left recto); Mr. Hervey; Earls of Gainsborough;
Jacques Petit-Horry, Paris
BIBLIOGRAPHY: Unpublished

Jak Katalan

Breathtaking in its magisterial use of wash, this previously unpublished sheet is remarkably finished for a preparatory drawing. Because of its unusual completeness, we have had a certain degree of difficulty situating it in Guercino's chronology, there being so few works with which to compare it.

The treatment of the wash may be likened to a study at Windsor (M-T, no. 100) of *St. Lucy,* which has been convincingly connected to a documented commission of 1640 that resulted in the painting now in S. Maria Forisportam, Lucca.[1] Certain analogies, especially regarding the quality of line (very thin and exhibiting a great deal of precision) may also be made with two other pen-and-wash drawings at Windsor, a *St. Francis in Meditation* (M-T, no. 113) for the well-known painting in San Giovanni in Monte, Bologna, of 1645,[2] and an *Atlas* (M-T, no. 120), one of a series of studies at Windsor for the painting now in Florence, Museo Bardini, of 1646.[3]

No painting of the 1640s conforms exactly to the dramatic composition set forth in the exhibited *St. Francis.* Nicholas Turner has suggested in conversation that the drawing may be related to the *Stigmatization of St. Francis* of 1646 at Cesena, Chiesa dell'Osservanza (fig. 44a).[4]

For an earlier representation of *St. Francis,* connected to the 1632-1634 altarpiece at Piacenza, see cat. no. 28. See also the previous entry.

44a

1.   Salerno, no. 187.
2.   Salerno, no. 224.
3.   Salerno, no. 230.
4.   Salerno, no. 229.

45

Saint Jerome and the Angel

Pen and brown ink, on laid paper
240 x 216 mm.
Lined
Slight foxing; corners torn (partially repaired) and signs of glue stain
Inscribed in graphite, lower left recto: *45*
PROVENANCE: Casa Gennari; Francesco Forni; Hon. Edward Bouverie, M.P. (d. 1810); by descent to his nephew, Mr. Hervey; the Earls of Gainsborough; Gainsborough sale: Christie's, London, 27 July 1922, probably from lot 81 (68 drawings); Sir Robert Witt; Helen C. Seiferheld Gallery, N.Y. (advertisement in *Burl. Mag.* 103 [Dec. 1961], p. xxviii, repr.); purchased in 1968
BIBLIOGRAPHY: *Drawing and the Human Figure: 1400 - 1964,* exh. cat., The University of Iowa, Art Department, 1964, no. 46, repr.; Robert Hobbs, *The University of Iowa Museum of Art: 101 Masterworks,* exh. cat., Iowa City, 1986, repr. (as "St. Matthew and the Angel")

The University of Iowa Museum of Art, University Purchase, 1968.67

A fine example of Guercino's more classicizing approach to the human figure in the late period, this sheet may be compared with a drawing of the *Guardian Angel* at Windsor (M-T, no. 101), which was made as a preparatory study for a painting of 1641 representing the same subject (Fano, Museo Civico Malatestiano).[1] The Fano picture has the distinction of being celebrated in a poem by Robert Browning ("The Guardian Angel," 1885).

Guercino's linear treatment begins to have a certain angularity and abstractness (less descriptive—more geometric and arbitrary) in the 1640s. The artist also continues a trend that began in the early 1630s of designing his compositions with greater planarity (compare cat. no. 4 of 1618 in which the picture space is quite deep and the figures are solidly modelled and three-dimensional). The overall effect is one of precision and clarity, conforming quite closely to the new *chiarezza* and harmony of color one finds in Guercino's paintings of these years.

1. Salerno, no. 196.

46

Saint John the Evangelist in Meditation

Pen and brown ink, on laid paper
222 x 200 mm.
Laid down
Inscribed in pen and brown ink, upper left corner of
recto: *10.P.* (notation often found on drawings with a
Casa Gennari provenance; cf. Mahon, "Casa Gennari,"
1968)
PROVENANCE: Casa Gennari (characteristic mount; see
Mahon, 1967, p. 20); F. Forni; E. Bouverie; Mr. Hervey; the
Earls of Gainsborough; private collection(s); sale:
Sotheby's, London, 27 June 1974, lot 26, p. 16, repr. p. 46;
Yvonne Tan Bunzl, London (*Old Master Drawings and
French Drawings of the 19th Century,* London, 1975, no.
18, repr.)
BIBLIOGRAPHY: Robert Flynn Johnson and Joseph R.
Goldyne, *Master Drawings from the Achenbach
Foundation for Graphic Arts, The Fine Arts Museums of
San Francisco,* Geneva: Richard Burton, S.A., n.d.
(1985 ?), no. 1, color repr.; Bagni, 1988, no. 190, repr.;
M-T, under no. 588, fig. 33

The Fine Arts Museums of San Francisco,
Achenbach Foundation for Graphic Arts, purchase,
1976.2.19

Cat. no. 46 is a fine example of the later evolution of Guercino's "gravure style," which began early in his career in drawings like the Manning *Infant Christ Holding a Bird, and Saint Joseph* of c. 1621 (for a full discussion, see cat. no. 11). Though it may be that this hatching and/or line-and-stipple technique was initially linked to drawings destined for Guercino's personal engraver, G.B. Pasqualini (see cat. nos. 75 and 75A and figs. 75a and 75b), the artist very frequently used it in the late 1630s and 1640s for other purposes, as in drawings like the *St. John,* which may have been made as a preparatory drawing for a painting or as an independent work.

As Mahon and Turner explain in their lengthy study of a red-chalk copy of the San Francisco sheet preserved at Windsor (M-T, no. 588), a Bolognese printmaker named Domenico Bonaveri (d. 1731), the likely author of the copy, made a series of eleven engravings of half-length figures after designs by Guercino, including cat. no. 46.[1] The series must have been completed before the fall of 1719, since the copper plates are listed in a Gennari inventory of 31 October of that year.

The red-chalk copy was probably made by Bonaveri for the purpose of executing his engraving, which reverses the composition and leaves out the important inscription on the first page of St. John's gospel shown in Guercino's drawing: *INPRINCIPIO ERAT VERBVM* (In the beginning was the Word). Another print, in the same sense as Bonaveri's copy and the exhibited sheet, was etched by Richard Dalton, the Royal Librarian to King George III. The print was wrongly attributed to Francesco Bartolozzi by A. Calabi.[2]

Drawings of the later 1640s like Guercino's *St. John* (c. 1645-1650) have an arresting calmness and stability that seem almost neo-classical in feeling. They stand in stark contrast to the pulsating rhythms and *vibrato* effects of light and shadow in comparable sketches of the mid-1620s, such as the *Man Reading at a Table* in the Fogg Art Museum (cat. no. 79).

1. For a discussion of Bonaveri's career and illustrations of his engravings after Guercino, see Bagni, 1988, pp. 126-51.

2. For further particulars, see M-T, under no. 588.

IN PRINCIPIO ERAT VERBVM.

109

47

Saint Joseph and the Christ Child, with a Vase of Lilies

Pen and dark brown ink, brown and gray-brown wash
231 x 222 mm.
Stained; laid down
PROVENANCE: Charles Fairfax Murray (note by Platt on
the verso); Dan Fellows Platt (L. Suppl. 750a, lower left
verso)
BIBLIOGRAPHY: Lynes, p. 95, no. 77; DeGrazia, 1969,
no. 8; Gibbons, no. 306

The Art Museum, Princeton University
Bequest of Dan Fellows Platt, 49-25

Exhibiting the tranquility of mood and softness of touch that often characterize Guercino's late style, this sheet, which might be dated to c. 1645-1650, seems to relate to two other drawings of the same subject. The first of these, in pen and wash, is in the Mahon Collection (Mahon, 1967, no. 40; Mahon-Ekserdjian, no. 40, color pl. vi). The second, in pen and ink, is untraced (photo, Witt Library); it once belonged to William Mayor and bears his stamp (L. 2799, lower right recto).[1]

Unlike the Princeton sheet, which features a rather centralized composition, the two other studies show the figures in far more active poses and facing to the right. It is this more active pose that is taken up in a previously unknown picture recently discovered in the north of England. The canvas, which is currently being restored, has been linked by Mr. Aidan Westin-Lewis of the Witt Library, Courtauld Institute of Art, University of London, to the three drawings just mentioned. Until the picture has been thoroughly cleaned and properly examined, there is no point in speculating on its authorship. I certainly agree, however, that the work is very Guercinesque and may indeed be connected in some way to the three sheets.[2]

1. According to the photo at the Witt Library, the sheet measures 288 x 231 mm. See Mahon-Ekserdjian, under no 40. For another drawing of *St. Joseph with the Infant Christ*, this one in the Willumsen Collection, Frederikssund, Denmark, see Fischer, 1984, no. 45, pl. 37. The sheet is drawn in a technique similar to the Princeton drawing and may be related to the drawings mentioned above. Its composition is the least close to that shown in the recently discovered painting.

2. I thank Mr. Westin-Lewis for sharing his promising discovery with me and look forward to his eventual publication of the painting.

48

A Sibyl with a Book, Seated before a Standing Putto Leaning on a Vase

Red chalk, on ivory laid paper
240 x 357 mm.
Inscribed on verso in brown ink: *Guercino*
PROVENANCE: Christopher Head (according to Vasari Society, 1911-1912, see below); Colnaghi & Obach, London, 1914 (according to a typewritten label affixed to the back of the frame); Frederick Keppel & Co., N.Y., no. I 5430 (printed label with this name and stock number appears on back of frame, just above the typewritten label mentioning Colnaghi; it is partly covered by an old loan sticker from the Fogg Art Museum: TL 16963.3, inscribed *JONES*); Paul J. Sachs, Cambridge, Mass.; by descent to Mrs. Soma Weiss, Cambridge, Mass. (later Mrs. Victor O. Jones)
BIBLIOGRAPHY: *The Vasari Society for the Reproduction of Drawings by Old Masters,* Series I, Part VII, Oxford and New York: University Press, 1911-1912, no. 13, repr. (as *Consolation:* Allegorical Subject, with incorrect dimensions)

Private Collection

In the 1640s and early 1650s, Guercino made a number of extremely noble paintings of Sibyls, the ancient prophetesses who foretold the coming of Christ. In several of them, like the *Phrygian Sibyl with a Putto* of 1647, which was recently discovered and exhibited in London,[1] a woman in classical garb sits with her hand on a book while a nude putto stands before her on a table. The putti in these paintings, who sometimes have wings, typically gesture at inscriptions on large stone tablets (as does the one in the London picture) or hold up scrolls identifying the name of the Sibyl.

The exhibited sheet, a masterpiece of Guercino's late period, is not connected to any of the known pictures, all of which are in a vertical format. Nonetheless, it is clear from the *all'antica* hairstyle and clothing of the woman, her thoughtful pose and curious expression, the presence of a book—faintly sketched—in her elegant left hand (she seems to be turning the page, perhaps an allusion to the new era approaching), and the knowing gaze of the putto leaning on a classical urn, that Guercino's drawing represents the inspiration of a Sibyl, perhaps intended for depiction in a painting.

The softness and luminosity of the red chalk is exceptional in this work. By using a light touch in certain areas, like the chest of the putto, Guercino gives the viewer the impression of light bathing the forms and blurring their edges and contours. Based on the handling and conception of the drawing, we should like to suggest a dating of around 1635-1645.[2]

1. Not in Salerno. Oil on canvas, 1.146 x .96 m. Hazlitt, Gooden & Fox, London, sale cat., *Italian and the Italianate,* 20 June - 20 July 1990, color repr. *Libro dei Conti,* p. 327: 21 May 1647: "Dal Sig. Girolamo Bolognetti si è ricevuto ducatoni N. 70 per il quadro della Sibilla Frigia fatta all'Ill.mo Sig. Ambasciator di Bologna che risiede a Roma, fanno—scudi 87. e mezzo."

2. I extend my warmest thanks and deepest appreciation to William Robinson for bringing this virtually unknown drawing to my attention and for arranging to have it lent to the exhibition.

113

Oiled black chalk, heightened with white chalk, on
oatmeal paper
352 x 256 mm.
Several small holes around head; laid down on three sides
PROVENANCE: Earl of Gainsborough (according to
Bresler), and therefore, Casa Gennari-E. Bouverie
previously; E. Parsons & Sons, London, 1922; purchased
from F.H. Bresler Co., Milwaukee (attributed to Tintoretto)
BIBLIOGRAPHY: Minneapolis, 1971, no. 4, repr.

Mr. and Mrs. Benton Case, Jr.

Representations of God the Father abound
in Guercino's paintings. Although they appear in a variety of iconographic contexts,
Guercino's depictions of God usually conform
to a specific physiognomic type: flowing
white hair and beard, broad and wrinkled
forehead, long nose with flaring nostrils, large
eyes with a stern, powerful gaze.

In many of Guercino's works, the *Padre
Eterno* peers down from the cloud-filled
upper half of a large altarpiece. However,
there are several instances in which Guercino
made a *sopraqquadro*—literally, a picture to
be placed on top of another picture or altarpiece—that featured God the Father all alone
or in the company of a dove or little angel.
For example, the *Padre Eterno* of 1646 in the
Pinacoteca at Bologna (fig. 49a)[1] was specifically made to surmount a picture of the *Cir-
cumcision* (Lyons, Musée des Beaux Arts),[2] a
huge altarpiece commissioned that same year
by the nuns of the Bolognese church of Gesù
e Maria.

The carefully drawn head shown here
does not match up exactly with any of the
known images of God painted by Guercino.
Given its large size and precise treatment, it
is, however, almost certainly preparatory for a
painting or *sopraqquadro* that included the
Padre Eterno. The expression and facial type
of the figure in the drawing are unmistakable
in this regard. Moreover, the costume, a kind
of cape which has a single closure below the
neck, is used for virtually all of Guercino's
depictions of the Creator. The style of the
drawing would indicate a date in the middle
of the 1640s, very near, in fact, to the time of
the 1646 *Padre Eterno* in the Bologna Pinacoteca.

1. Inv. no. 42. Salerno, no. 235.
2. Salerno, no. 233.

49a

115

50

Helmeted Warrior with Two Separate Studies of His Head, and Two Other Studies

(Study for *Hersilia Separating Romulus and Tatius,* Paris, Louvre, 1645)

Pen and brown ink, on laid paper
200 x 215 mm.
Inscribed in ink, lower right recto, *859;* notes on the verso, in Platt's hand
PROVENANCE: Casa Gennari; Francesco Forni; Hon. Edward Bouverie; Mr. Hervey; the Earls of Gainsborough (sale: London, Christie's, 27 July 1922, either multiple lots 84 or 85); E. Parsons & Sons, London (stockbook no. 29, "A Warrior & four other heads"); Dan Fellows Platt, 1924 (L. Suppl. 2066b, verso); Benjamin West Society, Swarthmore College (stamp, recto); Colnaghi, New York
BIBLIOGRAPHY: Colnaghi, New York, 1984, no. 16, repr.; M-T, under no. 115

Janet Mavec

This unusual sheet formerly in the Platt Collection is a study for the bearded leader depicted on the left side of Guercino's painting of *Hersilia Separating Romulus and Tatius* ("the Sabine women intervening to make peace between the Romans and Sabines"), now in the Louvre, inv. no. 85 (fig. 50a).[1] The picture—the third of four large paintings of Roman historical subjects completed by Guercino for the Secretary of State to Louis XIII, Louis Phélypeaux de La Vrillière—was paid for on 8 July 1645 (*Libro dei Conti,* p. 326). It was subsequently sent to Paris where it joined works by Poussin, Reni, Cortona, and other great masters in the large Galerie of La Vrillière's palace, now the Banque de France.[2] The importance and subsequent influence of this commission would be hard to exaggerate. Neoclassical history paintings of the late eighteenth century such as Jacques-Louis David's *Rape of the Sabines* and the *Oath of the Horatii* owe a significant debt to Guercino's highly structured and noble images.[3]

Having defined the general composition for his picture in a very finished pen-and-wash drawing preserved in the Uffizi (fig. 50b),[4] Guercino turns here to the difficult problem of working out the specific attitude, physiognomy, and costume of one of his main protagonists. With rather schematic penstrokes, he blocks out the position of the upper body, which strides forward, much as it does in the painting, with the extended left arm bearing the oval-shaped shield. The head and helmet are shown in profile to emphasize the frieze-like, "antique" character of the depiction and to increase the warrior's severity.

Using parallel lines, or hatching, like that employed by engravers, Guercino models the forms and determines the placement of lights and darks. This hatching technique, which is often used by Guercino in sketches of the 1630s and 40s (e.g., cat. nos. 30 and 53), has sometimes confused connoisseurs, who have taken its occurrence as an indication that a particular sheet is a copy or forgery made in response to reproductive prints, such as those etched by Bartolozzi after Guercino's drawings (e.g., fig. 22b).[5] Bartolozzi, in fact, may have intended to reproduce the exhibited drawing in a print. A pen-and-ink copy of Guercino's sketch (fig. 50c), probably made at Casa Gennari in 1763 when the printmaker accompanied the British Royal Librarian, Richard Dalton, to Bologna, is now in the Al-

50a

117

50b

50c

bertina, where it is attributed to Bartolozzi.[6] Though such cases of copies after prints are common, the authenticity of a given drawing cannot be decided solely on the basis of these parallel lines, since such gravure-style hatching is often a perfectly genuine aspect of Guercino's own draftsmanship.

The two studies to the right of the sheet offer alternatives for the angle of the warrior's head and reconsider the proper amount of facial hair: these heads perhaps have more personality than that of the central figure, but they are no substitute for the compositional strength of the profile view, which is the one Guercino ultimately translated into paint. Contrary to the opinion of Mahon and Turner, who describe the two heads on the left as

further studies for the central warrior, it seems clear from the open-mouthed expression and the glance—into the picture rather than across it—that these heads are preparatory studies for one (or two) of the secondary warriors who stand immediately adjacent to the central character in the Uffizi sketch, but who were subsequently abandoned and replaced by a single Sabine woman facing towards the left in the painted version of the subject.[7]

1. Salerno no. 226, repr. See Paris, 1988, no. 86, color repr.; and Loire, 1990, no. 9., repr.

2. For the history of the commission, which included a fourth work by Guercino (*Mucius Scaevola*) that was completed but never delivered, see Paris, 1988, esp. pp. 29-46; Salerno no. 248; M- T, under no. 138; and Mahon,

"Le Guerchin et la France," pp. 13 ff., in Loire, 1990. An autograph drawing for the figure of Mucius Scaevola, formerly assigned to School of Guercino, is in the Art Museum, Princeton, Gibbons, no. 376; inv. 49.49. It was so identified by Denis Mahon and Nicholas Turner.

3. See Rosenblum, 1962.

4. Inv. no. 10746-s. Johnston, 1970, pl. XXX and p. 86; Johnston, 1973, no. 86, fig. 59. Cf. also Paris, 1988, p. 247 and M-T, under no. 574. For a black-chalk study at Windsor for the figure of Hersilia (and for references to two other related drawings), see M-T, no. 115.

5. See also our discussion under cat. nos. 11, 75-76.

6. Inv. 1390, Stix-Fröhlich-Bum, I, pl. 198, no. 456.

7. A very Guercinesque black-chalk drawing in Dresden (1854, inv. C529.95.394; photo, Hertziana Library, Rome) of a beardless, muscular nude man striding towards the right with an oval shield on his left arm and a sword in his right hand would appear to be by one of Guercino's collaborators or students. It may have been drawn as an academic exercise based on the striding figure in the *Sabines*.

51
Silvio Discovering the Wounded Dorinda Supported by Linco
(Study for the painting, Dresden, Gemäldegalerie, 1646-1647)

Pen and brown ink, brown wash
289 x 275 mm.
Foxed; lined
PROVENANCE: Charles Fairfax Murray; purchased by J.
Pierpont Morgan in London, 1910
BIBLIOGRAPHY: Stampfle-Bean, 1967, no. 45; *Disegni,*
no. 158; Artioli-Monducci, pl. 54

The Pierpont Morgan Library, New York, I, 101g

As Stampfle and Bean have noted, this poetic drawing is a study for a picture now in Dresden (fig. 51a),[1] which was commissioned by Count Alfonso of Novellara in 1646 and completed by Guercino in 1647. The subject, which makes obvious allusions to Cupid's marksmanship, represents an episode from Giovanni Battista Guarini's pastoral drama, *Il Pastor Fido,* first published in 1590, and performed countless times throughout the seventeenth century. In this scene Silvio has accidentally wounded the nymph Dorinda, whom he has mistaken for a wolf because of her disguise. Her faithful shepherd Linco comes to her aid as the smitten Silvio, gesturing with one hand to his heart, offers her the bow so that she might take her revenge on him.

1. Salerno, no. 240.

51a

52

Two Studies for the *Vision of Saint Philip Neri*
(Bologna, Santa Maria in Galliera, 1646-1647)

Pen and brown ink, brown wash
145 x 237 mm.
Light foxing
PROVENANCE: J. Theodor Cremer; sale: Sotheby's, Amsterdam, 17 Nov. 1980, lot 133; sale: C.G. Boerner, Düsseldorf
BIBLIOGRAPHY: Stampfle-Bean, 1967, no. 43; Salerno, under no. 243

Elmar W. Seibel, Boston

Few drawings could demonstrate better than cat. no. 52 the intensity and velocity of Guercino's search for perfection as a designer. Throughout his early and mature years, as well as in the late period—even after the death of Guido Reni in 1642 and Guercino's subsequent rise to the status of *caposcuola* in Bologna—the master was never content with his first sketches. He was his own harshest critic and continually adjusted and corrected his designs, sometimes on the same sheet (as in the exhibited sketch, on the right side) but more frequently by making new drawings from scratch on separate pieces of paper.

For paintings like the *St. William of Aquitaine* of 1620, this process could lead to the production of dozens of drawings (see cat. no. 9), each one more adventurous than the last. In Guercino's later years, as Mahon has noted,[1] the excited and dynamic initial sketches continued to be made, but were more quickly succeeded than in the past by harmonious and equilibrated drawings that correspond compositionally rather closely to the paintings they prepare (unlike in early

52a

Guercino). As evident in a marvelous pen-and-wash drawing formerly in the Janos Scholz Collection and now in the Morgan Library (fig. 52b),[2] Guercino has compressed and distilled the forms that were so nervous and ecstatic in the Seibel drawing and has predicted to a significant degree the restraint and symmetry of the 1647 altarpiece in Santa Maria in Galliera, Bologna (fig. 52a) for which both sheets are preparatory.[3]

As previously mentioned, the design of this work may recall—in a general way—the Seattle sketch of the *Ecstasy of St. Teresa* (cat. no. 31), which Guercino decided not to use for his altarpiece of 1634. In that project, one finds a far more radical split between the initial design and the final outcome than in the *St. Philip*. It should be pointed out in passing that many of the changes Guercino makes as he works out his designs for a given painting are motivated by iconographic concerns and cannot be attributed singlemindedly to a general notion of "style."

Even in its highly classicizing form, the *Vision of St. Philip Neri* still maintains a great deal of the spiritual energy one associates with the earlier Guercino. But this spirituality no longer takes the form of action; in the late style it is conveyed through beauty. Much of what Guercino has to say in these late paintings comes through subtle manipulation of color and elegant *contrapposti* of attitudes. Due to his preoccupation with color, it is quite understandable why he turns again and again to red and black chalk in the later years. In many ways, these drawings, for example, cat. nos. 57, 60, and 61, are more revealing of his ultimate goals in the paintings than the sketches in pen and ink.

52b

1. See *Disegni*, pp. 27-38. Cf. also Stone, 1989, pp. 300 ff.

2. Inv. 1977.49. 252 x 290 mm. Stampfle-Bean, 1967, no. 44.

3. Salerno, no. 243.

121

53
Andromeda Chained to the Rock
(Study for the painting, Genoa, Palazzo Balbi Senarega, 1648)

Pen and brown ink, on laid paper
196 x 239 mm.
Acid ink corrosion, especially in the area to the left of the face; previously backed by another sheet (on the verso of which is a fragment of a list in pen and brown ink with figures). The drawing has been restored for the 1991 exhibition: the backing, which caused considerable wrinkling of the original sheet and losses in the area of Andromeda's drapery, has been removed.
PROVENANCE: Dan Fellows Platt; purchased from Schaeffer Galleries, N.Y.
BIBLIOGRAPHY: Lynes, p. 88, no. 56, pl. vi, fig. 12

Robert and Bertina Suida Manning

The *Libro dei Conti* lists two paintings of *Andromeda,* one in 1648 and another in 1660.[1] The latter is lost, but the former is almost certainly to be identified with the picture in the Balbi Senarega Collection in Genoa which depicts *Andromeda Chained to the Rock and Threatened by a Sea Monster, as Perseus Comes to Her Rescue* (fig. 53a).[2]

The drawings previously connected to this project (in the Brera, Milan and the Graphische Sammlung, Stuttgart)[3] are not as convincing in their relationship to the painting as cat. no. 53, which on the basis of style alone can be comfortably dated to the 1640s, arguably the second half of the decade. Though the Manning drawing does not illustrate the monster and the flying Perseus shown on the right side of the canvas, the general attitude of the female figure and her gesture are reasonably close to the final composition.[4]

1. For references, see M-T, under no. 485.

2. Salerno, no. 254.

3. See M-T, under no. 485. No connected drawings are listed by Salerno, under no. 254.

4. An equally beautiful but untraced pen drawing of the same subject (195 x 250 mm.) is reproduced in a photograph at the Witt Library. The sheet, which comes from the collection of J.P. Mariette (L. 1852), is stylistically very much in tune with the exhibited work and the Genoa painting. It shows the nude *Andromeda* standing before a comparable rock with her feet and left arm in chains; she leans over a ledge to the left and looks up over her left shoulder toward the right (at Perseus, who is not shown). The sea monster, which is lacking in the Manning sheet, is nicely described in this work in the lower right corner. The photograph states that the drawing was sold at the Boussac Sale, Galerie Petit, Paris, 10-11 May 1926, cat. no. 85, repr. on p. 41.

53a

124

54

Three Studies of a Putto

(Study for *Saint Margaret of Cortona,* Rome, Vatican Pinacoteca, 1648)

Red chalk
273 x 199 mm.
Excellent condition
PROVENANCE: Casa Gennari (characteristic mount, L. Suppl. 2858c; cf. Mahon, 1967, p. 20); F. Forni; E. Bouverie; Mr. Hervey; Earls of Gainsborough; sale: Christie's, London, 23 Nov. 1971, lot 100; Harry Michaels; sale: Christie's, London, 7 July 1981, lot 50, color repr.
BIBLIOGRAPHY: Unpublished

Private Collection

As Denis Mahon has said (cf. Christie's catalogues), this sensitive sheet represents three studies for the putto in the upper left corner of Guercino's *Saint Margaret of Cortona,* an altarpiece of 1648 formerly at Cesena and now in the Vatican.[1]

Studies like the exhibited drawing, which have multiple heads on the same page, are not infrequent in Guercino's later oeuvre (see also cat. nos. 50 and 61). They testify to the fact that even in the artist's late period he continued to treat every pose and design as an experiment whose outcome he could not predict.

The central child in this sheet is situated in such a way that it is hard to envision him flying horizontally across the top of a painting as he does in the altarpiece itself. I would propose that this study and its companions—however idealized their rendering—were done from life and were subsequently adapted for use in the Cesena *St. Margaret.*

(See the following entry.)

1. Salerno, no. 253. The painting was paid for by Alessandro Martinelli of Cesena (*Libro dei Conti,* 17 June 1648).

Black chalk, on buff paper
275 x 340 mm.
Repairs; creases along borders
Inscriptions and erasures in lower left corner of recto
PROVENANCE: sale: Sotheby's, New York, 16 January
1985, lot 134, color repr.
BIBLIOGRAPHY: Unpublished

Dr. Carlo M. Croce

The large and austere black-chalk drawing of a *Flying Putto* in the Croce Collection (cat. no. 55) should be compared to the three studies depicted in cat. no. 54. Complete with wings and indications of a cloud, this child is much more abstract and idealized than the putti in the red-chalk sheet just examined. Unlike cat. no. 54, this drawing was probably done without the aid of a model.

In the 1640s and 1650s, after a hiatus of about a decade in which he used pen and red chalk almost exclusively, Guercino returned to the use of black chalk for certain subjects like head studies and half-length putti. These are usually drawn with oiled charcoal, called *carboncino,* as in cat. nos. 49 and 55, although he sometimes used a graphite-like *matita nera,* as, apparently, in cat. no. 62. In his early days, Guercino employed oiled black chalk for academic nudes (see cat. nos. 63-65), figures of various types (see cat. nos. 77-78, 86), and occasionally for draperies.[1]

Previously unconnected, cat. no. 55 may, in fact, be related to a figure of a flying putto with wings who gestures with his right hand and leans on a cloud with his left in the lower center of a small *Assumption of the Virgin* painted in 1654-1655 (Ackland Art Museum, Chapel Hill, University of North Carolina).[2] The connection should be considered tentative, since the torso of the putto in the painting is turned further downwards, his head is shifted to one side and tilted down, and, most significantly, his right arm is bent ninety degrees and gestures toward the upper right corner of the scene. However, I am struck by the resemblance of the heads and faces and by a terribly subtle detail that is perhaps only visible when studying the drawing in the original. A group of wavy lines begins just to the left of the navel and at a certain point rises upwards on a diagonal. It goes past the right hip (now a single, un-broken line), and trails off like curls of smoke towards the left side of the sheet. These faint lines are Guercino's shorthand for the putto's drapery, which in the painting performs a similar spiral in the same location. It should also be borne in mind that the figures are similarly illuminated from the left side. In all events, the drawing should be dated to c. 1650.

1. As in a sheet in the Fachsenfeld Collection for a work of 1618-1619. See *Disegni,* no. 39.

2. Salerno, no. 312.

Red chalk, on laid paper
197 x 140 mm.
Excellent condition
PROVENANCE: Lord Northwick (according to Weiner; thus, probably also Casa Gennari, F. Forni, E. Bouverie); Private Collection, New Haven; Mia N. Weiner, *Old Master Drawings,* exh. sale cat., New York, Fall 1987, no. 25, color repr.
BIBLIOGRAPHY: Unpublished

Private Collection

Drawings like this serious-looking High Priest or Rabbi in an exotic costume were probably hoarded in artists' studios. Such heads served the painter when a supporting cast of characters was needed for a biblical subject.

Not connected to any known painting by Guercino, this fine study is more worked up than most and may also have been intended for engraving.[1] The strong horizontal line across the bottom edge is a finishing touch which would otherwise be hard to explain.

The style and technique of this work should be compared to the large head of *God the Father* in oiled black chalk with white highlights in the Case Collection, exhibited here as cat. no. 49. Both studies should be dated to c. 1645.

1. This suggestion was made by Denis Mahon (cf. Weiner, 1987, under no. 25).

130

Studies for the *Assumption of the Virgin*
(Detroit Institute of Arts, 1650)

57 The Assumption of the Virgin (r.)
   Study of a Putto Looking Down (v.)

Red chalk, on laid paper
305 x 223 mm.
Excellent condition
PROVENANCE: Casa Gennari; F. Forni; E. Bouverie; Mr.
Hervey; 1st Earl of Gainsborough (?); Lord Northwick;
A.P. Oppe; Yvonne ffrench, London (until May 1967)
BIBLIOGRAPHY: A.H. Scott-Elliot, *Exhibition of Works
from the Paul Oppé Collection: English Watercolors and
Old Master Drawings,* exh. cat., Royal Academy, London,
1958, no. 383; Frederick J. Cummings, "The *Assumption of
the Virgin* by Guercino," *Bulletin of the Detroit Institute of
Arts* 51, nos. 2 & 3 (1972), pp. 52-62, figs. 3-4; Salerno,
under no. 270

{H,O}

Mr. and Mrs. Morton B. Harris

58 The Apostles at the Tomb

Red chalk, on laid paper
287 x 206 mm.
Excellent condition; edges stained by old mat or frame
WATERMARK: Anchor
PROVENANCE: Casa Gennari; F. Forni; E. Bouverie; Mr.
Hervey; Earls of Gainsborough; sale: Sotheby's, London,
23 Nov. 1971, lot 103, repr.; Baskett & Day, London,
Exhibition of Drawings, 28 Nov. - 12 Dec. 1972, no. 9,
repr.
BIBLIOGRAPHY: Unpublished. Mentioned in
Cummings, 1972, p. 62, n. 15

Private Collection

The ten-foot high altarpiece of the *Assumption of the Virgin* now in the Detroit Institute of Arts (fig. 57a)[1] was first identified by Denis Mahon,[2] who connected it to the following description by Malvasia under the year 1650: "Un'Assonta con gli Angioli & Apostoli in lontananza al sepolcro della B.V. tavola d'altare in Napoli [an Assumption with Angels, with the Apostles in the distance near the tomb of the Virgin—altarpiece in Naples]."[3] Guercino's *Libro dei Conti* also records this work (payments on 14 May and 25 October 1650, for a total of 437 scudi or about 350 ducats) and confirms the destination as Naples.[4]

A well-preserved example of the flickering luminosity and ethereal abstraction of Guercino's late drawing style, the Harris sketch (recto) exhibited here as cat. no. 57 represents a preliminary compositional study for the Detroit painting. As one can see by comparing the sketch to the altarpiece, Guercino went on to make several revisions. The most important of these concerns the positions and attitudes of the two large angels who form a kind of cartouche base for the figure of the Virgin. In classic Guercino fashion, the angel on the right-hand side of the Harris drawing has been drafted for duty on the left side of the painting. The change necessitated only a slight adjustment to the angel's head, which instead of looking down, now looks up over the left shoulder to address the Madonna. The angel on the left side of the Harris sheet was rejected altogether. No doubt at least one or two further studies were required to develop a new design for the angel on the right side of the painting, whose wings now face into the center of the composition.

Guercino also reworked the attitude of the putto who appears in the upper left corner of the Harris recto. In the painting, instead of looking down, he flies upward on a swift diagonal. His sturdy companion on the right

57a

side of the canvas is perhaps presaged by a squiggle or two on the right side of the drawing's recto. On the verso, one finds a delightful study for the figure in a highly finished style, which one should compare to the "broken" quality of line and the relative absence of shading or modelling on the recto. Here, again, the function of the drawings has dictated to an appreciable degree the handling they receive. The *Putto,* who corresponds quite closely to the final version, no doubt came at an advanced stage in the design process, perhaps even after the initial figures were blocked out on the canvas. The general compositional sketch on the recto, by contrast, did not necessitate such detail; its function was more schematic. For two other studies of putti, see cat. nos. 54-55.

Cat. no. 58, a very moving representation of the *Apostles at the Tomb,* accords perfectly with the style of Guercino drawings of the

57: recto

57: verso

early 1650s such as the Harris sheet. As Mahon has suggested, cat. no. 58 may be connected to the Naples project, which is the only late painting representing an *Assumption with Apostles* recorded by Malvasia or the account book.[5] Based on the scene depicted in the drawing, one can hypothesize that instead of placing the apostles at the tomb *in lontananza* (in the distance), as Malvasia says and as Guercino actually painted them in a wonderful bit of classicizing landscape along the lower edge of the canvas, the artist at first may have considered situating medium-size figures of the apostles in the middle distance and placing one full-size apostle (St. Peter ?) in the foreground. The large apostle in the drawing stares transfixed at a miraculous sight overhead, which is clearly that of the ascendant Virgin, who has risen from the the tomb where the other apostles—not yet aware of the assumption—have gathered to mourn. This was more or less how Guercino painted the scene in 1623 in a large painting now in the Hermitage, Leningrad (for references and a related drawing, see Suppl. no. 226, repr.). Owing to the higher price such a picture inevitably would have cost (since Guercino charged by the figure), it is possible that the client decided to eliminate the traditional scene from the foreground and to make do with just the Virgin, two large angels, and two putti (the equivalent of three and a half figures at 350 ducats).

Guercino may have made cat. no. 58 before the details of the commission were finalized. It is even conceivable that the Harris drawing also predates the decision to eliminate the large figures from the bottom half of the painting. The putto and two angels on the recto all glance down to something happening below them. I doubt that Guercino would have constructed such an image if he knew that the tomb scene below was going to be invisible to anyone standing four feet away from the altarpiece.

For a similar case in which a composition was substantially changed after sketches had been made, see cat. no. 30.

1. Inv. 71.1. 3.080 x 2.198 m. Founders Society Purchase, Robert H. Tannahill Foundation Fund and Josephine and Ernest Kanzler Founders Fund. Salerno, no. 270.

2. See Cummings, 1972.

3. Malvasia, II, p. 269.

4. Salerno, no. 270. The name of the church is not given.

5. Mahon's opinion is stated in the Christie's catalogue, 1971, p. 35, under no. 103 and is repeated by Cummings, 1972, p. 62, n. 15.

58

59
Endymion Sleeping
(Study for the lost painting, 1650)

Pen and brown ink, brown wash
211 x 248 mm.
Lined
PROVENANCE: Casa Gennari; F. Forni; E. Bouverie; Mr.
Hervey; Earls of Gainsborough; sale: Christie's, London,
27 July 1922, one of five multiple lots; A.G.B. Russell,
Lancaster Herald (L. Suppl. 2770a, lower right recto);
purchased in New York in 1968
BIBLIOGRAPHY: Russell, 1923, p. 34, pl. V; Mahon, 1967,
p. 8, n. 11; Jacob Bean, *Metropolitan Museum of Art
Bulletin* (Feb. 1969), p. 315, repr.; Bean, 1979, no. 238,
repr.; Salerno, under no. 247; M-T, under no. 215

{O,C}

The Metropolitan Museum of Art, New York,
Purchase, 1968, Rogers Fund, 68.171

Guercino is known to have made five paintings of *Endymion,* but only one of them was full-length.[1] This was the *Endimione figura intera* paid for in March of 1650 by Don Antonio Ruffo of Messina (*Libro dei Conti,* p. 331). Denis Mahon has suggested that the sensuous nude represented in the exhibited sheet is likely to be a preliminary study for the Ruffo picture, which is lost and otherwise visually undocumented.[2] One can imagine from the heroic structure of this beautifully preserved work what an important painting Guercino must have created.

For another commission from Don Antonio Ruffo, see cat. no. 62.

1.   For a complete discussion, see Salerno, under no. 247 and M-T, under no. 215.

2.   Mahon, 1967, p. 8, n. 11.

Red chalk

270 x 295 mm.

Laid down on Barnard mount; top corners cut

PROVENANCE: George Earl Cholmondeley (according to Rogers); John Barnard (L. 1419, his mount with initials in script, lower right recto of mount; inscriptions on verso of mount); Lenglier (L. 1670, script on verso of mount); Baron D. Vivant-Denon (L. 779, lower right recto); Buhler (according to present owner); unidentified collector's mark in black ink, *JC* in a circle, lower right recto of mount (perhaps the same stamp as on the verso of a Franceschini drawing in the Metropolitan Museum of Art, New York; see Bean, 1979, no. 184, who gives the collector as J. Cantacuzène, Paris); Private Collection, Paris

BIBLIOGRAPHY: Charles Rogers, *A Collection of Prints, in Imitation of Drawings . . .*, London, 1778, II, p. 115 (as "Chastity burning the arms of Cupid" in the collection of Cholmondeley), repr. (engraved in the same sense by W.W. Ryland, 1762); L.J.J. Dubois, *Description des objets d'arts qui composent le cabinet de feu de M. Le Baron V. Denon . . .*, Paris, 1826, p. 134, no. 453 ("Dessin de la sanguine, representant l'Hymen brûlant les armes de l'amour"); not listed in *Monuments des Arts,* 1829

Private Collection, New Haven, Connecticut

This majestic late Guercino which has not been reproduced since 1762 may have been made as a presentation drawing or intended for a print. It is not connected to any known painting. Few late drawings by the master could compete with its high degree of finish and grand design. The exquisite landscape background is perhaps the most beautiful and extensive by the artist in a red-chalk drawing of a historical subject.[1]

The drawing represents a familiar theme in Seicento art, the punishment of Love by Chastity. Diana the huntress, the goddess of the moon, the nightime companion of the ever-sleeping, ever-youthful Endymion (see the previous entry), is also the goddess of Chastity. She is depicted here in high-topped sandals or buskins (as described in classical literature) putting a torch to Cupid's armaments of love: the bow, arrows, and quiver. To her left, Cupid cries in defeat.

On the basis of style, the work should be dated to c. 1650 or perhaps slightly earlier. If the drawing had been made into a painting, it might have looked something like the *Venus Mourning the Dead Adonis* commissioned by Cardinal Mazzarin in 1647 (formerly Dresden, destroyed).[2]

An equally finished red-chalk study in the Morgan Library of a *Magdalen Praying in a Landscape* (Suppl. no. 136, repr.) should be compared to the exhibited sheet both for the style of the drapery and the handling of the figure as well as for the treatment of the landscape. This elegant work, which has not been connected to a painting, may have been made as a presentation drawing.

1. I thank the owner for providing me with references relating to this highly important drawing. Some of his notes were based on material furnished by Denis Mahon. I would also like to thank Nicholas Turner for verifying citations of Rogers and Denon.

2. Salerno, no. 237.

139

61

Three Studies of a Madonna Mourning

(Study for *The Entombment of Christ,* The Art Institute of Chicago, 1656)

Red chalk, on ivory laid paper
168 x 272 mm.
PROVENANCE: P. & D. Colnaghi & Co. Ltd., London
(*Old Master Drawings,* exh. sale cat., 28 June - 21 July
1984, no. 21, repr.)
BIBLIOGRAPHY: Unpublished

William D. Shorey

According to Guercino's account book, the large *Entombment of Christ* now in the Art Institute of Chicago (fig. 61a) was commissioned by an anonymous "Cavaliere Veneziano" in 1656.[1] The painting later passed into the Colonna Collection in Rome.[2] Not in the traditional upright format of an altarpiece, this extremely restrained, tightly composed work may have been used for private devotion in a palace.

Three drawings have been related to the Chicago picture. A complete compositional sketch in red chalk which reverses the position of Christ was sold at Christie's, London on 5 July 1983, lot 97 and is now in an Italian private collection.[3] On the verso of the sheet is a study in black chalk for a painting of *Santa Francesca Romana* (Turin, Galleria Sabauda), which Guercino painted in 1656-1657.[4] Another fine red-chalk study, this one concentrating on just the figure and expression of the *Dead Christ* (fig. 61b) was sold at Sotheby's, London on 2 July 1984, lot 81 and is now in an American private collection.[5] This drawing continues the idea set forth in the ex-Christie's sheet of showing Christ facing towards the right. Just under Christ's right armpit, one can see a faint sketch of the right hand of one of the mourners.

Compared to the two drawings just mentioned, the unpublished drawing in the Shorey Collection would certainly seem to have come much later in the evolution of the design.[6] The Madonna in the center is used with little variation in the final work. The other two studies both imply that Christ's head is located in the right half of the composition, just as in the Chicago painting. The weeping Madonna on the left, shown in profile, was eventually adopted by Guercino for the pose of Mary Magdalen. In the painted work Guercino has removed her veil (usually reserved for the Madonna) and turned the figure's head in the direction of the viewer.

Her left hand still holds a handkerchief, but this has been lowered.

The exhibited drawing should be compared to the handling of line in the Harris sketch (cat. no. 57, recto), which Guercino made in 1650 for an *Assumption of the Virgin* now in Detroit. The Shorey drawing might be said to evince a similar if not greater fragility of touch. The sheet is somewhat faded, but drawings of this type were lightly sketched in the first place. An analogous study with comparable red-chalk technique and handling of the figures was employed by Guercino in *Two Studies of St. Catherine of Alexandria,* the verso of a sheet in Dublin, National Gallery of Ireland (*Disegni,* no. 169: verso). This sketch and the compositional drawing on the recto are studies for a painting of the *Madonna di Soriano with the Magdalen and St. Catherine of Alexandria,* which Guercino made for Bolzano in c. 1655.[7]

1. Wilson L. Mead Fund, 1956.128. Photo courtesy of the Art Institute of Chicago. 1.467 x 2.212 m. See Salerno, no. 317. *Libro dei Conti,* p. 337.

2. See *Dipinti,* no. 99, with extensive commentary and references on the provenance of the painting.

3. Salerno, under no. 317.

4. Salerno, no. 315.

5. Mentioned by Salerno, under no. 317. Dimensions: 159 x 267 mm. Inscribed lower right corner in ink: *guarchino.* Upper right corner made up. The drawing has been restored since coming into the collection of the current owner, whom I should like to thank for providing me with a new photograph.

6. Not mentioned in Salerno, under no. 317. The connection to the Chicago painting was first made by Denis Mahon (according to the Colnaghi catalogue of 1984).

7. Salerno, no. 314.

61a

61b

62

A Cosmographer with a Globe and Compass

(Study for the lost painting, 1660)

Black chalk
260 x 193 mm.
Foxed, stained, and pasted to old mount
PROVENANCE: Count Cesare Massimiliano Gino
(according to crayon-manner print [in the same sense as
drawing] by Giuseppe Zaoli [Faenza, c. 1760 - ?]: *Ex
insigni collectione Comitis Cesari Maximiliani Gini*; see
Augusto Calabi, *La Gravure italienne au XVIII siècle*,
Paris, 1931, plate LXXXI); William Bateson (L. Suppl.
2604a, lower center verso); Dan Fellows Platt (L. Suppl.
750a, lower left verso, and 2066b, center verso), bought at
Parsons in 1929
BIBLIOGRAPHY: Lynes, p. 112, no. 131; Jakob
Rosenberg, "Rembrandt and Guercino," *Art Quarterly* 7,
no. 2 (Spring 1944), pp. 129-34, fig. 1; DeGrazia, 1969, no.
33; Varriano, 1974, no. 40; Gibbons, no. 256; M-T, under
no. 228

The Art Museum, Princeton University
Bequest of Dan Fellows Platt, 48-709

Jakob Rosenberg was the first to connect the exhibited drawing formerly in the Platt Collection with a lost painting of a *Cosmographer* commissioned in 1660 by the extraordinary art *amateur* Don Antonio Ruffo of Messina.[1] The picture, as described in the following passage from an inventory of the Ruffo gallery, would seem to correspond in several details to the drawing: "Cosmografo con un turbante turchino in testa che considera un mappamondo tenuto con la mano sinistra sopra un tavolino e con la destra va accennando. . . ."[2] From documents published by Vincenzo Ruffo ("La Galleria Ruffo del Sec. XVII in Messina," *Bollettino d'arte* 10 [1916]), we learn that Guercino's *Cosmographer* was ordered specifically as a companion piece for no less a picture than Rembrandt's *Aristotle Contemplating the Bust of Homer* (New York, Metropolitan Museum of Art) of 1653. The *Aristotle,* one of Rembrandt's most celebrated works, arrived in Messina in 1654, two years after it had been ordered.[3]

In a famous letter to Ruffo, which we will quote in the translation by Ruth Magurn, Guercino enquires about certain details relating to the unusual commission. It seems that in the initial correspondence, Rembrandt's picture was merely described as a "half-figure." The subject and composition of the work were not mentioned. Guercino obviously could not paint a pendant without more facts at his disposal.

Earlier in the same letter, Guercino refers to an apparent request by Ruffo that he paint the pendant in his *prima maniera gagliarda* or "early style." Ruffo obviously knew Guercino's paintings very well (he had commissioned several works from him in the recent past, including the lost *Endymion* of 1650 discussed under cat. no. 59) and was aware of the change in style that had occurred in the master's art over the course of what was now

a fifty-year career. He must have felt that the Reniesque colorism of the late style was ill-suited to Rembrandt's chiaroscuro in the *Aristotle* and consequently asked Guercino to try to repeat his dark, deeply shadowed manner of the early period.[4] Though the artist could not turn back the stylistic clock that had brought him from the *St. Albert* of 1618 (see cat. no. 4) to the *Assumption* of 1650 (see cat. nos. 57-58), he was at least willing, if only in words, to try to please his patron. Since there is no record of the painting, we cannot know if Guercino actually accomplished this stylistic backflip. However, the Princeton drawing exhibited here leaves little doubt that the general composition was fully in keeping with Guercino's *ultima maniera.*[5]

From Bologna on 13 June 1660, Guercino writes:

> As for the half-figure of Rembrandt which has come into your hands, it cannot be other than complete perfection, because I have seen various works of his in prints which have come to our region. They are very beautiful in execution, engraved with good taste and done in a fine manner, so that one can assume that his work in color is likewise of complete exquisiteness and perfection. I sincerely esteem him as a great artist.
>
> Then as to the half-figure which you desire from me as a companion piece to that of Rembrandt, but to be done in my first broad manner [*ma della mia prima maniera gagliarda*], I am quite ready to agree, and to carry it out according to your orders. Will you, therefore, kindly send me the measurements, both the height and the breadth of the painting, so that I, on my part, shall not fail to use the same dimensions, and as much as my poor ability will allow, you yourself will see expressed in this picture.
>
> If you would also, on the occasion of sending me the measurements, be willing to honor me with a little sketch of Rembrandt's picture, done by some painter, so that I could see the disposition of the half-figure, I should consider it the greatest favor, and

should be better able to make a counterpart, as well as to place the light in the right place. I shall wait also for the subject whch I am to represent, in order to be able to conform more closely to your wishes.[6]

Ruffo apparently never informed Guercino of the subject of Rembrandt's painting nor did he instruct the Italian artist what to paint (as Guercino specifically requested). It is no wonder that after receiving the sketch on 18 August,[7] Guercino wrote back (on 6 October) to Don Antonio with the mistaken idea that Rembrandt's *Aristotle* was a "Physiognomist." This was not an unreasonable conclusion, since the artist's only clue to the iconography seems to have been a sketch of a man with his hand on a bust. Guercino decided that an appropriate symmetry could be made by evoking the subject of a Cosmographer.[8]

As Seymour Slive has noted, it is remarkable that Guercino had the sensitivity to admire Rembrandt's etchings and that Ruffo had the breadth of taste to commission pendants from Northern and Southern artists.[9] Guercino's enthusiasm for Rembrandt as expressed in the first paragraph of the letter has usually been discussed only in very general terms. But a pen drawing in an American private collection of *Susanna and an Elder* (Suppl. no. 204, repr.) may document a specific response by Guercino to Rembrandt's early etchings of figures such as the *Naked Woman on a Mound* of c. 1631.[10]

The Cento master's accolades for the Dutchman's virtuosity were not written to flatter an eclectic connoisseur. Guercino's own works, like the Chicago study for *Jacob's Blessing* (see cat. no. 8), the Baer drawing for *Esther and Ahasuerus* (see cat. no. 41), or the *Man Reading at a Table* (cat. no. 79), issue from a mind and aesthetic that could not help but understand and admire much of what Rembrandt had to say. One is curious to know if Rembrandt ever saw any of Guer-

cino's drawings and, if so, what he might have thought of them.[11]

1. Under 9 October 1660, one finds the following entry in the account book: Dalli Signori Davia si è ricevuto ducatoni 160 per pagamento del rame dipinto, e la mezza figura del Cosmografo, che furono fatti per l'Illmo Sig. D. Antonio Ruffi [sic] di Messina . . . (*Libro dei Conti*, pp. 340-41). It is incorrectly listed by Malvasia, II, p. 271, under 1661.

2. "A Cosmographer with a Turkish turban on his head, considering a geographical globe held with his left hand on a table, while he points to it with his right" (as quoted and translated in Rosenberg, 1944, p. 130). The inventory was originally published in Ruffo, 1916 (see below).

3. Rosenberg, 1944, p. 129.

4. For an interpretation of this strange request by Ruffo, see Mahon, 1947, p. 105 f., n. 178.

5. For a discussion of Guercino's other drawings of astronomers or cosmographers, one of which is known only through a print by C.M. Metz, see M-T, under no. 228. For two other drawings of astronomers at Princeton, see cat. no. 36 and Suppl. no. 88.

6. Rosenberg, 1944, p. 130.

7. See Rosenberg, 1944, p. 130.

8. Rosenberg, 1944, p. 130. A third picture, commissioned from the Neapolitan painter Mattia Preti in 1661, was added to the group. Preti's work, which is also lost, represented *Dionysius of Syracuse*. See Rosenberg, 1944, p. 132.

9. Seymour Slive, *Rembrandt and his Critics: 1630 - 1730*, The Hague: Martinus Nijhoff, 1953, pp. 60 ff.

10. This observation was made by Jonathan Bober, in conversation.

11. While on the subject of Guercino in Holland, it is a little-known fact that several plates from Guercino's *Drawing Manual* of 1618, engraved by Oliviero Gatti and later reissued by Bernardino Curti, were pirated by Crispijn van de Passe for his *'t Light der Teken in Schilderkonst* (Amsterdam, 1643). See the reprint with commentary by Jacob Bolten (Soest, Holland: Davaco Press, 1973). On Guercino's *Drawing Manual*, see Stone, 1989, pp. 269-78.

145

Oiled black chalk with white chalk highlights, on gray-brown paper
572 x 427 mm.
Corners made up; minor losses
PROVENANCE: Hugh Blaker, London; Sir Colin Anderson, London; Lady Anderson, London; sale: Christie's, London, 9 Dec. 1986, lot 48; Hazlitt, Gooden & Fox, Ltd. (presented by John Morton Morris), London, exh. sale, *European Drawings,* 23 Nov. - 9 Dec. 1988, no. 26, repr.
BIBLIOGRAPHY: Unpublished

{H}

The J. Paul Getty Museum, 89.GB.52

In seeming harmony with critical attitudes established in Florence and Rome, the Accademia dei Desiderosi (later the "Incamminati")—the important school founded in Bologna by the Carracci in the late sixteenth century—regarded the rendering of nude and semi-nude figures in frontal and foreshortened poses as the *sine qua non* of artistic practice. The Carracci's actual treatment of the nude, however, was anything but traditional in the context of late-Cinquecento painting.

The Carracci and their followers reinvented the practice of drawing after the live model as a necessary corrective to the excesses and artificiality of Mannerism. Whereas the Mannerists often drew their ornamental *figure* from the imagination or in explicit dialogue with Michelangelo, Raphael, and antique statuary, the Carracci insisted on the actuality of the model's appearance, even—and this was the truest test—when the figure was placed in a fancy artistic pose. Like Correggio and Tintoretto before them, they were especially sensitive to the play of natural light over the surfaces of the human body. Their nudes often have a roughness and directness of observation that seem almost modern in comparison with the aestheticism and polish given such studies by members of the Florentine Accademia del Disegno, that bastion of Michelangelism inaugurated by Giorgio Vasari in 1563, some two decades before the formation of the Bolognese Academy.

Guercino did not attend the Carracci's lessons but he was certainly familiar with their methods. In fact, he initiated his own *Accademia del Nudo* in Cento in 1616 (see cat. no. 10). Guercino's nude sketches—typically in oiled black chalk and roughly datable to the early and Roman periods—explore a wide range of postures, physical types, and problems of foreshortening and shading. Though he seems to have responded in certain drawings (e.g., the *Standing Nude with Arms Raised* at Oxford, Ashmolean Museum)[1] to the more classically posed studies of Annibale, many of Guercino's sketches (cf. cat. no. 64) are inspired by the nudes of Pietro Faccini (c. 1562 - 1602). Faccini's drawings are unusually vibrant and are characterized by strong lighting effects, faceted and angular draperies reminiscent of Federico Barocci, and an expressionistic warping of the figure no doubt in emulation of his teacher Ludovico Carracci.[2] Guercino removes some of Faccini's hyperactivity but retains his black-chalk technique (often with white highlights) and the intensity of his contrasts between light and shadow.

Since their function was largely academic and since they rarely made encore appearances in preparatory sketches or paintings, Guercino's nude studies are notoriously difficult to date. Cat. nos. 64 and 65 are exceptions to this general rule. More typical is cat. no. 63, a major acquisition recently made by the Getty Museum, which has not been connected to any known composition. Figures like the one depicted in this marvelous, large sheet were probably made without a particular image or project in mind. Comparison of the Getty *Seated Young Man* with the figure of *Lazarus* in the painting of c. 1619 now in the Louvre (Salerno, no. 56) would suggest an approximate dating of c. 1619-21 for this excellent drawing.

1. *Disegni,* no. 253. See Mahon-Ekserdjian, no. V, color frontispiece.

2. As Mahon discovered among Malvasia's manuscript notes, the Bolognese cleric Padre Don Antonio Mirandola, Guercino's discoverer and protector during the early period, showed the young artist a group of Faccini's drawings. See *Disegni,* p. 44; and Marzocchi, 1984, pp. 383, 386. On Pietro Faccini, see DeGrazia, 1984, pp. 374 ff., with further bibliography.

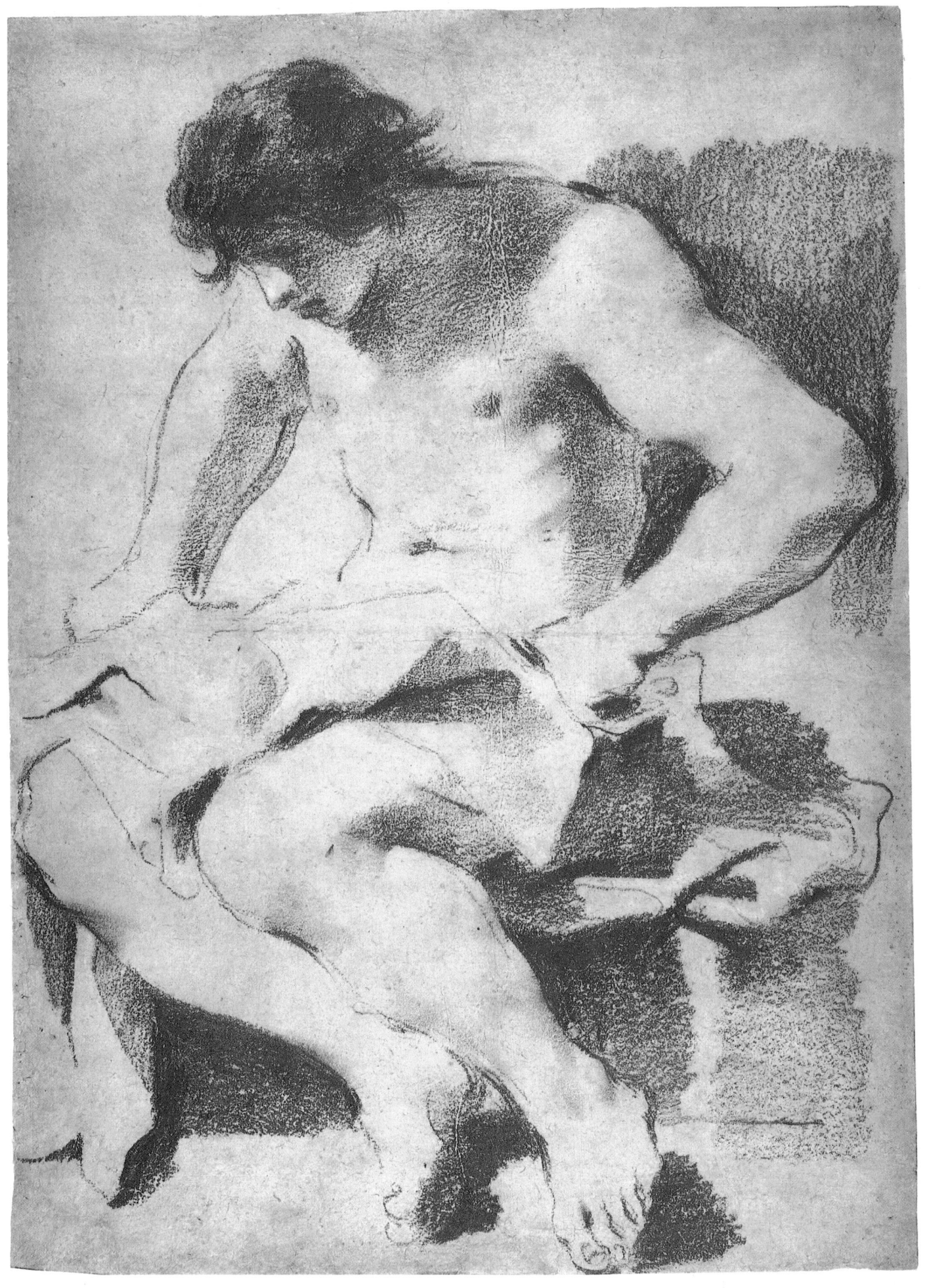

147

Pen and oiled black chalk, on brown paper
442 x 548 mm.
Vertical crease down the center where sheet was once folded
Inscribed on back of lining sheet (removed): *N. 12.*
PROVENANCE: Lord Somers; Swiss Private Collection; Paul Drey Gallery, N.Y.
BIBLIOGRAPHY: *Recent Acquisitions and Promised Gifts: Sculpture, Drawings, Prints,* exh. cat., National Gallery of Art, Washington, D.C., 1974, no. 32, repr. (entry by Diane DeGrazia)

{H,O}

National Gallery of Art, Washington, D.C., Ailsa Mellon Bruce Fund, 1973.30.1

When it has been possible to relate one of Guercino's nude studies to a figure depicted in a compositional sketch or a painting, scholars have queried whether the study was made (and the model posed) specifically for the task or whether, as seems to be more likely, it is not simply a case of a ready-made image from a life session being pressed into service at a later date when needed. The question has arisen only occasionally, however, since most of Guercino's nude studies are unconnected.

An oiled-black-chalk drawing in Paris, École des Beaux-Arts (*Disegni,* no. 35), a purposeful life study for the figure of Marsyas in the *Apollo and Marsyas* in the Pitti Palace in Florence of 1618 (Salerno, no. 47), represents a very rare instance in which Guercino posed a nude specifically for a painting. The majority of his studies—like cat. no. 63—were done as academic exercises and were not made to fit into a composition. The drawing exhibited here as cat. no. 64 is also of this common type, except that it was eventually adopted for a repoussoir figure in a compositional study.

Previously unconnected, cat. no. 64 is the source for a nude figure seen from behind in a drawing of c. 1618 in the Albertina, Vienna, representing *Souls in Purgatory Supplicating the Madonna of Loreto* (fig. 6a). Cat. no. 6 (Ottawa, National Gallery of Canada), a revised sketch of the Vienna sheet, shows this figure once again, but this time without the left foot tucked under the extended right leg.

The exhibited nude study, just as DeGrazia hypothesized, would seem to date from c. 1618. She has also put forth the plausible theory that a similar nude study in Genoa (*Disegni,* no. 249) might in fact be a rendering of the same figure from the same life session but seen from the front.[1]

Unlike the Paris *Marsyas,* the nude boy studied in the Washington and Genoa sheets would appear to be posed in a very general way, without regard to any specific compositional design or narrative. When devising his *Souls in Purgatory* (see cat. no. 6), a composition which demanded an interesting array of foreshortened nude figures, Guercino probably turned to his cache of academic nude studies and selected one or two for the large figures in the foreground.

1. For references to an excellent copy of this sheet, possibly by Carlo Gennari (1712-1790) and now in the Fogg Art Museum, Harvard University, Cambridge, Mass. (inv. 1956.14), see *Disegni,* no. 249.

149

65
Seated Male Nude

Oiled black chalk, on faded blue paper
476 x 401 mm.
PROVENANCE: Zettler Collection; Zettler sale: Hirsch, Munich, 5 March 1921, no. 138, repr.; Mathias Komor, N.Y. (see L. Suppl. 1882a); Mr. and Mrs. Joseph Henry Grand, St. Louis
BIBLIOGRAPHY: Neilson, 1972, no. 27, repr.

Evalyne S. Grand

65a: verso

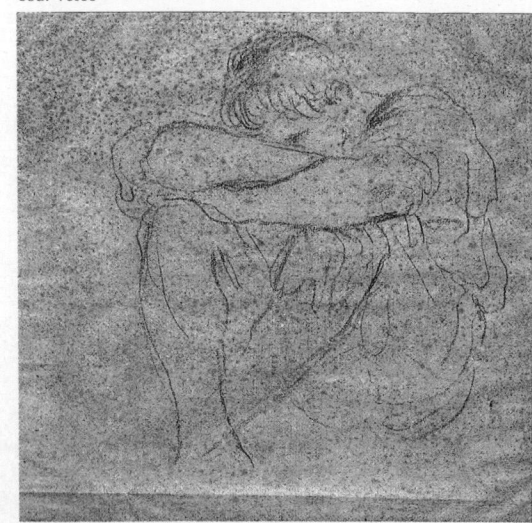

Like the Paris drawing which Guercino executed specifically for the Pitti Palace *Apollo and Marsyas* of 1618 (see the previous entry), cat. no. 65—one of Guercino's most romantic nude studies—seems to have been made with a particular composition in mind. Unlike the figures posed in cat. nos. 63 and 64, that depicted in cat. no. 65 is endowed with a precise mood. This sense of feeling distinguishes it from the average Academy drawing.

A double-sided sheet in black chalk preserved in the Nationalmuseum, Stockholm (inv. 1120/1863) develops further the pose of the figure studied in the Grand drawing.[1] On the recto of the Stockholm sheet (fig. 65a: recto) the seated boy (now clothed) appears in the midst of what seems to be a partial compositional study for an undocumented *Resurrection* or *Transfiguration*. The boy's legs have been inverted with respect to the Grand *Nude* (the left leg now crosses in front of the right leg) and the arms and hands are situated in a different manner. The head is slightly raised and cocked to one side. The light, however, strikes the figure in exactly the same fashion (from the right side of the sheet) as in the Grand drawing.

On the verso of the Stockholm sheet (fig. 65a: verso), Guercino made a quick sketch—not much more than an outline, really—of the Grand *Nude*. This study probably preceded the one on the recto, since it merely adds a bit of clothing to the figure in cat. no. 65 and raises his head just enough to reveal part of the left eye.

Two copies, both of fairly low quality, exist of the Grand *Nude*. The first is a pen-and-wash drawing in the collection of the Earl of Leicester at Holkham Hall.[2] The second, in black chalk on gray-brown prepared paper, is in the J.F. Willumsen Museum, Frederikssund, Denmark.[3]

On the basis of style, the Stockholm sheet

and the Grand *Nude* may be tentatively dated to c. 1620-1623.

1. Dimensions: 395 x 325 mm. Prov.: N. Tessin. See *Italienska Barockteckningar*, exh. cat., June - August 1965, Nationalmuseum, Stockholm, 1965, p. 22, no. 96 (not repr.). I thank N. Turner for bringing this sheet to my attention.

2. See A.E. Popham, *Old Master Drawings at Holkham Hall* (prepared for publication and introduced by C. Lloyd), text and microfiche, Chicago University Press, 1986, p. 72, no. 154 (Microfiche, pl. 2F11). 212 x 174 mm. Popham also mentions the connection with the Stockholm and Grand drawings.

3. See Fischer, 1988, p. 41, no. 57, pl. 48. 229 x 169 mm.

945, 3

1120

152

65a: rec°

66

Wooded Landscape with Two Grave Robbers, an Exhumed Body, a Hidden Onlooker, and a Flying Devil

Pen and brown ink, on laid paper
90 x 182 mm.
Some minor cracking, especially on left side
Inscribed in ink, lower right recto: *Guercin*
PROVENANCE: Sotheby's, London, 25 June 1970, lot 49;
Martin & Sewell, London, exh. sale cat., *Old Master Drawings (Presented by Lorna Lowe and Adolphe Stein)*, 1971, pp. 14-15, no. 67, repr.
BIBLIOGRAPHY: Bagni, 1985, no. 10, repr.

Private Collection

Guercino painted several stunning landscapes in his youth (Salerno, nos. 19-20, 28), but after going to Rome, where he executed a landscape fresco in the Casino Ludovisi in 1621 (Salerno, no. 83, fig. 5), he seems to have become too busy filling orders for altarpieces and history paintings to produce any further examples. Throughout his career, however, he drew landscapes of every variety, both for his own enjoyment and no doubt to give away as gifts. It has recently been said that more landscape sheets are known by his hand than by any other Italian artist of the Seicento, including specialists like his compatriot Grimaldi.[1]

Guercino's landscape drawings are among the most beautiful and majestic in Baroque art. They do not seem to have been used for the backgrounds of history paintings but were made as independent, highly finished works in their own right. Many of the scenes depicted in these drawings are made up of landscape motifs seen in the area around Guercino's native Cento.[2] These often have the idyllic, poetic flavor of Giorgione, Titian, and especially Domenico Campagnola. Other sheets are the products of the artist's imagination and response to masters like Niccolò dell'Abate, Paul Brill (who also executed a fresco in the Sala dei Paesaggi in the Casino Ludovisi in 1621), Agostino Tassi (Guercino's quadratura partner in Rome), and Adam Elsheimer. Guercino's handling of line is often very precise and has an ornamental quality which reflects still other sources in this genre: Northern prints. The Carracci Academy members, especially Annibale and Domenichino, were equally influential, although their sketches of nature (sometimes not much more than a detail of a single tree or a rough outline of a vista with classical buildings) are rarely as elaborate as Guercino's.

Guercino's landscape drawings have always been popular. Fourteen of them were etched in a suite of prints by Jean Pesne (1623 - 1700) and published in Paris in c. 1685 with a frontispiece designed by Cesare Gennari.[3] Until recently, the fourteen original drawings were preserved together at Chatsworth. Some have now left the collection. An anonymous eighteenth-century forger made deceptive copies after the prints (he seems not to have had access to the originals). For nearly three centuries, these clever fakes have been bought and sold as autograph Guercinos. There is scarcely a museum in Europe or America which does not have at least one of these pen drawings.

The fakes after Pesne, like the etchings themselves, are in reverse of the original compositions. However, the faker also availed himself of a second edition of the fourteen landscapes. The Bolognese printmaker Ludovico Mattioli, before his death in 1747, made a complete group of engravings after Pesne's etchings. Mattioli's set is in reverse of Pesne's, which means that the fakes after Mattioli's edition are in the same sense as Guercino's originals! The faker also produced pastiches of these compositions and created "new" designs based on Guercino's style, making it even more difficult to spot his handiwork. Only recently have scholars, notably Prisco Bagni, studied the problem in depth and published enough of the faker's work to alert dealers and collectors to his often monotonous handling of line and flat renderings of spatial recession.[4] In original Guercino landscapes—such as those shown here, especially cat. nos. 68, 70, and 72—the sense of movement in zigs and zags through a panoramic terrain is breathtaking. The faker would never have been able to handle the wind-blown tree depicted in cat. no. 69 with anything like the virtuosity of Guercino's pen.

Because they are so finely crafted and unrelated to his paintings, Guercino's landscapes

153

are very difficult to date. It is likely, however, that cat. nos. 66 and 67 were done in Guercino's early period. Cat. no. 66 is a kind of picturesque mystery tale; cat. no. 67, a charming, utterly direct scene of recreation in the countryside. Both drawings are unusual in taking an interior view of a landscape and in depicting proportionally large figures. In the majority of Guercino's landscape drawings, it is the distant or bird's-eye view which is utilized. Both sheets may reflect Guercino's landscape and genre scenes created in 1615-1617 for Casa Pannini in Cento.[5] It was for this large decorative project that Guercino designed the *Venus and Cupid in a Chariot* shown here as cat. no. 2.

As James Byam Shaw has pointed out, cat. no. 66 may have been designed as part of a series. A sketch of a *Landscape with a Fisherman* in the Frits Lugt Collection, Paris, has virtually the same dimensions (90 x 186 mm.) as the exhibited sheet and is drawn in the same style.[6] It bears an identical inscription (*Guercin*) in the lower right corner. A third drawing, this one representing a *Man Fishing with a Net* and measuring 93 x 187 mm., may also belong to the group.[7] Perhaps Guercino intended to have these sheets and others like them reproduced by Pasqualini.[8]

For a copy of this sheet at Windsor, see M-T, no. 582.

8. A much larger drawing in the British Museum of *Angelica and Medoro in a Landscape* (inv. P.p. 4-63), while obviously not for this hypothetical series, is worth comparing to cat. no. 66, particularly in terms of its treatment of the foliage. Cf. also another sheet in the British Museum, *Disegni*, no. 197, of a *Man and Child Seated on a Mound in the Center of a Landscape* (inv. F.f. 2 - 142). This work was etched in reverse by Charles Knapton in 1735 when in the collection of Arthur Pond. For particulars on the Pond-Knapton print series, see under cat. no. 11.

1. See M-T, pp. 101-3, who provide an useful introduction to Guercino's landscapes, which we have partially summarized below.

2. See Bagni, 1984 and Bagni, 1985.

3. See Bagni, 1985. See also M-T, pp. 105-7, under no. 246.

4. For a complete discussion of the faker's landscapes, see Bagni, 1985. See also M-T, pp. 101-3. The faker is also responsible for copies and derivations after Guercino's figural compositions. We have cited a few examples of these: cf. especially under cat. nos. 22 and 23. Prisco Bagni is currently preparing a thorough study of this aspect of the forger's production.

5. See Bagni, 1984.

6. James Byam Shaw, *The Italian Drawings of the Frits Lugt Collection,* 3 vols., Paris, 1983, no. 339, repr. on pl. 390.

7. Sotheby's, London, 2 July 1984, lot 56, repr. on p. 80.

Pen and brown ink, brown wash, on laid paper
178 x 248 mm.
Foxed; some darkening and cracking due to acid ink
PROVENANCE: Mr. Milton McGreevy
BIBLIOGRAPHY: *Nelson-Atkins Museum of Art Bulletin*
4, no. 6 (1965), no. 19, repr.

The Nelson-Atkins Museum of Art, Kansas City, Missouri,
Bequest of Mr. Milton McGreevy, 81-30/31

This intimate landscape may be tentatively dated to c. 1617 - 1621 (see the previous entry). For a drawing (private collection) of c. 1623 - 1630 depicting a comparable subject but with large figures in a vertical format, see Bagni, 1984, p. 194, no. 156, repr. The handling of the log and the treatment of the bathing figures in this second sheet are similar to those in the Kansas City drawing.

68
Landscape with a Road and Figures

Pen and brown ink, on a sheet made up of three separate pieces of cream laid paper
266 x 467 mm.
Small losses at bottom edge
WATERMARK: Crown and eagle within a circle (on two sheets), (Heawood 1258)
PROVENANCE: Robert Lehman, New York
BIBLIOGRAPHY: *European Master Drawings from the Fogg Art Museum,* Tokyo, National Museum of Western Art, 1979, no. 39, repr.; Bagni, 1985, no. 11, repr.; Bober, 1988, no. 57, color repr.

Fogg Art Museum, Harvard University,
Cambridge, Massachusetts,
Gift of Robert Lehman, 1943.1873

For a similar landscape in the Fogg Art Museum, see Suppl. no. 29, repr. Cf. also the large sheet in the Collection of the Duke of Devonshire at Chatsworth (*Disegni,* no. 206), which was etched by Pesne (no. 2).

Pen, brown ink and iron gall ink, on ivory laid paper
277 x 430 mm.
Mild foxing; some acid ink corrosion around base of large
tree; wrinkled along top border
Stamped on verso: *OBERLIN*
WATERMARK: Circle enclosing illegible object
PROVENANCE: Dan Fellows Platt (L. Suppl. 750a and
2066b); American Private Collection, from which
purchased, 1942
BIBLIOGRAPHY: Wolfgang Stechow, *Catalogue of
Drawings and Watercolors in the Allen Memorial Art
Museum, Oberlin College,* Oberlin, 1976, no. 161, repr.;
Bagni, 1985, no. 8, repr.

{H,O}

Allen Memorial Art Museum, Oberlin, Ohio,
Friends of Art Fund, 1942,   42.126

161

70

Landscape with a View of a Fortified Port

Pen and brown ink, on laid paper
290 x 432 mm.
Excellent condition
PROVENANCE: Art market, Amsterdam; sale: Sotheby's,
London, 23 March 1972, lot 121; art market, N.Y.
BIBLIOGRAPHY: Bagni, 1985, no. 18, repr.; *J. Paul Getty
Museum Journal* 14 (1986), p. 236, no. 175; Goldner,
1988, no. 17

{H}

The J. Paul Getty Museum, 85.GA.408

A similar scene with fortifications is represented in a drawing with a Casa Gennari provenance now in the University of Michigan Museum of Art. See Suppl. no. 33, repr.

71

Landscape with a River and Boat, and a Dog Swimming to Shore

Pen and brown ink, brown wash
262 x 422 mm.
PROVENANCE: Colnaghi, London; purchased in 1937
BIBLIOGRAPHY: A.E. Popham and K.M. Fenwick,
*European Drawings in the Collection of the National
Gallery of Canada,* Ottawa, 1965, no. 78, repr.; Bagni,
1985, no. 25, repr.

{O,C}

National Gallery of Canada, Ottawa / Musée des
Beaux-Arts du Canada, Ottawa,   4359

72

Landscape with a Waterfall

Pen and brown ink, on laid paper
288 x 427 mm.
PROVENANCE: Galerie Sabrina Forster, Düsseldorf, sale
cat., *Italienische Zeichnungen,* 1989, no. 6, repr.
BIBLIOGRAPHY: Unpublished

National Gallery of Art, Washington, D.C.,
Ailsa Mellon Bruce Fund, 1989.34.1

For an equally spectacular panoramic
view, compare the sheet formerly at Chatsworth (and etched by Jean Pesne) which was
recently on the London art market (sale:
Christie's, London, 3 July 1984, lot 20).

Pen and brown ink, brown wash, on laid paper
200 x 278 mm.
Considerably damaged from acid ink corrosion. Flaking
and cracking, especially at lower center of sheet.
Recently restored and relined by the Conservation
Laboratory of the National Gallery of Art
PROVENANCE: Casa Gennari (characteristic mount; cf.
Mahon, "Casa Gennari," 1968, p. 356, n. 44); F. Forni; E.
Bouverie; Mr. Hervey; Earls of Gainsborough; Archibald
G.B. Russell, Lancaster Herald (L. 2770a, lower left recto);
sale: Sotheby's, London, 22 May 1928; Durlacher, N.Y.;
John Nicholas Brown, Providence, Rhode Island
BIBLIOGRAPHY: Russell, 1923, pp. 22, 59, pl. XVIII (with
previous bibl.); McComb, 1934, fig. 33; Bagni, 1985, no.
34, repr.

National Gallery of Art, Washington, D.C.,
Gift of Nicholas Brown, J. Carter Brown and Angela B.
Fischer: Tenants in Common, 1986.59.1

One of Guercino's most romantic landscapes, cat. no. 73 is exceptional for its bold
use of wash. A similar configuration of rocks
and mountains is depicted in a very beautiful
pen drawing of a *Landscape with a Natural
Bridge* in the Tunnard Collection (260 x 419
mm.), which was exhibited at Vassar in 1961.
See *Centennial Loan Exhibition (Drawings
from Alumni Collections)*, Vassar College Art
Gallery, Poughkeepsie, New York, 1961, no.
35, repr.

Brush and brown wash, on blue paper
258 x 372 mm.
Inscribed in brown ink, lower left of mount in an old hand, possibly Italian: *4* [...] (number four followed by two brief words, illegible)
PROVENANCE: Casa Gennari (characteristic mount but with red ink rather than black; cf. Mahon, "Casa Gennari," 1968, p. 356, n. 47); F. Forni; E. Bouverie; Mr. Hervey; 1st Earl of Gainsborough (?); Lord Northwick (according to Russell); William Bateson (L. Suppl. 2604a, lower right recto of mount); Janos Scholz, New York
BIBLIOGRAPHY: Russell, 1923, pp. 22, 51, pl. XIV; "Italian Drawings from the Collection of Janos Scholz," *Metropolitan Museum of Art Bulletin* (May 1965), Part II, p. 340, repr.; Stampfle-Bean, 1967, no. 50; Moir, 1974, no. 57, repr. (with further bibl.); Westin and Westin, 1975, no. 19, repr.; Feinblatt, 1976, no. 96, repr. (with extensive list of exhibitions); Charles Ryskamp, ed., *Eighteenth Report to the Fellows of the Pierpont Morgan Library, 1975-1977,* New York, 1978, pp. 247-48.

The Pierpont Morgan Library, New York,
The Janos Scholz Collection, 1975.36

Arguably Guercino's masterpiece in the landscape genre, cat. no. 74 ranks with the finest sheets of Claude Lorrain and Rembrandt. The "Chinese" quality of the trees and figures is the result of Guercino's virtuoso brush-and-wash technique. This is the master's only landscape executed without the use of the pen. Its only rival is cat. no. 73, a drawing with an almost identical provenance, which has only a few pen lines and nearly the same amount of wash.

The volcano depicted here may be based on prints or drawings of Mt. Vesuvius. So far as we know, Guercino never travelled to Naples.

75   Saint Luke
Pen and brown ink, gray-brown wash
175 x 149 mm.
Laid down
PROVENANCE: William Bates (L. 2604, lower right recto,
overlaps mount)
BIBLIOGRAPHY: Unpublished

J.F. McCrindle, Princeton, New Jersey

75A   Saint Luke
Giovanni Battista Pasqualini (1595 - 1631)
Engraving after the drawing by Guercino
180 x 152 mm.
BIBLIOGRAPHY: Bertelà, 1973, no. 814, repr.; Bagni,
1988, no. 14, repr.

The Metropolitan Museum of Art, New York,
Harris Brisbane Dick Fund, 1953, 53.600.2306

A number of Guercino's early drawings—for example, cat. no. 11—employ a hatching/line-and-stipple technique like that used by printmakers. It is probably not a coincidence that some of these sheets were reproduced by Guercino's Centese companion and personal engraver, Giovanni Battista Pasqualini (1595 - 1631). We have hypothesized earlier that Guercino may have intentionally made certain drawings in this "gravure manner" to facilitate their transfer to engravings. For a complete discussion with references, see under cat. no. 11.

Cat. no. 75, *St. Luke,* is a previously unpublished example of an autograph drawing which we believe Guercino designed specifically for Pasqualini. Cat. no. 75A is a fine impression of Pasqualini's print based on the drawing. The print is part of a series of the *Four Evangelists* (see Bagni, 1988, nos. 11 - 14, repr.), datable to the same approximate moment as the drawing—c. 1618-1619.

We are fortunate in being able to identify and illustrate here yet another unpublished preparatory drawing for the *Evangelist* group, a pen-and-ink study in the Albertina, Vienna (fig. 75a),[1] designed for Pasqualini's *St. Mark* (fig. 75b).[2] It should be noted that Pasqualini added vertical hatching lines in the small area between the margin of the sheet and St. Mark's head and eliminated the little clump of vegetation Guercino had placed half-way up the wall.[*]

[*] Prisco Bagni's important new book on the forger of Guercino's figural drawings (*Il Guercino e il suo falsario: i disegni di figura,* Bologna: Nuova Alfa Editoriale, 1990) did not reach me until after the Catalogue had gone to press. I will only mention here that the drawing in the Biblioteca Comunale at Forlì of *St. Mark* (189 x 160 mm.), assigned by Bagni to the forger (Bagni, 1990, no. 7), cannot be after the print by Pasqualini, since it includes the little outgrowth on the wall and a group of loose, diagonal lines just below it, which are present only in Guercino's drawing in Vienna. Perhaps the Forlì sheet, which is in the same sense as the Vienna drawing, is not by the faker after all, but is instead a working copy (a

trace ?) made by Pasqualini directly from Guercino's original. The forger's sources, as mentioned under cat. no. 66, were typically prints and not actual drawings.

1. Inv. 2332, SB. 390. 210 x 170 mm. I thank Konrad Oberhuber and Veronika Birke for their help in securing a photograph of this important drawing in the Albertina.

2. Bertelà, no. 813; Bagni, no. 12. 184 x 155 mm.

75a

75b

173

174

Io. Franciscus Barberius Centensis Inu   Io. Bapt. Pasqualinus Centensis sculpsit.

76   Saint Anthony of Padua
Pen and brown ink, brown wash
136 x 115 mm.
Laid down
Badly foxed and stained; acid ink corrosion; mat stain
across top; small losses top center
PROVENANCE: Carl König, Vienna (L. 583, on verso of
mount); Anton Schmied, Vienna (see L. Suppl. 2330b);
Private Collection
BIBLIOGRAPHY: Unpublished

Private Collection

76A   Saint Anthony of Padua
Etching
150 x 115 mm. (plate)
In bottom margin: *S. ANTON.º DA PADOA / Io. Franc.
Cent. inu. Fe.*
Second state with the address of Rossi: *alla Pace / Jo:
Jocomo Rossi form. Romae*
BIBLIOGRAPHY: Adam Bartsch, *Le Peintre Graveur,*
XVIII, Vienna, 1818, p. 362, no. 1; *Disegni,* no. 254 (with
additional bibl.); Bertelà, 1973, no. 10 (i/ii), before the
address of Rossi; Salerno, p. 16, fig. 7; Bagni, 1988, no. 2,
repr.

Private Collection

Guercino, who relied on engravers like Pasqualini (see the previous entry) to reproduce his works, made only two prints in his lifetime, the *St. Anthony of Padua* exhibited here (cat. no. 76A) and an *Infant St. John the Baptist Seated in a Landscape* (*Disegni,* no. 255).[1]

One wonders if the motivation for these two etchings might not have been Pasqualini's death in 1631. Perhaps the loss of his publisher spurred Guercino to try to make his own prints. As beautiful as the results obviously were, Guercino was not compelled to make any further examples. The etchings, in any case, are approximately datable to c. 1630- 1640.

No drawing is known for the *St. John* but a somewhat damaged sheet in an American private collection exhibited here as cat. no. 76 has every appearance of being a preliminary sketch by the master for his own etching of *St. Anthony.*[2] In the print, Guercino made several important adjustments to his original design. In fact, we might hypothesize that he made at least one revised sketch before picking up the etching needle.[3]

Looking at the drawing in reverse in order to compare it more effectively with the etching, it should be noted that the saint's left elbow rests on a pedestal and that the lilies are held upright with the left hand. In the etching, by contrast, the lilies make an elegant diagonal across the composition and are held in the right hand. The pedestal has been eliminated and a landscape added. Perhaps the most significant change in the etching is the least obvious: Guercino has lowered Anthony's arms, thereby creating a sense of height which is lacking in the drawing.

1.   Bartsch, XVIII, p. 363, no. 2. See also Salerno, p. 15, fig. 6; Bagni, 1988, no. 3, repr.

2.   I thank William Robinson for bringing this drawing to my attention. I would also like to thank Veronika Birke for her help in tracing the provenance of the sheet.

3.   This suggestion was made to the author by Sir Denis Mahon.

S. ANTON°. DA PADOA

Io. Franc. Cent. inu. Fe. alla Pace
Jo: Jacomo Rossi form Rome

Oiled black chalk, heightened with white, on brown paper
358 x 258 mm.
Inscribed on verso in pen and brown ink: *Guer⁰L₄₅*
PROVENANCE: Casa Gennari; F. Forni; E. Bouverie; Mr.
Hervey; Earls of Gainsborough; German Private
Collection; Walter Hugelshofer, Switzerland; Janos Scholz,
New York
BIBLIOGRAPHY: Detroit, 1965, no. 108, repr. (with
previous bibl. and exhibitions); Varriano, 1974, no. 32,
repr.; Westin and Westin, 1975, no. 18, repr.; Charles
Ryskamp, ed., *Nineteenth Report to the Fellows of the
Pierpont Morgan Library, 1978-1980,* New York, 1981,
pp. 174-75.

The Pierpont Morgan Library, New York,
The Janos Scholz Collection, 1979.7

Some of Guercino's most unusual and appealing drawings are sketches of everyday life: beggars and poor folk (cat. nos. 77, 80-81), tradesmen (cat. no. 78), figures in casual or meditative poses (cat. no. 79), scenes of regional literature and comic theatre (cat. nos. 82-83), and many other types.

The Carracci and their immediate followers ostensibly made such drawings in the hope that insights gained from observing nature directly would lead them to a new, more accessible style in history painting. Of course, they also made them for fun. Like Passerotti before them, Annibale and Agostino also made genre and satirical paintings, but this was something Guercino apparently never attempted himself.

Nearly a generation later, Guercino found the practice of genre drawings well-established, but he was not necessarily concerned with its original function or context. For him, genre drawings were worth executing for their own sake and for their entertainment value. One cannot help but notice the sincere humanity and "down-home" flavor of many of Guercino's sketches. Looking at drawings like cat. nos. 80 and 82, it is easy to understand why the artist left Rome in 1623 and returned to a "piccolo paese" to continue his career. He seems genuinely to have enjoyed the provincial community where he grew up and learned to paint.[1]

Guercino's genre drawings range in technique from bold studies in oiled black chalk (cat. nos. 77-78) to very rapid sketches in pen or pen and wash (e.g., cat. no. 81). The fact that he did not customarily use red chalk for these drawings is significant. It demonstrates that this medium had such strong associations with *finezza* and elegance that a genre drawing so executed would be a kind of contradiction.

Guercino's drawing technique, as we have mentioned several times in our discussion of

his preparatory drawings (e.g., cat. nos. 40-42), can be modal. The outrageously vulgar scatological scene depicted in cat. no. 84, formerly in the Scholz Collection, is drawn in a rustic, purposely *rozzo* style to give it special character. This ability to express humor by and through linear treatment is the province of caricature, a field in which Guercino was brilliantly skilled. See our discussion of his portraits and caricatures below (cat. nos. 85-92).

1. For an full discussion of Guercino's genre drawings in which this very astute observation concerning Guercino's "roots" has been made, see M-T, pp. 110-11.

179

Oiled black chalk, heightened with white, on brown paper
403 x 279 mm.
Fragment of an inscription in light brown ink, lower left
recto (illegible)
PROVENANCE: Jan van Rijmsdijk; John Thane (L. 1544,
script, above stamp of Egerton); Thomas Dimsdale (see L.
2426); Sir Thomas Lawrence; Francis Egerton, 1st Earl of
Ellesmere (L. Suppl. 2710b, lower right recto, in black);
sale: Sotheby's, London, 11 July 1972, lot 95, repr. (as a
"Fisherman"), (*Catalogue of the Ellesmere Collection of
Drawings by the Carracci and other Bolognese Masters
Collected by Sir Thomas Lawrence,* with additional bibl.);
Thos. Agnew & Sons, London, exh. sale, 12 March - 10
April 1974, no. 5, repr.
BIBLIOGRAPHY: P. Tomory, *The Ellesmere Collection of
Old Master Drawings, exh. cat., Leicester Museums and
Art Gallery, Leicester,* 1954, no. 105; *Master Drawings
from the Collection of the National Gallery of Art and
Promised Gifts,* exh. cat., Washington, D.C., 1978, repr. on
p. 71

National Gallery of Art, Washington, D.C.,
Pepita Milmore Memorial Fund, 1974.102.1

In this fine sheet, Guercino takes up the tradition established by Annibale Carracci in his celebrated suite of drawings of Bolognese streetvendors and tradesmen, the *Arti di Bologna*. The drawings, reproduced in competent etchings by Simon Guillain, were published in 1646 together with a fragment of a theoretical text written in the early Seicento by Monsignor Agucchi.[1] Guercino has certainly also profited from looking at Annibale's black-chalk figure studies and early paintings like the *Boy Drinking* (New York, Sharp Collection), recently shown in Bologna, Washington, and New York.[2]

Like his academic nude studies and landscapes, Guercino's genre and figure drawings are difficult to date. It may, however, be safe to assign this sheet, which has such stark, heavy outlines, to Guercino's pre-Roman period.

1. See Mahon, 1947, Appendix I. See also Marabottini, 1966, with commentary and a full set of illustrations.

2. *The Age of Correggio and the Carracci,* exh. cat., National Gallery of Art, Washington, D.C., Bologna: Nuova Alfa Editoriale, 1986, no. 84, color repr.

181

Pen and brown ink, brown wash, on beige laid paper
230 x 210 mm.
Inscribed in brown ink, lower right: *Guercino*
PROVENANCE: Charles A. Loeser
BIBLIOGRAPHY: Mongan-Sachs, no. 263, fig. 134;
Detroit, 1965, no. 107, repr.; Varriano, 1974, no. 49, repr.;
Oberhuber, 1979, no. 30, repr.; *European Master
Drawings from the Fogg Art Museum, Tokyo, National
Museum of Western Art,* 1979, no. 38, repr.; Kristen A.
Mortimer, *Harvard University Art Museums. A Guide to
the Collections,* Cambridge and New York, 1986, no. 267,
repr.; Bober, 1988, no. 56, color repr.

Fogg Art Museum, Harvard University,
Cambridge, Massachusetts,
Bequest of Charles A. Loeser, 1932.233

For a similar composition in a different
(and later) drawing style, see cat. no. 46. The
Fogg sheet, which contains virtuoso passages
of wash and energetic flourishes of the pen,
may be tentatively dated to c. 1625-35.

183

Pen and brown ink, brown wash, on laid paper
278 x 211 mm.
Lined
PROVENANCE: A. Grahl (L. 1199, lower right recto); Mrs.
Josephine Steen, Berkeley, California
BIBLIOGRAPHY: Neilson, 1972, no. 30, repr.; M-T, under
no. 553

The Saint Louis Art Museum,
Purchase, 1954, 66:54

The subject of this wonderful sheet makes one think of Netherlandish prints and paintings rather than the usual Italian artistic sources. Since Guercino was familiar with Rembrandt's etchings (see under cat. no. 62), we suspect he also knew the works of other Dutch masters like Buytewech and van Ostade. It was not until the eighteenth century that masters like Giuseppe Maria Crespi and Piazzetta—both avowed admirers of Guercino—would make such themes popular in Italy.

A Cavalier and a Dwarf Beggar

Pen and brown ink, on laid paper
234 x 255 mm.
WATERMARK: Encircled dove
PROVENANCE: Dan Fellows Platt (L. Suppl. 750a, verso), purchased from E. Parsons & Sons, London in 1925; Mrs. Platt; Museum purchase, 1950
BIBLIOGRAPHY: Lynes, p. 106, no. 111; Spark, 1949, no. 130; Norfolk, 1950, no. 23; Zafran, 1979, no. 18, repr. (as School)

{H}

The Chrysler Museum, Norfolk, Virginia, 50.48.94

Given the precise if rigid handling of line in this sheet—unusual in Guercino's genre drawings—we may be permitted to suggest a date sometime in the 1630s. The previous assignment of this sheet to Guercino's School (by Zafran, 1979) does not seem to take into account the problems of modality in Guercino's drawings. The stiff lines are used by the artist to add a certain level of frank, unadorned realism to the scene. The suavity of line typical of Guercino's works in the 1630s (see cat. no. 31), we believe, is absent on purpose.

Pen and brown ink, brown wash
257 x 394 mm.
Lined
Slight staining; three very small losses at lower right corner
Inscribed by the artist in pen and brown ink at upper left:
Sicut mat. (Positively mad); on a block at the left: *DAI
DAI / AL' MAT. / LÈ AMATĨI P CHÈ LÀ / MANGIA
DEL CERVEL' / D' GAT' AL LOV*
(Go on! Give to the madman! He went mad because he
eats cat brain[s] like a wolf [glutton].)
PROVENANCE: Sir Joshua Reynolds (L. 2364, lower left
recto); Lord Palmerston (according to Fairfax Murray);
Charles Fairfax Murray; purchased by J. Pierpont Morgan
in London, 1910
BIBLIOGRAPHY: Fairfax Murray, I, no. 101, repr. (as "A
Satire on Gambling"); Stampfle-Bean, 1967, no. 38, repr.
(with additional bibl.); *Disegni,* no. 242 (as a "Village
Madman"); Roli, 1972, no. 23, repr.; Varriano, 1974, no.
26; Cazort-Johnston, no. 52, repr.

The Pierpont Morgan Library, New York,   I, 101

Cat. no. 82 is a very provocative work whose meaning remains obscure. It may depict a proverb, legend, or comic tradition of strictly local origin. A stylistically similar drawing in Windsor of a *Street Scene with a Vendor* (M-T, no. 278) contains an inscription of the same variety. This work has been decoded by Mahon and Turner (as a quack selling chicken blood as a cure for cuts) and assigned to c. 1618-1619. Such a date would seem appropriate for the Morgan sheet. Indeed, I have often been tempted to place it in 1619, at about the time Guercino designed the *Samson Seized by the Philistines* now in the Metropolitan Museum, New York. The Morgan drawing's motifs are not unlike those in Guercino's *Samson* sketch in Haarlem, Teylers Museum (see under cat. no. 7).

The Morgan and Windsor drawings cause one to wonder whether Guercino may have intended to produce a series of local, farcical images such as those made later in the century by his follower Giuseppe Maria Mitelli. Though these scenes lack the sophistication of Mola and Bernini, they are very compelling and often display true wit. They might be more appreciated by art historians and collectors if their subject matter were better understood. The results of Mahon and Turner's investigation of the *Quack* are very encouraging; however, much new research still needs to be done on the iconography of these "regional" genre scenes.

189

Pen and brown ink, brown wash, on two joined pieces of
laid paper
288 x 263 mm.
Laid down on thick sheet
Bottom right corner missing and shading has been filled
in on the secondary support; some foxing and
discoloration; acid ink corrosion; trimmed at bottom and
possibly across the top
Inscribed in pencil, lower left recto: *Guerchin*
PROVENANCE: Sir Peter Lely (L. 2092, lower right recto,
cropped); L.D. Lempereur (L. 1740, lower right recto on
shaded portion of support); Lionel Lucas (L. Suppl. 1733a,
lower right recto); Claude Lucas; sale: Christie's, London,
9 Dec. 1949, no. 75
BIBLIOGRAPHY: Detroit, 1965, no. 106, repr. (with
previous bibl.); Varriano, 1974, no. 33, repr.

Worcester Art Museum,
Worcester, Massachusetts, 1951.21

Possibly a scene culled from the popular
theatre of the period, the Worcester sheet
may be very tentatively dated to c. 1620-1630.

191

Pen and dark brown ink, on ivory laid paper
191 x 318 mm.
Minor losses
PROVENANCE: From an old album of caricatures
(dispersed) perhaps belonging to the Odescalchi family
(see below: Brown, University, 1971, under nos. 17 and
21, and notes); Janos Scholz, New York
BIBLIOGRAPHY: Department of Art, Brown University
(various authors), *Caricature and its Role in Graphic
Satire,* exh. cat., Museum of Art, Rhode Island School of
Design, Providence, 1971, no. 17 (as "Scatological
Scene"); Varriano, 1974, no. 27

The Pierpont Morgan Library, New York,
The Janos Scholz Collection, 1990.29

Drawings like this one must have been more plentiful in Guercino's graphic oeuvre. Because of their nature, some were probably not preserved. Such sheets were surely a source of inspiration for the Roman artist Pier Francesco Mola, who applied aspects of Guercino's satire and caricature style to a wide range of subjects, many having to do with the Roman clergy.

See also under cat. no. 77.

Pen and brown ink, on cream laid paper
172 x 147 mm.
WATERMARK: Partial (unidentifiable)
PROVENANCE: Sir Joshua Reynolds (L. 2364, lower right recto); P.O. Dubaut (see L. Suppl. 2103b); Pietro Scarpa, Venice
BIBLIOGRAPHY: Margaret P. Morgan, in Oberhuber, 1977, no. 19, repr.; Spike, 1984, no. 27, repr.

Private Collection

Caricatures or *caricature* derive their name from "ritratti carichi," literally, "loaded portraits." Agostino Carracci made some of the first caricatures in Western art and all of the members of the Carracci school were familiar with them and their didactic function. On one level, caricatures challenged the draftsman's control over his own style. It took tremendous skill to draw badly and to deform the body once an artist had for years practiced making only the most beautiful forms. These satirical, "loaded" portraits tested the artist's ability to capture a character's personality or peculiar physiognomy quickly, in a few penstrokes.

These drawings also required something from the viewer, and this is perhaps the reason for their great popularity. The viewer had to deconstruct the image. The drawings were not complete until the beholder had mentally taken stock of the distance between the exaggeration on the sheet and the truth it referred to or suggested.

On another, more philosophical level, caricatures taught important art-theoretical lessons. In a kind of inversion of the Neoplatonic ideal held sacred by certain artists and theorists in the sixteenth century, that truth is revealed by and through beauty, caricatures revealed "truth" through gross distortion and creative ugliness. Such ideas were essential to Agostino and Annibale Carracci, to Bernini, and perhaps even to Guercino. Baroque artists and poets never tired of analyzing such visual or conceptual paradoxes.

In some cases, it was God who made the caricatures. The artist merely had to make a selection and "copy" what he saw. As Mahon and Turner have recently noted after consultation with medical historians and physicians, Guercino was a keen student of physiognomies and often accurately portrayed men and women (see cat. no. 91) with strange diseases and medical conditions.[1] There seems to be little in the natural world which did not catch Guercino's eye and result in a drawing.

The sheets exhibited here range from a light-hearted sketch of a self-important individual with the chain of the Golden Fleece around his neck (cat. no. 85),[2] to an uncanny study of an aged, emaciated man with a funny hat (cat. no. 92), a kind of walking skeleton. Cat. no. 90, one of a group of sheets (cat. nos. 87-91) exhibited here from the famous album of caricatures once owned by Sir Joshua Reynolds and now preserved at Princeton, owes its central idea—the relationship between human and animal physiognomy and personality—to Giambattista della Porta's seminal treatise on physiognomy, *De Humana Physiognomonia* (Vico Equense, 1587). Bernini also seems to have used (and abused) this text as a springboard for his ingenious satires of popes and cardinals.[3]

1. See M-T, pp. 117-18, who provide a complete introduction to Guercino's caricatures, many of which are preserved at Windsor.

2. The idea raised by Spike (based on a comparison with a portrait medallion) that this sheet might represent Vincenzo Gonzaga II, Seventh Duke of Mantua (1594-1627) with the chain of the Knights of the Golden Fleece (even though Gonzaga was never so decorated) does not seem convincing in light of the fact that the sitter is portrayed in an extremely casual, if not satirical, manner. Moreover, Guercino visited Mantua only once, in 1620 (see under cat. no. 9), but the style of this drawing would argue for a date approximately five to ten years later. After a consultation on this subject, Denis Mahon and I agree that this work is likely to be a lampoon of a local worthy of Cento and not a portrait of a major Italian ruler. The chain of the Golden Fleece, we believe, was included as an ironic twist.

3. For Bernini's caricatures, as well as for a thought-provoking study of the whole issue of social satire in the Seicento, see Irving Lavin, "Bernini and the Art of Social Satire," in *Drawings by Gianlorenzo Bernini from the Museum der Bildende Kunst Leipzig*, exh. cat., Princeton University Press, 1981, pp. 27-54.

Oiled black chalk, with traces of white chalk heightening, on laid paper
400 x 299 mm.
PROVENANCE: Casa Gennari; Francesco Forni; Hon. Edward Bouverie, M.P. (d. 1810); by descent to his nephew, Mr. Hervey; the Earls of Gainsborough; Gainsborough sale: Christie's, London, 27 July 1922, probably from lot 81 (68 drawings); Sir Robert Witt, London (L. Suppl. 2228b, on verso) until 1951 (see Mahon, "Casa Gennari," 1968, esp. p. 355, n. 38); Thomas Carr Howe, San Francisco, 1951-1981
BIBLIOGRAPHY: Robert Flynn Johnson and Joseph R. Goldyne, *Master Drawings from the Achenbach Foundation for Graphic Arts, The Fine Arts Museums of San Francisco,* Geneva: Richard Burton, S.A., n.d. (1985 ?), no. 2, color repr. (as a "Kneeling Nun")

The Fine Arts Museums of San Francisco,
Achenbach Foundation for Graphic Arts,
Gift of Mr. and Mrs. Thomas Carr Howe in honor of
Elizabeth S. Tower,   1981.2.38

The costume of this figure, which would seem to be a normal dress (with a bodice across the lower part of the chest) surmounted by a tent-like shawl, probably necessitates a modification of the previous identification of this corpulent woman, which described her as a kneeling nun.

Caricatures by Guercino in black chalk are extremely rare. A unique example in red chalk, recently on the London art market and now in an American private collection, is noted and illustrated in the Supplement (see Suppl. no. 222).

197

87

Boy in a Large Hat
(Page from *The Reynolds Album of Caricatures*)

Pen and brown ink, brown wash
165 x 121 mm.
Small losses; some acid ink corrosion
Laid down on page of 18th-century album: *Album of
Caricatures*— album in brown leather with
gold-embossed spine, containing 36 leaves to which are
attached 22 or 23 drawings presumably by Guercino and
7 or 8 by imitators (see Suppl. nos. 61-83). Some pages
have been cut out and reinserted (see Lynes, esp. p. 33;
Bean, 1966, p. 36; and Gibbons, I, p. 104).
Title page: *DIVERSE CARICATURE DISEGNATE / A
PENNA E AQUARELLA / DI GIO: FRANCESCO
BARBIERE / DETTO IL GUERCINO / DA / CENTO.*
(Probably by the same 18th-century Bolognese hand as
the sheet [*DIVERSI DISEGNI . . .*], also formerly in the
Platt Collection and now at Princeton, which we have
used as our Frontispiece. Neither Lynes nor Gibbons
discusses this second sheet, which at one time may have
actually been bound into a volume of Guercino drawings.
Perhaps it has the same provenance as the Princeton
caricature album.)
PROVENANCE: According to a series of notations in four
different hands on the flyleaf of the album: Sir Joshua
Reynolds; John Palmer, Lt. Col.; W.E. Price (one notation
explains that Price's wife, Anne Palmer, was the great
niece of Sir Joshua); Clara J. Pearce (sister of Ann Palmer);
Savile Gallery, London; Dan Fellows Platt (L. Suppl.
2066b, lower left inside front cover), bought through
Holoway in 1928
BIBLIOGRAPHY: *International Studio* 91 (Nov. 1928), p.
54, repr.; Lynes, p. 79, no. 25; Max Kozloff, "The
Caricatures of Giambattista Tiepolo," *Marsyas* 10
(1960-1961), fig. 10, opp. p. 17; Bean, 1966, no. 45;
DeGrazia, 1969, no. 34 (entire album); Roli, 1972, no. 48,
repr.; Gibbons, no. 280

{H,O}

The Art Museum, Princeton University
Bequest of Dan Fellows Platt, 48-1294

88

Unshaven Man in a Cap with His Hands Crossed on His Chest

(Page from *The Reynolds Album of Caricatures*)

Pen and brown ink, brown wash
259 x 161 mm.
Slight stains and soiling
Laid down; separated from album in 1964 and matted
apart
PROVENANCE: See cat. no. 87
BIBLIOGRAPHY: Lynes, p. 83, no. 41; Bean, 1966, no. 47;
DeGrazia, 1969, no. 34 (entire album); Gibbons, no. 295

{H,O}

The Art Museum, Princeton University
Bequest of Dan Fellows Platt, 48-1309

201

89

Monk Seated on a Low Bench, Reading

(Page from *The Reynolds Album of Caricatures*)

Pen and brown ink, brown wash
192 x 152 mm.
Slight stains and losses at corners
PROVENANCE: See cat. no. 87
BIBLIOGRAPHY: Lynes, p. 84, no. 44; DeGrazia, 1969,
no. 34 (entire album); Gibbons, no. 298

The Art Museum, Princeton University
Bequest of Dan Fellows Platt, 48-1312

203

90

Two Men in Broad-Rimmed, High-Crowned Hats

(Page from *The Reynolds Album of Caricatures*)

Pen, brown and iron gall ink, brown wash
206 x 176 mm.
Creased lower right; minor stains and soiled, especially
along right edge
Laid down
Inscribed in ink in lower left recto of page in an
18th-century hand: *Questa caricatura somiglia
moltissimo Barone Stosch* (this caricature very much
resembles Baron Stosch). As Bean, 1966, p. 36, notes,
Philip von Stosch (1691-1757) arrived in 1715 in Rome
where he served Cardinal Alessandro Albani
PROVENANCE: See cat. no. 87
BIBLIOGRAPHY: Lynes, p. 86, no. 51; Bean, 1966, p. 36;
DeGrazia, 1969, no. 34 (entire album); Gibbons, no. 305

{H,O}

The Art Museum, Princeton University
Bequest of Dan Fellows Platt, 48-1319

91
Woman with Deformed Lips
(Page from *The Reynolds Album of Caricatures*)

Pen and brown ink, brown wash
167 x 165 mm.
Verso: Landscape
Soiled along right edge
Partially laid down; separated from album in 1964 and
matted apart
PROVENANCE: See cat. no. 87
BIBLIOGRAPHY: Lynes, p. 82, no. 34; Bean, 1966, no. 46;
DeGrazia, 1969, no. 34 (entire album); Gibbons, no. 288

{H,O}

The Art Museum, Princeton University
Bequest of Dan Fellows Platt, 48-1302

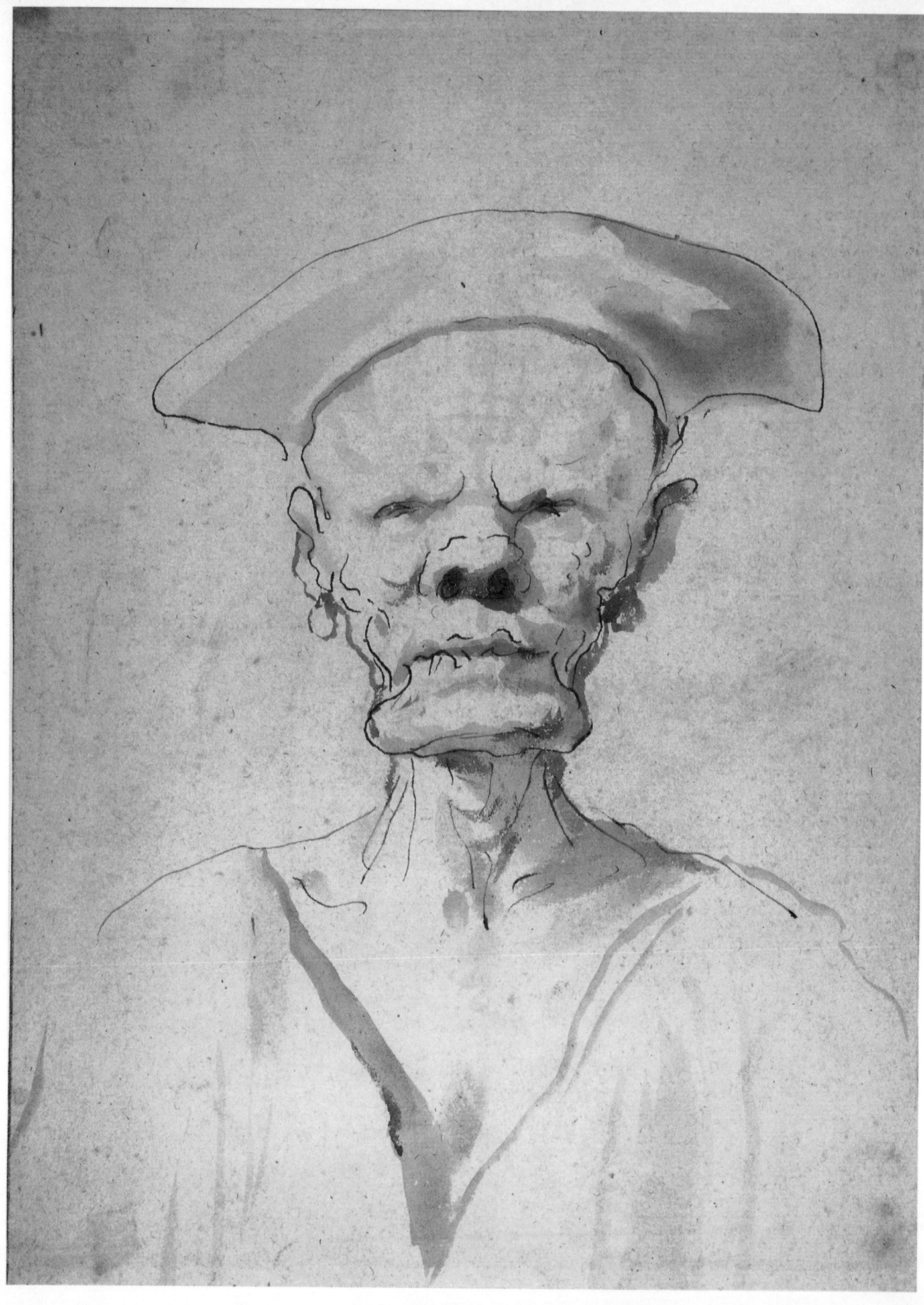

Pen and brown ink, light brown wash, on cream laid
paper
292 x 208 mm.
Excellent condition, perhaps slightly faded
PROVENANCE: Colnaghi, London; purchased in 1984
BIBLIOGRAPHY: Diane Karp *et al., Ars Medica: Art,*
Medicine, and the Human Condition, exh. cat.,
Philadelphia Museum of Art, 1985, no. 93, repr.

Philadelphia Museum of Art,
SmithKline Beckman Corporation Fund,   1984-77-1

A similar drawing, brought to our attention
by Diane DeGrazia, is now in the collection
of Mr. Edmund P. Pillsbury, Fort Worth, Texas
(fig. 92a).[1]

1. Pen and ink; 304 x 230 mm. Prov.: unidentified collector's mark (lower left recto); sale: Sotheby's, London,
20 May 1985, lot 484, repr. on pl. 10 (as Bolognese, 17th
century); Mia N. Weiner, N.Y., exh. sale cat., *Old Master*
Drawings, 5 - 23 Nov. 1985, un-numbered, repr. on loose-
leaf page.

92a

SUPPLEMENT

GUERCINO DRAWINGS IN NORTH AMERICAN COLLECTIONS

A Selective Checklist

Supplement Plates begin on p. 229.
Drawings without references in bold type and braces are not illustrated.
Credit Lines are given only for those drawings illustrated in the Supplement.
Works are in pen and ink, unless otherwise noted.
I.   Drawings in museums are arranged alphabetically by location and then by inventory number.
II.   Drawings in private collections are listed by the name of the collector. Where permitted, the location of the collection is also given.

SUPPLEMENT

GUERCINO DRAWINGS IN NORTH AMERICAN COLLECTIONS

A Selective Checklist

I. Drawings in Museums

U.S.A.

ARKANSAS
Little Rock
Arkansas Arts Center Foundation Collection
1   Study for Ahasuerus. 1984.27.2 **[cat. no. 42]**

CALIFORNIA
Berkeley
University Art Museum, University of California, Berkeley
2   King David. 1967.29 (241 x 292 mm.) **[Plate H]**
Corners lost and repaired.
Prov.: Oswald Hughes-Jones, London; sale: Sotheby's,
London, 7 July 1966, lot 12; Charles E. Slatkin Gallery, N.Y.,
1966. Bibl.: Juergen Schulz, *Master Drawings from California
Collections,* exh. cat., Berkeley, 1968, no. 28:105, repr.
    A late drawing, perhaps of the 1640s. An early treatment
of this subject, in pen and wash, is in the British Museum,
F.f.2- 136.

Los Angeles
Los Angeles County Museum of Art
3   Two Putti. 54.12.6, L.A. County Funds. (168 x 162 mm.)
black chalk **[Plate A]**
     See cat. nos. 19-21.
4   Christ Among the Doctors (?). 64.24 **[cat. no. 18]**
5   SS. John the Baptist and John the Evangelist. M.78.25
[cat. no. 27]

Malibu
The J. Paul Getty Museum
6   Christ Among the Doctors. 84.GG.23 **[cat. no. 17]**
7   Landscape with a View of a Fortified Port. 85.GA.408
[cat. no. 70]
8   Seated Young Man Looking Downwards. 89.GB.52 **[cat.
no. 63]**

Sacramento
Crocker Art Museum
9   Warrior Running with His Arms Outstretched. 1981.50
(231 x 210 mm.) red chalk **[Plate F]**
Bibl.: Sven H.A. Bruntjen Fine Arts, *Twelve Drawings,* sale cat.,

Woodside, California, Winter 1981, no. 3, repr.
A drawing of the late 1640s or early 1650s.

San Francisco
The Fine Arts Museums of San Francisco
Achenbach Foundation for Graphic Arts
10   St. John the Evangelist. 1976.2.19 **[cat. no. 46]**
11   A Kneeling Woman with Rosary Beads. 1981.2.38 **[cat. no. 86]**

Stanford
Stanford University Museum of Art
12   Madonna and Child. 60.44.206, Gift of Mrs. M. C. Sloss.
(127 x 130 mm.) **[Suppl. Frontispiece]**
Upper right corner stained.
Inscription in lower left corner in pen and ink: *2 P. Do*
[probably "Dol." (as in the Montreal *Warrior,* listed below),
but edge is cut immediately after the "o"].
Prov.: Casa Gennari (characteristic inscription).
    A very fine drawing, probably of the early 1630s. The
wire-like lines for the contours of the drapery and the style of
the hatching are similar to two drawings at Windsor of *Alex-
ander the Great* (M-T, nos. 59-60), which have been connected to a lost work of 1631. The style and treatment of
subject in the Stanford drawing may also be compared to a
study at Windsor of the *Madonna and Child Seated* (M-T, no.
62), which was made in preparation for the Giroldo Chapel
*Martyrdom of SS. John and Paul, with the Madonna and
Child Above,* Toulouse, Musée des Augustins (fig. 24a), commissioned in 1627 and completed in 1632 (for a full discussion, see cat. nos. 24-26). The Stanford sheet depicts the
Child's reaching gesture and his position relative to the Madonna in a scheme not dissimilar to that used in the Giroldo
Chapel painting itself, although in the latter the Infant Christ
looks down more directly than he does in the drawing. The
relationship of the Madonnas is not close, however, and any
connection between the Stanford drawing and the 1632 painting must remain tentative.

CONNECTICUT
Hartford
Wadsworth Atheneum
13   The Vision of St. Francis (?). 1948.122, Goodwin Fund,
1948. (151 x 156 mm.) **[Plate J]**
Prov.: William Mayor (L. 2799, lower right recto).
    An early drawing, probably in relation to a lost altarpiece.
From the photograph, it would appear that the face of the   213

saint has been retouched by another hand. I thank Andrew Blume for bringing this drawing to my attention, and Jean Cadogan, Curator, for her assistance.

HAWAII
Honolulu
Honolulu Academy of Arts
14   Joseph and Potiphar's Wife. 13.427 **[cat. no. 29]**

ILLINOIS
Chicago
The Art Institute of Chicago
15   Jacob Blessing the Sons of Joseph. 1922.484 **[cat. no. 8]**
16   Bearded Man Seated at a Table. 1922.486, Leonora Hall Gurley Memorial Collection. (189 x 233 mm.) red chalk on buff paper **[Plate H]**
Rubbed.
Bibl.: Joachim, Microfiche, 3D12.
   A late drawing, perhaps of the 1650s.
17   St. Francis Receiving the Stigmata. 1922.492 **[cat. no. 28]**
18   Christ on the Cross. 1927.7754 **[cat. no. 13]**
19   Martyrdom of St. Bartholomew. 1960.832 **[cat. no. 33]**

INDIANA
Notre Dame
The Snite Museum of Art, University of Notre Dame
20   An Angel Sheathing the Flaming Sword, with Saints Roch and Sebastian in a Landscape. On extended loan as a promised gift from Mr. John D. Reilly. L.88.60.1 **[cat. no. 30]**
21   *Extensive River Landscape with Figures and a Village in the Distance.* On extended loan as a promised gift from Mr. John D. Reilly. L.90.19.1 (169 x 263 mm.) **[Plate O]**
Laid down.
Inscribed on verso of mounting paper: *By Guercino/Kaye Dowland/1870/No. 909.*
Prov.: Kaye Dowland (L. 691); sale: Sotheby's, London, 2 July 1990, lot 3, repr.
   Attribution confirmed by Mahon and Turner. Perhaps a view of the countryside near Cento. A similar scene is depicted in M-T, no. 239, at Windsor.

IOWA
Iowa City
University of Iowa Museum of Art
22   St. Jerome and the Angel. 1968.67 **[cat. no. 45]**

MAINE
Brunswick
Bowdoin College Museum of Art
23   Battle Scene. 1930.197, Museum Purchase. (227 x 296 mm.) **[Plate N]**
Bibl.: Becker, 1985, no. 55, repr.
   A study connected with Guercino's frescoes of c. 1614 in the Casa Provenzale at Cento. See cat. no. 9.
24   Ceres (?). 1956.24.221, Gift of Miss Susan Dwight Bliss. (229 x 171 mm.) red chalk **[Plate F]**
Laid down on canvas.
Bibl.: Becker, 1985, no. 168 (as School), repr.
   A very beautiful and sensitive but quite damaged late drawing, attributed here to Guercino. Because of its canvas lining, the sheet might possibly have a Casa Gennari provenance (this is only a suggestion mentioned to me by N. Turner, who notes that many drawings were preserved in this manner in the Gennari collection; see M-T, p. xx).

MASSACHUSETTS
Cambridge
Fogg Art Museum, Harvard University
25   Man Reading at a Table. 1932.233 **[cat. no. 79]**
26   Thin Man with Big Ears. 1932.251, Bequest of Charles A. Loeser. (252 x 200 mm.) **[Plate G]**
Prov.: Count Gelozzi (L. 545. upper left recto); Klinkosch (L. 577); von Wurtzbach-Tannenberg (L. 2587); Charles A. Loeser.
Bibl.: Mongan-Sachs, no. 266, fig. 135.
27   Landscape with a Road and Figures. 1943.1873 **[cat. no. 68]**
28   David with the Head of Goliath. 1965.385, Bequest of Meta and Paul J. Sachs. (254 x 206 mm.) **[Plate D]**
Prov.: Miss Mabel Tupper to Paul J. Sachs.
Bibl.: Mongan-Sachs, no. 267 (as inv. 140.1931); Varriano, 1974, no. 8.
29   Landscape with a River and Boats. 1969.104, Bequest of Austin A. Mitchell. (280 x 423 mm.) **[Plate O]**
Prov.: Dan Fellows Platt, purchased in 1936; Austin A. Mitchell.
Bibl.: Lynes, no. 4, fig. 4 (detail); Bagni, 1985, no. 12, repr.; Bober, 1988, fig. 43.

Northampton
Smith College Museum of Art
30   Young Woman and a Monk. 1949: 16-2, Purchased. (185 x 248 mm.) **[Plate H]**

Bibl.: Varriano, 1974, no. 35, repr.

Not connected with any known work, the drawing probably dates to the 1630s.

South Hadley
Mount Holyoke College Art Museum
31   Christ Among the Doctors. P.Riv.1.1954 **[fig. 17b: recto; fig. 17b: verso]**

Worcester
Worcester Art Museum
32   Domestic Conflict. 1951.21 **[cat. no. 83]**

MICHIGAN
Ann Arbor
University of Michigan Museum of Art
33   Landscape with Town Gate and Ramparts. 1970/2.28, Gift through the Estate of Edward Sonnenschein, Chicago. (171 x 262 mm.) **[Plate O]**
Prov.: Casa Gennari; F. Forni; E. Bouverie, Mr. Hervey; Earls of Gainsborough; E. Parsons and Sons, London.
Bibl.: Mary Cazort Taylor, *European Drawings from the Sonnenschein Collection and Related Drawings in the Collection of the University of Michigan Museum of Art,* exh. cat., Ann Arbor, 1974, no. 30, repr.
34   Esther before Ahasuerus. 1978/2.41 **[cat. no. 40]**

Detroit
Detroit Institute of Arts
35   Flying Putto and a Fragment of a Seated Man, Facing Left. 1947.359, Gift of C. Edmund Delbos. (150 x 138 mm.) red chalk **[Plate C]**
Prov.: Dan Fellows Platt (L. Suppl. 750a, verso), purchased 1920; C. Edmund Delbos.
Bibl.: Lynes, p. 101, no. 97; Ann Sutherland Harris, *Italian Drawings in the Detroit Institute of Arts,* in preparation (as "Flying Putto and the Arm of an Old Man, 1640s").

This drawing has not been connected to a painting by Guercino. In her entry (in preparation) for the Detroit sheet, Harris notes that flying putti are usually situated far away from any seated figures in Guercino's compositions and, thus, the two figures shown in this drawing were probably not meant to appear so close together in the final design. However, based on the glance of the putto and the position of the torso and nose (?) of the second figure, it seems to

me that the putto is actually looking at the man. The drawing may, in fact, be a preliminary study for an unusual composition in which the figures are to be seen in close proximity. Moreover, one may well question the description of the partially cut-down figure on the right as an "Old Man." I read the light, horizontal lines running in short dashes across the torso and across the upper half of the biceps of the seated figure as Guercino's "shorthand" for armor. Similar treatment of armor may be found in the red-chalk Windsor study (M-T, no. 107) for Guercino's painting of 1643 for M. La Vrillière, *Veturia and Volumnia Beseeching Coriolanus to Spare Rome* (Caen, Musée des Beaux-Arts; Salerno, no. 204), and in the stunning red-chalk study of *Erminia* in the Stiftung Ratjen, Vaduz, Liechtenstein (Stiftung Ratjen. *Italienische Zeichnungen des 16. - 18. Jahrhunderts,* exh. cat., Munich, 1977, cat. no. 72, color repr.), which should be connected to the painting of *Erminia and the Shepherd* of 1648-1649 in the Minneapolis Institute of Arts (Salerno, no. 256, who does not mention the drawing). An oiled-black-chalk sketch of *Erminia* (wearing her helmet and a suit of armor) in the Albertina (Stix-Spitzmüller, no. 232), which like the Ratjen sheet shows the figure in reverse of the pose used in the painting, should also be related to the 1648-1649 project.

Between October of 1648 and October of 1649, Guercino painted a pair of large canvases for General Barone Mattei. The first picture, now lost, is described by Malvasia, II, p. 267, as a *Venere con Amore.* The pendant, which was begun a few months later, is described in Guercino's account book (*Libro dei Conti,* p. 330) as *Marte con un'Amoretto* and has been identified as the picture now in the Cincinnati Art Museum (Salerno, no. 257). In the *Mars,* a flying cupid with wings is situated in the upper left corner of the composition near a seated Mars, who occupies the entire center of the picture and looks toward the right (presumably in the direction of the lost *Venus* with which he formed a pair), although his legs are extended toward the left. The cupid bisects a triangular wedge of curtain that covers the left quarter of the canvas. Flying toward the left but looking back to the right toward the figure of Mars, he plunges an arrow which he holds in his right hand into a heart which he holds in his left. The gesture refers, of course, to Love's triumph: Venus's beauty (in the lost painting) renders Mars peaceful and oblivious to the battle taking place in the background.

The establishment of a connection between the severely

cropped drawing illustrated here and the Cincinnati *Mars* depends on the following observations: 1) the sheet can be dated to around 1649 and the man can be identified as a warrior through comparison to the Stiftung Ratjen *Erminia* drawing; 2) the orientation of the two figures in the sheet, which has already been noted to be unusual, does not differ to an unacceptable extent from the grouping in the corresponding painting (the discrepancy between sketch and final version is typically quite marked in Guercino); and 3) it is very possible that the putto in the Detroit drawing is holding a heart in the right hand (I do not believe the putto is holding up a curtain) and a bow (and arrow ?) in the left. There are no known drawings for the *Mars* composition, and so it is not possible to test this hypothesis any further than has been done here.

36   Pope Gregory the Great. 1965.61, Gift of Mr. and Mrs. Lawrence A. Fleischman. (200 x 162 mm.)
[Plate M]
Prov.: Casa Gennari (characteristic mount); F. Forni; E. Bouverie; Lord Northwick (according to Harris); William Bateson (L. Suppl. 2604a, on lower right recto, in black ink);
sale: Sotheby's, London, 23-24 April 1929, no. 59 (with Northwick cited as previous owner, according to Harris);
E. Parsons & Sons, London, according to inscription on verso; purchased from Parsons in 1931 by Dan Fellows Platt (L. Suppl. 750a, verso of mount in lower left corner, in gray ink); Schaeffer Gallery, N.Y., 1964; purchased in 1965 by Mr. and Mrs. Lawrence A. Fleischman, Detroit.
Bibl.: Lynes, p. 109, no. 119; Detroit, 1965, no. 111, repr.

A fine example of Guercino's hatching style in a "close-up" study. This drawing is preparatory for the head of Pope Gregory the Great in the altarpiece of *Saint Gregory the Great Saving Souls in Purgatory*, Bologna, San Paolo Maggiore (Salerno, no. 242), painted in 1643-1647. See also M-T, no. 357.

MINNESOTA
Minneapolis
Minneapolis Institute of Arts
37   Two Putti Covering a Cartouche on the Base of a Pediment with a Tapestry Showing a Seated Man in a Landscape Playing a Lute. 70.50, The John R. Van Derlip Fund, 1970. (105 x 212 mm.) **[Plate H]**
Laid down.
Prov.: John Barnard (d. 1784); Lord St. Helens (inscribed on mount); P & D Colnaghi, London (*Exhibition of Old Master

and English Drawings,* 2 June - 26 June 1970, no. 18, pl. VII [plate mistakenly captioned as pl. VI, no. 21]).
Bibl.: *Minneapolis Institute of Arts Bulletin,* 1971.

An early drawing, c. 1621, possibly for a print or book illustration.

MISSOURI
Kansas City
Nelson-Atkins Museum of Art
38   St. Augustine with a Child. 44-29/2, Nelson Fund. (308 x 238 mm.) pen and wash **[Plate B]**
Prov.: Casa Gennari (characteristic mount, similar to Mahon, 1967, p. 20, example 5); F. Forni; E. Bouverie (?); Lord Northwick (?) [see Mahon, *loc. cit.*] L'Abbé Thuélin; sale: Drouot, Paris, 11 Dec. 1930, no. 20; purchased from J.W. de Rehling Quistgaard.

A preparatory study, with some compositional differences, for a painting of the same subject, executed in 1635 and now in Madrid, Prado (Salerno, no. 157, who notes related drawings in the Fachsenfeld collection published by Thiem).

39   Landscape with Bathers. 81-30/31 **[cat. no. 67]**

Saint Louis
Saint Louis Art Museum
40   The Louse Hunters. 66.54 **[cat. no. 80]**

NEW JERSEY
Princeton
The Art Museum, Princeton University
41   A Cosmographer with a Globe and Compass. Gibbons, no. 256; 48-709 **[cat. no. 62]**
42   Profile Bust of a Bearded Man in Fur-Edged Cap. Gibbons, no. 257; 48-710
43   Seated Man, Writing. Gibbons, no. 258; 48-711 **[cat. no. 37]**
44   Head of a Bearded, Balding Man, Looking Down. Gibbons, no. 259; 48-712
Bibl.: Varriano, 1974, no. 51; Reed-Wallace, 1989, cat. no. 66, repr.
45   Head of a Clean-Shaven Young Man in Profile. Gibbons, no. 260; 48-713
Bibl.: Varriano, 1974, no. 54.
46   Young Man, Shown Half-Length, Wearing a Large Soft Hat. Gibbons, no. 261; 48-714
47   Bearded Monk in Three-Quarter Length. Gibbons, no. 262; 48-715
Bibl.: Varriano, 1974, no. 46.

48 Profile of an Unshaven Pope. Gibbons, no. 263; 48-716
Bibl.: Varriano, 1974, no. 50.

49 Head and Shoulders of a Young Soldier Wearing a Helmet. Gibbons, no. 264; 48-718

50 Seated Woman, Reading a Book, with Two Putti Holding Hourglasses (*Allegory of Memoria*). Gibbons, no. 265; 48-722 **[cat. no. 14]**

51 Head and Shoulders of a Young Soldier in a Helmet and) Armor. Gibbons, no. 266; 48-725

52 Bearded Man with a Celestial Globe (An Astronomer). Gibbons, no. 267; 48-726 **[cat. no. 36]**

53 Couple Conversing. Gibbons, no. 268; 48-727
Bibl.: Mahon, "Casa Gennari," 1968, p. 356, n. 43; Roli, 1972, no. 30; Varriano, 1974, no. 34.

Mahon has made the suggestion that this sheet is a preliminary idea for the painting of 1624 in Boston, Museum of Fine Arts, depicting *Semiramis at Her Toilet Receiving a Messenger* (Salerno, no. 102). See also M-T, under no. 114. A fine pen study for the head of Semiramis (Paris, École des Beaux-Arts, no. 151) was recently shown at the Louvre. Cf. Loire, 1990, no. 34, repr.

54 Windy Landscape with Figures and a Flock of Sheep. Gibbons, no. 269; 48-729

55 Woman and Child. Gibbons, no. 270; 48-731

56 Cephalus and Procris. Gibbons, no. 271; 48-733
Bibl.: Varriano, 1974, no. 25. Cf. M-T, nos. 112; 207. See also Suppl. no. 155 (Chrysler Museum).

57 Martyrdom of St. Bartholomew. Gibbons, no. 272; 48-734 **[cat. no. 32]**

58 Arrest of Christ. Gibbons, no. 273; 48-744 **[cat. no. 15]**

59 The Visitation/verso. Gibbons, no. 274; 48-745 **[cat. no. 26]**

60 Madonna and Child with St. Dominic (?) Gibbons, no. 275; 48-1267 **[cat. no. 1]**

*   *   *

Guercino and Imitators. Album of Caricatures, once owned by Sir Joshua Reynolds, with additions from the collection of Platt. Gibbons, 276-305; 48-1290 - 48-1319. Those caricatures attributed here to Guercino are listed below.

61 Man in a Turban, in Right Profile. Gibbons, no. 276; 48-1290

62 Man in a Wide-Brimmed Hat, Seen Frontally. Gibbons, no. 278; 48-1292

63 Head of a Young Man in a Hat. Gibbons, no. 279; 48-1293

64 Boy in a Large Hat. Gibbons, no. 280; 48-1294 **[cat. no. 87]**

65 Bespectacled Cleric, Reading. Gibbons, no. 281; 48-1295

66 Bearded Monk. Gibbons, no. 282; 48-1296

67 Two Caricatured Male Heads in Caps. Gibbons, no. 283; 48-1297

68 Heads and Shoulders of Two Men in Large Hats, Facing Right (recto). Gibbons, no. 284 (as School); 48-1298 red chalk.
Probably by the master himself.

69 Two Standing Men (Dwarfs?). Gibbons, no. 285; 48-1299

70 Young Bearded Man with Receding Hair. Gibbons, no. 286; 48-1300

A copy of this head appears on a sheet in the British Museum by the Florentine artist, Livio Mehus (1630-1691). See M-T, no. 296 and fig. 30.

71 Youth with a Slanting Nose, in Left Profile. Gibbons, no. 287; 48-1301

72 Woman with Deformed Lips (recto). Gibbons, no. 288; 48-1302 **[cat. no. 91]**

73 Man with a Long Upper Lip, in Left Profile. Gibbons, no. 289; 48-1303

74 Beggar with a Child on his Shoulder. Gibbons, no. 290; 48-1304

75 Bearded Man in a Cap with Ear Flaps, Full Face. Gibbons, no. 291; 48-1305

76 Scowling Elderly Man with a Full Beard, Full Face. Gibbons, no. 292; 48-1306

77 Unshaven Monk in Left Profile. Gibbons, no. 294; 48-1308

78 Unshaven Man in a Cap, with His Hands Crossed on His Chest, in Left Profile. Gibbons, no. 295; 48-1309 **[cat. no. 88]**

79 Man with His Arms Behind His Back, Standing at a Table with a Keg on It. Gibbons, no. 296; 48-1310

80 Group of Figures Around a Woman and a Child. Gibbons, no. 297; 48-1311

81 Monk Seated on a Low Bench, Reading. Gibbons, no. 298; 48-1312 **[cat. no. 89]**

82 Woman in Left Profile. Gibbons, no. 304; 48-1318
Bibl.: Marangoni, 1959, no. 43, repr.

83 Two Men in Broad-Rimmed, High-Crowned Hats. Gibbons, no. 305; 48-1319 **[cat. no. 90]**

*   *   *

84 St. Joseph and the Christ Child, with a Vase of Lilies. Gibbons, no. 306; 49-25 **[cat. no. 47]**

85 Two Putti Holding the Sudarium Above the Head of St. John the Baptist. Gibbons, no. 307; 49-30
Bibl.: Varriano, 1974, no. 21.

86 St. Joseph with Flowering Staff. Gibbons, no. 308; 49-40

[cat. no. 39]

87 St. Jerome Kneeling and Reading. Gibbons, no. 309; 49-44
Bibl.: Varriano, 1974, no. 15.

88 Astrologer Measuring an Astrological Globe with a Compass. Gibbons, no. 310; 49-48
Bibl.: Varriano, 1974, no. 41; M-T, no. 228.

89 Young Man in a Tall Cap, Pulling Flax (?). Gibbons, no. 311; 49-53

90 Bearded Man in Profile. Gibbons, no. 312; 49-54

91 Heads of Two Children. Gibbons, no. 313; 49-185

92 Head of a Bearded Man in a Cap. Gibbons, no. 314; 48-704

93 St. Mary Magdalen. Gibbons, no. 315; 48-1266

94 Mountainous Landscape with a Damned River, a Town and Figures. Gibbons, no. 316; 49-16
Bibl.: Bagni, 1984, no. 31, repr.

95 Head and Profile of a Youth in Profile, Wearing a High Crowned Hat. Gibbons, no. 320; 49-56

96 St. Peter in Prison, Writing and Speaking to a Youth Outside. Gibbons, no. 321; 59-36
Bibl.: Varriano, 1974, no. 11.

Possibly connected to Guercino's painting of c. 1620 (New York, Private Collection) of *St. John the Baptist in Prison, Visited by Salome* (Salerno, no. 65).

97 Bust of a Man Weeping. Gibbons, no. 325 (as School); 48-705
Bibl.: M-T, under no. 639 (as by Guercino).

97a Lucretia. Gibbons, no. 367 (as School); 49-36 red chalk
Bibl.: M-T, under no. 726 (as the likely source for an offset at Windsor; as possibly by Guercino)

Though not in the best of condition, the drawing contains passages of drapery that might indicate Guercino's authorship. I concur with M-T that the attribution is difficult.

98 Soldier in a Helmet, Shown Three-Quarter Length. Gibbons, no. 376 (as School); 49-49 brush and wash
Bibl.: Nicholas Turner, Review of Gibbons, *Art Bulletin* 62, no. 3 (Sept. 1980), pp. 488-9.
See cat. no. 50, note 2.

99 Bust of a Bearded Man in a Turban. Gibbons, no. 384 (as School); 49-62 red chalk

I see no reason not to ascribe this drawing to the master himself. A late drawing, comparable to cat. no. 56.

100 Half-Length Portrait of a Young Woman in Formal Dress. Gibbons, no. 390 (as School); 49-68
Bibl.: Bagni, 1988, no. 193, repr. (as Guercino, for the print, in reverse, by Domenico Bonaveri).

NEW YORK
New York
The Cooper-Hewitt Museum
101 Study of Four Figures. 1931.66.39 **[Intro.]**

The Metropolitan Museum of Art
102 The Raising of Lazarus. Bean, 1979, no. 235; 68.68
[cat. no. 7]

103 Study for *The Investiture of St. William of Aquitaine*/verso. Bean, 1979, no. 236; 08.227.29 **[fig. 9b: recto]**

104 Seated Old Man with Right Arm Upraised/verso: Seated Nude Youth. Bean, 1979, no. 237; 1970.168 red chalk on blue paper
Bibl.: Cazort-Johnston, no. 54.

105 Endymion Sleeping. Bean, 1979, no. 238; 68.171 **[cat. no. 59]**

106 Two Studies of a Kneeling Male Figure. Bean, 1979, no. 239; 63.37

107 The Virgin Immaculate. Bean, 1979, no. 240; 68.172.2

108 Adoration of the Magi. Bean, 1979, no. 241; 08.227.30
[cat. no. 22]

109 St. Cecilia Playing the Organ. Bean, 1979, no. 242; 1971.221.1 red chalk

110 Youth in a Chariot with Attendant Young Woman. Bean, 1979, no. 243; 80.3.294

111 A Sibyl Holding a Scroll. Bean, 1979, no. 244; 12.56.11
Bibl.: Salerno, under no. 178; Washington, 1990, p. 54, repr. (entry by J. Winkelmann).

For the painting of the *Cimmeran Sybil* of 1638 (Reggio Emilia, Credito Emiliano), Salerno, no. 178, color repr.

112 Standing Youth Holding a Bowl. Bean, 1979, no. 245; 63.75.2 red chalk
Bibl.: Roli, 1972, no. 42.

113 Bust of a Man Facing Right. Bean, 1979, no. 246; 38.179.4

114 Half-Figure of a Nude Man Facing Right. Bean, 1979, no. 247; 1970.40

Possibly a figure study for the Christ in the painting of *Christ and the Samaritan at the Well* (Modena, Banco S. Geminiano e S. Prospero), completed in 1647 (Salerno, no. 249). This sheet is very close in style to a drawing at Windsor that is firmly connected to the painting (M-T, no. 127). A pen drawing of Christ in the Rijksmuseum, Amsterdam (inv. A2124) may also be related to this project. For a general compositional sketch (Paris, Louvre) for the picture, see Loire, 1990, no. 37, repr. A remarkably beautiful study in black chalk of a *Half-Length Figure of a Woman, Facing Left*, Otterlo, Rijksmuseum Kröller-Müller, inv. 359 kl 1 (see Nijmegen, 1988, no. 8, repr.), should now be connected with the Samaritan in Guercino's painting. Details of physiognomy and costume in the sheet are quite close to the painted version, although the comparison makes one wonder about the condition of the Modena picture, especially in the area of the Samaritan's eyes.

115 Boy Wearing a Plumed Hat, with Arms Upraised. Bean, 1979, no. 248; 1972.118.258

116 Fireworks in a Piazza. Bean, 1979, no. 249; 12.56.12
Bibl.: Roli, 1972, no. 19; Cazort-Johnston, no. 51.

117 SS. Francis of Assisi and Louis of France with Two Angels Holding a Crown. 1987.21, Harry G. Sperling Fund (235 x 163 mm.) **[Plate B]**
Prov.: J. P. Zoomer (L. 1511, stamp lower right recto); Earls of Wicklow; London, Art Market; Zurich, Private Collection; N.G. Stogdon, N.Y. and Artemis Fine Arts, London (*Drawings from the 15th to the 20th Century*, sale cat., Spring 1986, no. 8, pl. 27.).
Bibl.: Nicholas Turner, "Some Preparatory Drawings for Guercino's Altarpiece of *Sts. Francis and Louis of France* at Brisighella," *Master Drawings* 19, no. 2 (Summer 1981), pp. 164-66, pl. 35 (as Zurich, Private Collection).

Connected by Denis Mahon to the altarpiece of 1618 at Brisighella (Salerno, no. 40). See Turner, *op. cit.*, for two other drawings related to the composition and a complete discussion. Cf. also Stone, 1989, p. 311.

118 Half-Length Figure of a Morose Man. 1989.222 **[Intro.]**

The Pierpont Morgan Library
119 Holy Family. I,99 **[cat. no. 23]**
120 Landscape with a Walled Town. I,100.
Bibl.: *Disegni*, no. 211.
121 The Mocking of a Village Madman. I,101 **[cat. no. 82]**
122 Christ Crowned with Thorns. I,101b (308 x 241 mm.)
red chalk **[Plate C]**
Strips (approx. 15 mm. wide) have been added along the left and right margins. The left strip, especially in the area of the soldier's helmet, is badly rubbed.
Prov.: Sir Charles Greville (L. 549, lower right recto); Earl of Warwick (L. 2600, lower left recto); Charles Fairfax Murray; J. Pierpont Morgan.

The strips attached to the left and right margins of this somewhat rubbed drawing appear to have been added by the artist himself. The shading lines across the joints are continuous and the right hand of the soldier is shown twice in the

left strip. The strips could not have been added by a collector concerned with making the sheet fit into a frame, or for some other cosmetic reason. The artist may have begun the composition as a Christ alone, but then later decided to add the soldier, necessitating a wider sheet.

According to Malvasia, II, p. 271, the *Ecce Homo* of 1659 (Turin, Galleria Sabauda; Salerno, no. 332) began as a painting with a single figure of Christ for an important patron, Prince Ludovisi. Malvasia—perhaps bragging about his intimacy with the artist—says that he himself intervened in the matter and compelled Guercino to add the head of the *manigoldo* to the composition at no extra charge (it would normally have cost an extra 25 scudi). Salerno notes that in the *Libro dei Conti*, Guercino actually did charge the full rate for one and a quarter figures (125 scudi). In any case, the story of the addition of the soldier may be accurate and would provide an example of the type of situation that could have led to the widening of the Morgan drawing.

In the illustrated sheet, there are some hard passages in Christ's drapery that are perhaps not characteristic of the master himself. The face of the soldier, by contrast, is remarkably sensitive. I am unable to come to a firm decision on the authorship of this very interesting drawing, which may date to the 1640s (it is almost certainly not so late as 1659). For an example of an unquestionably autograph red-chalk drawing to which Guercino added a strip of paper, see Suppl. no. 233.

123 Martyrdom of St. Bartholomew. I,101e **[fig. 32b]**
124 The Visitation. I,101f **[cat. no. 25]**
125 Silvio Discovering the Wounded Dorinda Supported by Linco. I,101g **[cat. no. 51]**
126 Martyrdom of SS. John and Paul/verso. I, 101h **[cat. no. 24]**
127 The Virgin of the Rosary. IV,167.
Bibl.: Stampfle-Bean, 1967, no. 42, repr. See also M-T, no. 363.
128 Landscape with a River and Bathers. IV,168.
Bibl.: *Disegni*, no. 212; Roli, 1972, no. 61; Bagni, 1985, no. 24.
129 The Madonna del Carmine Presenting the Scapular to St. Albert. IV, 168a **[cat. no. 4]**
130 Flying Amorino. IV, 168b (203 x 225 mm.) red chalk **[Plate J]**
Prov.: Sir Charles Greville; Earl of Warwick (L. 2600, lower right recto); Charles Fairfax Murray; J. Pierpont Morgan.

A preliminary study for the second *angiolino* from the left in the top portion of Guercino's somewhat damaged altarpiece of 1636-1638 representing *Santa Francesca Romana* 219

(Verona, Santa Maria in Organo; Salerno, no. 173).

131 Study of Amorini. IV,168c (244 x 191 mm.) black chalk
[Plate A]
Prov.: same as Suppl. no. 130.

132 Study of a Seated Child, with an Extra Study of the Right Arm. IV,168d (230 x 191 mm.) red chalk [Plate M]
Prov.: same as Suppl. no. 130.

One of the best preserved red-chalk drawings by Guercino in an American collection, this sheet depicts a child (possibly studied from life) in an unusual seated pose. The separate study of the right arm makes it very clear that Guercino is not designing the type of Christ Child who sits in the Virgin's lap in the upper half of an altarpiece, and who looks down to make a blessing or to offer an object to saints gathered below. In the full study, the child is looking up (not down) and the gesture of the left arm is exclamatory and in response to something the child sees. The same type of gesture is given to the opposite arm in the separate study and is repositioned in front of the child's chest. It is this second sketch—in addition to the design of the left leg, the shape of the head, and the conception of the torso in the main study—which leads to a connection with the child in a painting of 1637-1638 representing *St. Joseph and the Christ Child* (Dublin, National Gallery of Ireland; Salerno, no. 171), originally one of a pair of paintings that hung in the third chapel on the right in San Giovanni in Monte, Bologna. In the painting the Infant looks up to the right rather than to the left, as in the drawing, but his expression is unchanged. His right arm is in virtually the same position as in the separate study and his left arm is only slightly lowered vis-à-vis the design in the main sketch. It is as if Guercino superimposed the separate study on the main sketch, lowered the left hand in the latter, and reversed the position of the head.

In the canvas, the upraised left hand holds a rose, which Mahon (*Dipinti,* no. 69) suggests may have been painted by Guercino's brother, the still-life painter, Paolo Antonio Barbieri.

133 Mother and Sleeping Child. IV, 168e pen and wash (235 x 362 mm.) [Plate N]
Prov.: Earl of Aylesford (L. 58, lower right recto); Charles Fairfax Murray; J. Pierpont Morgan.

134 Madonna and Child, with a Bird in Flight. IV, 168f (238 x 191 mm.) red chalk [Plate M]
Prov.: Charles Fairfax Murray; J. Pierpont Morgan.

135 Virgin and Child with a Book and a Pot of Pinks. IV,168g red chalk

Bibl.: Stampfle-Bean, 1967, no. 47; Westin and Westin, 1975, no. 20; Bagni, 1988, no. 133; cf. also M-T, no. 600.

136 Magdalen Praying in a Landscape. IV, 168h (259 x 207 mm.) red chalk [Plate A]
Prov.: Same as Suppl. no. 130.

An extremely finished drawing of the 1640s or early 1650s, in the same style as *Diana Burning the Instruments of Love* (cat. no. 60).

137 The Visitation. 1956.21 [fig. 25b]

138 Seated Nude Man. 1970.12, Gift of Mrs. Jacob M. Kaplan in Honor of Mr. Frederick B. Adams, Jr. on the Occasion of his Retirement as Director of the Library. (196 x 187 mm.) [Plate K]
Verso: letter referring to a portrait which is nearly finished, lacking only the last brush strokes and the varnish (according to *Report,* 1973, see bibl.).
Watermark: heraldic mountain of three peaks surmounted by a bird within a circle (close to Heawood 161)
Prov.: Mrs. Jacob M. Kaplan; H. Shickman Gallery, New York.
Bibl.: H. Shickman Gallery, *Exhibition of Old Master Drawings,* New York, 1966, no. 25, repr.; *Sixteenth Report to the Fellows of the Pierpont Morgan Library, 1969-1971,* ed. Charles Ryskamp, New York, 1973, p. 115.

139 Landscape with a Volcano. 1975.36 [cat. no. 74]

140 The Vision of St. Philip Neri. 1977.49 [fig. 52b]

141 Beggar Holding a Broken Jug. 1979.7 [cat. no. 77]

142 The Birdcatcher. 1979.8, The Janos Scholz Collection (248 x 128 mm.) [Plate Q]
Prov.: Janos Scholz, New York.
Bibl.: Varriano, 1974, no. 31; *Nineteenth Report to the Fellows of the Pierpont Morgan Library, 1978-1980,* ed. Charles Ryskamp, New York, 1981, p. 175.

143 Study of Three Putti. 1988.38 [Intro.]

144 Satirical Scene with Three Figures and a Chamber Pot. 1990.29 [cat. no. 84]

Poughkeepsie
Vassar College Art Gallery
145 Presentation at the Temple. 41.4 [cat. no. 21]

OHIO
Cleveland
The Cleveland Museum of Art
146 Venus and Cupid in a Chariot. 25.1188
[cat. no. 2]

Oberlin
Allen Memorial Art Museum, Oberlin College
147 Landscape with a Large Weathered Tree. 42.126 **[cat. no. 69]**
148 The Enraged Mars Restrained by Cupid. 58.154, R.T. Miller,
   Jr. Fund, 1958. (255 x 184 mm.) **[Plate B]**
   Watermark: close to Heawood 792
   (repr. on p. 82 of Stechow, 1976; see below).
   Prov.: Casa Gennari (characteristic mount); F. Forni;
   E. Bouverie; etc., L. Franklyn Gallery, London; purchased
   from Schaeffer Galleries, New York in 1958.
   Bibl.: Detroit, 1965, no. 105, with previous bibl.; Wolfgang
   Stechow, *Catalogue of Drawings and Watercolors in the Allen
   Memorial Art Museum, Oberlin College*, Oberlin, 1976, no.
   160, fig. 121; M-T, under nos. 55; 661-2.
      A drawing of the 1640s, now connected by Mahon and
   Turner along with four other studies (Frankfurt, Zurich, and
   two in London) to a lost painting, known only through an
   engraving by Giovannini (Salerno, no. 364, repr.).

PENNSYLVANIA
Philadelphia
Philadelphia Museum of Art
149 Study of a Figure Leaning on Stick. 50.95.1, Given
   Anonymously. (159 x 124 mm.) pen and brown ink, brown
   wash on laid paper **[Plate Q]**
   Condition is generally very good. Fold across the sheet near
   bottom edge; slight stains; loss in lower left corner.
   Inscribed on the verso, along the bottom, in ink (by
   Guercino ?): . . . *21 Agosto 1629 . .bre et doglia di . . sera
   mentre faceva il letto.*; inscribed in pencil on the top recto
   of the sheet, in an old French hand (Lagoy ?):
   *La servante du Guerchin dessiné par lui (comme il la ecrit
   derrière) le 21 aoust 1629 ayant la fievre et mal a tete le
   soir lorsquelle faisait son lit.* [Guercino's servant, drawn by
   him (as he notes on the reverse) the 21st of August 1629, in
   the evening, while suffering from a fever and headache as
   she was making his bed.]
   Prov.: Marquis de Lagoy (L. 1710); H. Danby Seymour
   (L. 176).
   Bibl.: *Masterpieces of Drawing*, Diamond Jubilee Exhibition,
   Philadelphia Museum of Art, exh. cat., 1950-1951, no. 46,
   repr. (noted in the Foreword [unpag.] by Carl Zigrosser).
      The writing on the verso could well be in Guercino's
   own hand, but there is no mention of a servant in the
   legible portion of the inscription and it is impossible to tell
   from the Italian whether the subject is masculine or feminine.

To complicate matters further, the figure leaning on a stick is
not positively a female, and the inscription may not even
refer to the image on the recto, although the date of 1629
seems to accord with the style of the drawing. For two
documented sheets of around this time, compare cat. nos.
25-26.
150 Caricature of an Emaciated Man. 1984.77.1 **[cat. no.92]**

TEXAS
Houston
Houston Museum of Fine Arts
151 Two Sorcerers. 70.21 **[fig. 36a]**

VIRGINIA
Norfolk
The Chrysler Museum
152 Three Studies for a Crucifixion. 50.48.87 **[cat. no. 12]**
153 The Martyrdom of St. James [r.]; Two Studies of the
   Executioner [v.]. 50.48.88, Museum Purchase. (200 x 260 mm.)
   [Plate H: recto]
   Bibl.: Zafran, 1979, no. 16, repr. (with provenance and a
   complete discussion, relating the drawing to a lost altarpiece
   of 1627). See M-T, nos. 46-7; Salerno, no. 118.
154 Bearded Man Carrying a Gun. 50.48.89, Museum Purchase.
   (177 x 183 mm.) red chalk **[Plate E]**
   Bibl.: Zafran, 1979, no. 14, repr. (with provenance). There is
   an offset of this sheet at Windsor (M-T, no. 752).
155 Cephalus Discovers the Mortally Wounded Procris. 50.48.90,
   Museum Purchase. (213 x 319 mm.) **[Plate N]**
   Bibl.: Zafran, 1979, no. 17, repr. (with provenance and a
   complete discussion relating the drawing to a painting of
   1644, formerly at Dresden [destroyed]). See also Salerno, no.
   212, and M-T, no. 112. Cf. Suppl. no. 56 (Princeton).
156 A Cavalier and a Dwarf Beggar. 50.48.94 **[cat. no. 81]**

WASHINGTON
Seattle
Seattle Art Museum
157 The Ecstasy of St. Teresa. 51.115 **[cat. no. 31]**
158 Standing Man in Profile/verso: The Virgin Mary Standing or
   Kneeling with her Hands Clasped, Facing Left. 55.66,
   Gift of Mrs. Charles M. Clark and the late Mr. Clark.
   (193 x 142 mm.) **[Plate D: recto]**
   Verso is considerably damaged.
   Inscribed in ink on verso, lower right: *No. 111. c.*; just below
   this and to the right, probably in another hand: *35.*

Prov.: Arthur Sambon, Paris (variant of L. Suppl. 125a, lower right recto).
Bibl.: Sambon, 1929, no. 67, repr. (recto); Mandowsky. 1980, no. 18.

The female on the verso may be a preliminary sketch, in reverse, for the figure of the Virgin in Pasqualini's print of *SS. Sebastian and Roch, with other Saints,* made in 1630 during the plague. For the print, see Bagni, 1988, no. 119, repr.

WASHINGTON, D.C.
National Gallery of Art
159 Seated Male Nude Seen from Behind. 1973.30.1 **[cat. no. 64]**
160 A Grain Merchant. 1974.102.1 **[cat. no. 78]**
161 Madonna and Child with SS. Gimignano (Protector of Modena), George, John the Baptist, and Peter Martyr. 1977.43.1, Andrew W. Mellon Fund (270 x 194 mm.) Black chalk on very thin, laid paper **[Plate A]**
Traces of a circular stain (from a wine bottle ?), upper right.
Inscribed *Guercino* in pen in an old hand (lower left recto).
Prov.: Pierre Crozat [?] (L. 474); Dr. Brendan O'Brien, Dublin; sale: Sotheby's, London, 10 Dec. 1968, lot 18.
Bibl.: *Dipinti, p.* 201; Salerno, under no. 288; Loire, 1990, p. 76, fig. 46.

A delicate compositional study for one of Guercino's most beautiful altarpieces of the late period. Painted in c. 1651 as a substitute for an altarpiece by Correggio at Modena, Guercino's picture, which was not delivered to the city until 1668, is now in the Louvre (Salerno, no. 288).

162 Rest on the Flight into Egypt. 1979.14.1 **[cat. no. 20]**
163 The Angel of the Annunciation. 1984.3.10, Julius S.Held Collection, Ailsa Mellon Bruce Fund. pen and brown ink, brown wash (216 x 175 mm.) **[Plate J]**
Prov.: Julius S. Held.
Bibl.: M. Milkovich, *Selections from the Drawings Collection of Mr. and Mrs. Julius S. Held,* exh. cat., State University of New York, Binghamton, 1970, no. 125, repr. (cropped).

A detail study for the angel in Guercino's altarpiece of the *Annunciation,* 1638-1639, Milan, Ospedale Maggiore, SS. Annunziata (Salerno, no. 177). See also M-T, nos. 94-7; 590, and Czére, 1989, no. 41 (for the compositional study at Budapest, illustrated by M-T as fig. 21). In addition to those studies for the figure of God the Father mentioned by M-T, two pen drawings, known to me from photographs at the Hertziana Library, Rome, may be related to the project: 1) Milan, Ambrosiana, inv. F268, no. 101; and 2) Moscow, private collection, inscribed lower right recto: *Guercino*

[Hertziana photo no. 246719]. Both sheets show the figure with his right hand raised in a blessing gesture and with his left hand holding a scepter. In the Ambrosiana drawing, the scepter is nearly upright, whereas in the Moscow sheet, it is held at a forty-five degree angle. It is not possible to confirm the autograph status of these sheets without first seeing them in the original. On the basis of old photographs, they would appear to be by the master himself.

164 Landscape with a Waterfall. 1989.34.1 **[cat. no. 72]**
165 Shepherds Peering into a Chasm. 1986.59.1 **[cat. no. 73]**
166 Amnon and Tamar. 1989.14.1, Ailsa Mellon Bruce Fund (190 x 262 mm.) red chalk on laid paper **[Plate I]**
Prov.: Casa Gennari; F. Forni; E. Bouverie (L. 325, lower left recto); etc.; sale: Bonhams, London, 16 June 1988, lot 11, repr.; sale: Hazlitt, Gooden & Fox, London (*European Drawings: Recent Aquisitions,* 23 Nov. - 9 Dec. 1988, no. 27, repr.).
Bibl.: Mentioned by Salerno under no. 263.

An important study in reverse of the final composition, which was executed in 1649 in two original and nearly identical versions: 1) Beverly Hills, California, private collection (Salerno, no. 263), purchased by Girolamo Bavosi, who intercepted the work, which was destined for another patron, Aurelio Zaneletti, and 2) Washington, National Gallery of Art (Salerno, no. 262), for Zaneletti, the original patron who paired this second version of *Amnon and Tamar* with a *Joseph and Potiphar's Wife* (Washington, National Gallery of Art; Salerno, no. 261), the pendant to the first version of *Amnon and Tamar.* For a complete discussion and illustrations, see cat. no. 29.

*   *   *

CANADA

ONTARIO
Ottawa
National Gallery of Canada / Musée des Beaux-Arts du Canada
167 Souls in Purgatory Supplicating the Madonna of Loreto. 6837 **[cat. no. 6]**
168 Landscape with a River and a Boat, with Figures on the Shore. 4259 **[cat. no. 71]**

Toronto
Art Gallery of Ontario / Galerie de l'Art d'Ontario
169 A Witch, bust length, Two Bats, and a Demon in Flight Behind. 86/194, Gift of the Trier-Fodor Foundation, 1986.

(118 x 257 mm.) pen and brown ink, brown wash **[Plate I]**
Inscribed on verso: *Vechia streia donatra / brutta inenperosa;*
and price: *ZZ—10—*.
Prov.: An unidentified armorial collector's mark (verso);
sale: Christie's, London, 9 Dec. 1986, lot 42, repr.

QUEBEC
Montreal
Montreal Museum of Fine Arts / Musée des Beaux-Arts de Montréal
170 Young Warrior with a Bow. Dr.946.82 (160 x 135 mm.)
pen and wash **[Plate L]**
Inscribed lower left recto: *8 P. Dol.*
Prov.: Casa Gennari (characteristic inscription).
Bibl.: See under M-T, no. 8.

    Related by Mahon and Turner to Guercino's altarpiece for
Carpi of the *Crucifixion of St. Peter* (Salerno, no. 52), painted
in 1618-1619.

II.   Drawings in Private Collections

Marcello Aldega - Margot Gordon, New York (formerly)
171 Boy in a Tall Hat, Holding a Pole with an Owl.
(226 x 155 mm.) **[Plate K]**
Watermark: Orsini arms.
Inscribed on the verso: *B. del Guercino . . . L 20—*.
Prov.: unidentified mark lower right recto;
sale: Christie's, London, 1 April 1987, lot 12.
Bibl.: Aldega-Gordon, *Old Master Drawings: XVI-XVIII
Century,* sale cat., New York, 1987, no. 20, repr. color.

W. M. Brady, New York (formerly)
172 A Landscape with a Man seen from Behind, Seated on a
Mound, Taking off his Shirt. (188 x 195 mm.) **[Plate P]**
Bibl.: *Old Master Drawings*, Oct. - Nov., 1990, no. 9,
repr. color.
    Datable to the 1630s or early 1640s.
173 Half-Length Study of Saint Helen. (183 x 153 mm.) **[Plate D]**
Prov.: Casa Gennari; etc.; C. R. Rudolf; sale: Sotheby's,
London, 4 July 1977, lot 115, repr.
Bibl.: *Old Master Drawings,* Oct. - Nov., 1990, no. 10, repr.
color.; M-T, under nos. 110-11.
    A preparatory study for Guercino's painting of 1644, *The
Finding of the True Cross,* S. Lazzaro dei Mendicanti, Venice
(Salerno, no. 209).

Prof. and Mrs. Jonathan Brown, Princeton, New Jersey
174 David with the Head of Goliath. (260 x 200 mm.) **[Plate N]**
Inscribed, lower right recto: *Guercino da Cento.*
Bibl.: *Princeton Alumni Collections: Works on Paper,* exh.
cat., The Art Museum, Princeton Univ., 1981, ill. on p. 53.
    A marvelous composition of the type often repeated by
the Guercinesque painter and etcher, Giuseppe Caletti of Ferrara. The sheet may be dated to the late 1620s or early
1630s.

Mr. and Mrs. Benton Case, Jr., Woodland, Minnesota
175 Head of God the Father. **[cat. no. 49]**

Dr. Carlo M. Croce
176 Study for the *Investiture of St. William of Aquitaine.*
[cat. no. 9]
177 A Flying Putto. **[cat. no. 55]**
178 Landscape with a Hunter. (255 x 408 mm.) **[Plate O]**
Prov.: Christie's, London, 4 July 1984, lot 39.
Bibl.: Bagni, 1985, no. 7.

Collection of Lisa Donneson and Henry Weisburg
179 The Prophet Hosea and an Angel. **[cat. no. 19]**

Evalyne S. Grand
180 Seated Male Nude. **[cat. no. 65]**

Mr. and Mrs. Morton B. Harris
181 Study for the Assumption of the Virgin/verso: Putto.
[cat. no. 57]

Mr. Jeffrey Horvitz
182 Profile Head of a Monk. (175 x 175 mm.) pen and wash
[Plate E]
Inscribed lower right recto: *10. P. Dol.*
Prov.: Casa Gennari (characteristic inscription; cf. Mahon,
"Casa Gennari," 1968, p. 356, note 49); F. Forni; E. Bouverie;
Mr. Hervey; Earl of Gainsborough (according to Russell);
A.G.B. Russell, Lancaster Herald (L. Suppl. 2770a, lower right
recto); sale: Sotheby's London, 22 May 1928; Mr. John
Nicholas Brown, Providence, R.I.
Bibl.: Russell, 1923, pl. XVII (with previous bibl.); *Italian
Art: 1200-1900,* exh. cat., Royal Academy, London, 1930, no.
651a; Hans Tietze, *European Master Drawings in the United
States*, New York: J.J. Augustine, 1947, no. 56, repr.;
Marangoni, 1959, no. 34, repr.

Jak Katalan

183 The Vision of St. Francis. **[cat.no. 44]**

184 Isaiah. (134 x 132 mm.) red chalk **[Plate E]**
Verso: fragment of a letter.
Prov.: Casa Gennari; Cav. Lamponi; Francesco Carandini;
Conte Lovatelli di Ravenna; purchased from Aldega-Gordon,
New York.

A fine study for Guercino's painting of *Isaiah* (Private
Collection; Salerno, no. 255), executed in 1648 for Marchese
Cospi.

Dr. Hilary Koprowski

185 The Temptation of Saint Francis. **[cat. no. 43]**

Collection of Michael and Margaret Korda

186 Martyrdom of St. Bartholomew. **[cat. no. 34]**

J.F. McCrindle, Princeton, New Jersey

187 Saint Luke. **[cat. no. 75]**

188 Joseph and Potiphar's Wife. (165 x 137 mm.) **[Plate K]**
Prov.: Baron D. Vivant-Denon (L. 779, lower left recto);
Baron de Malaussena (L. 1887, lower right recto); Carlos
Savelli, (L. 637, lower left recto); Jean de Vichet (L. Suppl.
1549); and an unidentified collector (H.L. [?], lower right
recto).
Bibl.: Varriano, 1974, no. 20.
Etched in reverse by Vivant-Denon (impression in the British
Museum).

Though this interesting drawing has certain features that
call to mind the work of the gifted but quirky Ferrarese
painter, etcher, and forger, Giuseppe Caletti, it deserves to be
considered as an autograph work by Guercino of c. 1625,
which may have been designed for a print. The extensive
parallel hatching which Guercino often employs in drawings
destined for reproduction might explain the somewhat odd
style of this sheet. The figure and costume of Joseph should
be compared to those of Semele in a drawing of *Jupiter and
Semele* at Windsor (M-T, no. 36), which was the subject of a
print by Pasqualini, dated 1626.

Robert and Bertina Suida Manning

189 Christ and St. Thomas. **[cat. no. 10]**

190 The Infant Christ Holding a Bird, and St. Joseph. **[cat. no. 11]**

191 Sisyphus. **[cat. no. 38]**

192 Andromeda Chained to the Rock. **[cat. no. 53]**

193 Bust of a Boy, Looking Down and to the Right.

(196 x 139 mm.) black chalk **[Plate F]**
Laid down.
Prov.: Spencer-Churchill; Dan Fellows Platt
(L. Suppl. 750a, verso).
Bibl.: Lynes, no. 153.

194 Half-Length Male Saint Looking Up and to the Left
(St. Francis ?) (120 x 94 mm.) **[Plate K]**
Laid down on old mount (English ?).
Inscribed lower right corner: *de M. Crozat.*
Prov.: E. Parsons & Sons, London; Dan Fellows Platt
(inscriptions on verso of mount), purchased in 1921.
Bibl.: Lynes, no. 128.

195 Head of a Girl wearing a Hat and Necklace. (86 x 86 mm.)
[Plate Q]
Prov.: Dan Fellows Platt, purchased 1934.
Bibl.: Lynes, no. 195.

196 Landscape with a Central Tree. (162 x 146 mm.) **[Plate O]**
Prov.: Casa Gennari; F. Forni; E. Bouverie; Mr. Hervey;
Earls of Gainsborough; Dan Fellows Platt, purchased in 1924.
Bibl.: Lynes, no. 8.

197 Man with a Tall Hat, with Arms Spread Wide.
(194 x 178 mm.)
Prov.: Dan Fellows Platt, purchased 1920.
Bibl.: Lynes, no. 148; Detroit, 1965, no. 109, repr.

198 Monk with a Book. (179 x 180 mm.) **[Plate P]**
Prov.: Casa Gennari; F. Forni; E. Bouverie; Mr. Hervey; Earls
of Gainsborough; Dan Fellows Platt (L. Suppl. 750a; 2066b),
purchased in 1928.
Bibl.: Lynes, no. 123.

199 Woman with Braids, Looking Left. (164 x 128 mm.) **[Plate E]**
Laid down.
Prov.: Dan Fellows Platt (L. Suppl. 750a), purchased in 1920.
Bibl.: Lynes, no. 193.

Mrs. Edward A. Maser

200 St. Roch with a Dog. (271 x 271 mm.)
Bibl.: Neilson, 1972, no. 33.

Janet Mavec

201 Helmeted Warrior with Two Separate Studies of his Head,
and Two Other Studies. **[cat. no. 50]**

Edmund P. Pillsbury, Fort Worth, Texas

202 Caricature of a Large-Nostrilled, Bare-Breasted Man Wearing a
Hat. **[fig. 92a]**

224

Private Collection

203 A Sibyl with a Book Seated before a Standing Putto Leaning on a Vase. **[cat. no. 48]**

Private Collection

204 Susanna and an Elder. (259 x 380 mm.) **[Plate I]**
Prov.: H. Page Cross; sale: Sotheby's, London, 5 July 1976, lot 79.

Private Collection

205 Martyrdom of St. Bartholomew. **[cat. no. 35]**
206 Portrait of a Man. **[cat. no. 85]**

Private Collection

207 St. Anthony of Padua. **[cat. no. 76]**

Private Collection

208 Esther before Ahasuerus. **[cat. no. 41]**

Private Collection

209 SS. Peter and Jerome/verso: St. Jerome. **[cat. no. 16]**
210 Three Studies of a Putto. **[cat. no. 54]**

Private Collection

211 Head of a High Priest or Rabbi. **[cat. no. 56]**
212 The Apostles at the Tomb. **[cat. no. 58]**
213 Wooded Landscape with Two Grave Robbers. **[cat. no. 66]**
214 Flora. (255 x 180 mm.) **[Plate F]**
Prov.: purchased from H. Shickman Gallery, New York.
An excellent drawing, probably of the 1640s.
215 Old Bearded Man Looking Downwards (St. Joseph ?).
(255 x 208 mm.) red chalk **[Plate J]**
Prov.: C.L. Chute, Esq., The Vyne, Basingstoke; sale: Sotheby's, London, 22 June 1949, multiple lot 1; sale: Sotheby's, London, 21 Nov. 1974, lot 70; H. Shickman Gallery, N.Y.

An offset of this very sensitive sheet, formerly in the Chute collection in England, is in the Royal Library at Windsor (M-T, no. 781, not repr.). I thank N. Turner for calling my attention to the provenance of the illustrated work, which may date to the 1640s or 1650s.
216 Study of the Infant Christ. (95 x 88 mm.) red chalk **[Plate P]**
Possibly a study for the Christ Child, seated on a book at the edge of a table, who gestures to the kneeling St. Anthony of Padua in Guercino's altarpiece of 1649-1651 in the Collegi-

ata at San Giovanni in Persiceto (Salerno, no. 274).
217 Two Studies of St. Francis in Prayer. (85 x 173 mm.)
[Plate H]
Prov.: Sotheby's, London, 6 March 1973, lot 103.
A rapidly executed sketch of c. 1640-1650.

Private Collection

218 Two Studies of Hercules Slaying the Hydra. **[cat. no. 5]**

Private Collection

219 Landscape with Mountains and Figures (269 x 424 mm.)
Bibl.: Bagni, 1985, no. 13, repr.
220 The Return of the Prodigal Son. (203 x 176 mm.) **[Plate L]**
Prov.: Christie's, London, 9 Dec. 1982, lot 45.
221 Study of a Girl, Turned to the Right, Holding a Dish.
(195 x 155 mm.) **[Plate D]**
Prov.: Casa Gennari; F. Forni; E. Bouverie; Mr. Hervey; the Earls of Gainsborough; sale: Christie's, London, 23 Nov. 1971, lot 104.

A copy of this drawing by Bartolozzi is in the Albertina (Stix—Fröhlich-Bum, no. 450, repr.).

Private Collection

222 Portrait of a Fruit Vendor. (261 x 192 mm) red chalk
[Plate P]
Prov.: sale: Sotheby's, London, 3 July 1989, lot 93, repr.

Private Collection

223 St. Jerome and the Lion. (254 x 212 mm.) red chalk
[Plate M]
Prov.: Casa Gennari; F. Forni; E. Bouverie (L. 325, lower left recto); etc.; sale: Sotheby's, London, 5 Dec. 1977, lot 81.
224 Seated Putto Holding a Flower. (185 x 137 mm.) red chalk
[Plate C]
Prov.: Casa Gennari; F. Forni; E. Bouverie (L. 325, lower left recto); George Salting; Sir Bruce S. Ingram (L. 1405a); Carl Winter (bears both his marks CW and GL); sale: Sotheby's, London, 5 Dec. 1977, lot 11.
225 Study of a Youth Holding a Piece of Drapery. (271 x 220 mm.) red chalk **[Plate G]**
Prov.: Casa Gennari; F. Forni; E. Bouverie (L. 325, lower left recto); etc.; sale: Sotheby's, London, 5 Dec. 1977, lot 55 repr. on p. 58.
226 Woman with her Hands Clasped on her Breast, Seated on a Cloud. (222 x 190 mm.) red chalk **[Plate L]**
Prov.: Sotheby's, N.Y., 14 Jan. 1987, lot 101, repr. on p. 74.

Possibly connected with the *Assumption of the Virgin* for the Tanari family of Bologna (Hermitage, Leningrad; Salerno, no. 99), which Guercino painted immediately upon his return to Cento from Rome in 1623. See M-T, pp. 18-19.

Private Collection
227 Cleopatra. **[Intro.]**
228 Dead Christ. **[fig. 61b]**
229 A Man Weighing Spices. (198 x 218 mm) **[Plate Q]**
Prov.: Baron D. Vivant-Denon (L. 779, lower left recto); A.N. Pérignon, Paris, 1 May 1826, lot 465; sale: Paris, Rheims & L., 11 June 1971, no. 10; Christie's, London, 30 March 1976, lot 12A; purchased from H. Shickman Gallery, N.Y.
　　Reproduced in reverse (lithograph by Vivant-Denon) in Pierre-Amaury Pineux-Duval, *Monuments des arts,* 1829.
230 St. John the Baptist. (238 x 195 mm.) red chalk **[Plate B]**
Prov.: P & D Colnaghi, London; Paul H. Ganz, New York; Kate Ganz, London.
Bibl.: Detroit, 1965, no. 110 (as the *Prodigal Son*); K. Ganz, *Italian Drawings 1500-1800,*
sale cat.: London, June-July 1987, no. 20, color repr.

Private Collection, New Haven, Connecticut
231 Diana Burning the Instruments of Love. **[cat. no. 60]**

Private Collection, Minneapolis, Minnesota
232 Lucretia. (195 x 170 mm.) **[Plate G]**
Bibl.: *Drawings and Watercolors from Minnesota Private Collections,* 1971, no. 3, repr.

Private Collection, New York
233 The Madonna and Child, and the Infant St. John the Baptist. (297 x 257 mm.) red chalk **[Plate L]**
On two joined sheets.
Inscribed on verso: *72.*
Watermark: encircled anchor under star.
Prov.: Casa Gennari; F. Forni; E. Bouverie (L. 325, lower left recto); Mr. Hervey; Earls of Gainsborough; Sir Max Michaelis, purchased c. 1922; sale: Christie's, London, 4 July 1989, lot 13, repr.
　　A highly finished drawing, perhaps for presentation, of the 1640s or early 1650s.

Private Collection, Toronto
234 Scene of Sacrifice. (285 x 420 mm.) **[Plate I]**
See cat. no. 22, note 4.

Private Collection, Chittenden, Vermont
235 Head of a Bearded Man, Looking Left. (252 x 191 mm.) red chalk **[Plate G]**
Inscribed in ink in an old hand, lower right recto: *dell' Guercino.*
Prov.: Arthur Sambon, Paris (variant of L. Suppl. 175a, lower right recto; similar, if not identical, stamp on the *Standing Man in Profile*, Seattle Art Museum, Suppl. no. 158).
　　A drawing of the late 1620s or early 1630s. Judging from photographs, the sheet is comparable to the *Head of an Old Woman (St. Anne?)* in a Swiss private collection, published by Turner and discussed in cat. nos. 19-21.

Janos Scholz, New York
　　see above: New York, Pierpont Morgan Library

Elmar W. Seibel, Boston, Massachusetts
236 The Vision of St. Philip Neri. **[cat. no. 52]**
237 The Triumph of Galatea. (204 x 260 mm.) pen and brown ink, brown wash; squared in black chalk **[Plate I]**
Top edge made up by Mariette.
Laid down on Mariette's distinctive blue mount, which he inscribed with the artist's dates.
Prov.: Pierre Crozat, according to Mariette; P.J. Mariette (L. 1852, lower left and right recto); Marquis de Lagoy (L. 1710, lower right recto); Hôtel Drouot, Paris, sale: Collection M.D., Part I, 14 May 1936, no. 43, repr. (according to Lurie); Colnaghi, London, *Old Master Drawings,* 1-19 July 1986, no. 15, repr. Bibl.: Lurie, 1963, p. 229, n. 14, fig. 13.
　　This important drawing has not been connected with a documented project. Based on style and the treatment of the subject, the sheet may be compared to Guercino's *Aurora* fresco of 1621 in the Casino Ludovisi in Rome. The motif of playful amorini was one Guercino employed in many of his Roman pictures.
238 Landscape with Bathers. (165 x 285 mm.) **[Plate N]**
Prov.: Jonathan Richardson Sr. (L. 2184, lower left recto).

Mrs. Richard L. Selle
239 Saint Barbara, a Bishop Saint, and another Male Saint. **[cat. no. 3]**

William D. Shorey
240 Three Studies of the Virgin. **[cat. no. 61]**
241 Study of Two Female Saints in Prayer. (194 x 200 mm.) red chalk **[Plate C]**

Prov.: Collection Mrs. Eric van Noorden; purchased from Thomas Agnew & Sons, London (*Master Drawings & Sculpture,* 8 Nov. Dec. 1989, no. 31, repr.).

In the Uffizi, Florence, there is a copy of this delicate drawing, which shows a portion of the composition along the bottom that was apparently cut from the original sometime after the Uffizi drawing was made (see Marangoni, 1959, no. 58, repr.). Another copy, also showing a larger portion of the composition than remains in the original, was exhibited in London with R.E.A. Wilson in 1933 (no. 13).

The two figures were perhaps preparatory for an altar-piece depicting the *Crucifixion* or the *Entombment* (the latter is more likely, since the female on the left is looking down and pointing with her right hand to something on the ground). The woman on the left has the type of physiognomy Guercino often used for St. Catherine. The saint on the right is almost certainly Mary Magdalen, who holds the ointment vase in her right hand. The sheet may be dated to the 1650s.

Mrs. A. Alfred Taubman, New York

242 Marcus Curtius Throwing Himself into the Flames.
(200 x 256 mm.) red chalk **[Plate I]**
Prov.: Collection Michel Gaud; his sale: Sotheby's, Monaco, 20 June 1987, lot 121.

136

131

3

161

229

148

117

38

230

230

PLATE C

35

224

122

241

231

158

28

221

232

173

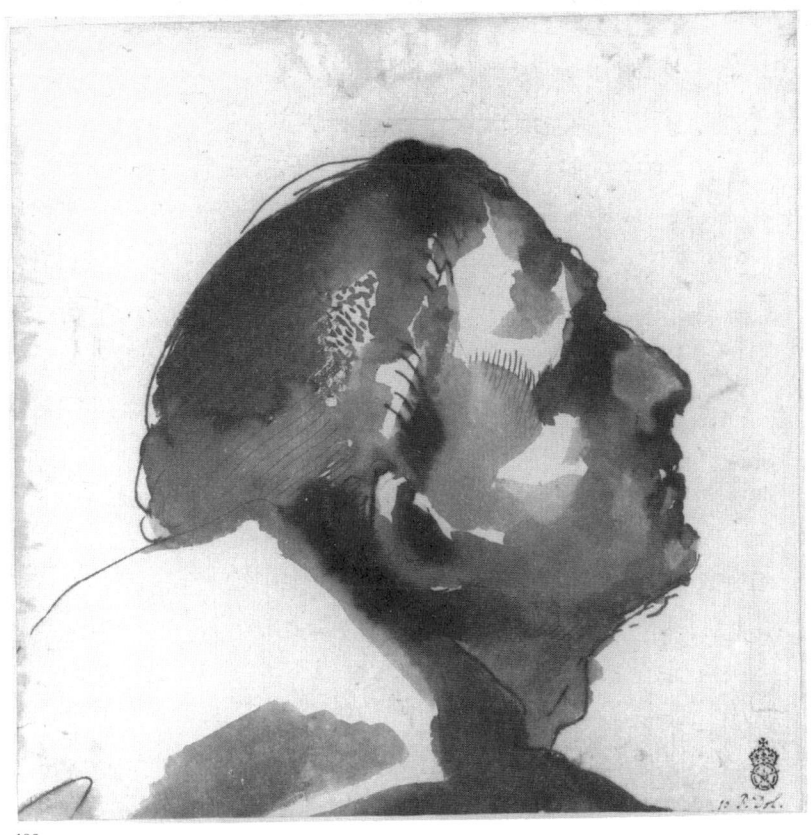

182

154

184

199

233

193

214

24

234

225

235

232

26

235

16

30

37

217

2

153

236

PLATE I

237

204

234

169

242

166

237

163

215

13

238

130

188

194

171

138

239

PLATE L

226

220

233

240

170

36

132

223

134

241

155

133

23

174

238

242

29

33

178

196

21

243

216

222

172

244

198

149

229

195

142

245

Bibliographic Abbreviations

Artioli-Monducci
Artioli, Nerio and Elio Monducci. *I Dipinti "Reggiani" del Bonone e del Guercino (pittura e documenti)*. Exh. cat., Reggio Emilia, Basilica della B.V. della Ghiara, 30 Jan. - 28 Feb. 1982. Second, corrected edition. Reggio Emilia, 1982.

Atti, 1861
Atti, Gaetano. *Intorno alla vita e alle opere di Gianfrancesco Barbieri detto il Guercino di Cento*. Rome, 1861.

Bagni, 1983
Bagni, Prisco. *Guercino a Piacenza. Gli affreschi della cupola della Cattedrale*. Bologna: Nuova Alfa, 1983.

Bagni, 1984
Bagni, Prisco. *Guercino a Cento. Le decorazioni di Casa Pannini*. Bologna: Nuova Alfa, 1984.

Bagni, 1985
Bagni, Prisco. *Guercino e il suo falsario. I disegni di paesaggio*. Bologna: Nuova Alfa, 1985.

Bagni, 1986
Bagni, Prisco. *Benedetto Gennari e la bottega del Guercino*. Bologna: Nuova Alfa, 1986.

Bagni, 1988
Bagni, Prisco. *Il Guercino e i suoi incisori*. Rome: Ugo Bozzi, 1988.

Bartsch
Bartsch, Adam. *Le Peintre-Graveur*. 21 vols. 2nd ed. Leipzig, 1854-70.

Baruffaldi
Baruffaldi, Girolamo. *Vite de' pittori e scultori ferraresi*. 2 vols. Ferrara, 1841-46.

Bean, 1966
Bean, Jacob. *Italian Drawings in the Art Museum, Princeton University. 106 Selected Examples*. Exh. cat. Princeton, 1966.

Bean, 1967
Bean, Jacob. "Publications Received: Denis Mahon, *Omaggio al Guercino*." *Master Drawings* 5, no. 3 (1967), pp. 304.

Bean, 1969
Bean, Jacob. "Guercino as a Draughtsman." Review of Mahon, *Disegni*. *Master Drawings* 7, no. 4 (1969), pp. 428-31.

Bean, 1979
Bean, Jacob. *17th Century Italian Drawings in the Metropolitan Museum of Art*. New York: Metropolitan Museum of Art, 1979.

Becker, 1985
Becker, David. *Old Master Drawings at Bowdoin College*. Exh. cat., Bowdoin College Museum of Art, Brunswick, Maine, 1985.

Bellori
Bellori, Giovan Pietro. *Le vite de' pittori, scultori e architetti moderni*. Rome, 1672; Edition E. Borea, Turin: Einaudi, 1976.

Berkeley, 1968
Schulz, Juergen, ed. *Master Drawings from California Collections*. Exh. cat., University Art Museum, University of California. Berkeley, 1968.

Bertelà, 1973
Bertelà, Giovanna Gaeta. *Incisori Bolognesi ed Emiliani del sec. XVII (Catalogo generale della raccolta di stampe antiche della Pinacoteca Nazionale di Bologna, Gabinetto delle Stampe)*. Bologna, 1973.

Bettagno, 1966
Bettagno, Alessandro. *Disegni di una collezione Veneziana del Settecento*. Exh. cat. Fondazione Giorgio Cini. Venice, 1966.

Bisogni, 1975
Bisogni, Fabio. "A Fragment of Guercino's Pesaro Altar." *Burlington Magazine* 117, no. 867 (1975), pp. 338-42.

Blunt, 1940
Blunt, Anthony. *Artistic Theory in Italy, 1450-1600*. London: Oxford University Press, 1940.

Blunt, 1956
Blunt, Anthony. *Handlist of the Drawings in the Witt Collection*. London: University of London, Courtauld Institute of Art, 1956.

Bober, 1988
Bober, Jonathan, et al. *The Famous Italian Drawings at the Fogg Art Museum in Cambridge*. Milan: Silvana Editoriale, 1988.

Bologna, 1956
Mostra dei Carracci. Exh. cat., Palazzo dell' Archiginnasio. Bologna, 1956.

Bologna, 1959
Maestri della pittura del seicento emiliano. Exh. cat., Palazzo dell' Archiginnasio. Bologna, 1959.

Bologna, 1984
Bologna 1584: Gli esordi dei Carracci e gli affreschi di Palazzo Fava. Exh. cat., Pinacoteca Nazionale. Bologna: Nuova Alfa, 1984.

Borea, 1975
Borea, Evelina. *Pittori bolognesi del seicento nelle gallerie di Firenze.* Exh. cat., Galleria degli Uffizi. Florence: Sansoni, 1975.

Bottari, 1966
Bottari, Stefano, et al. *Guercino, Disegni.* Florence: La Nuova Italia, 1966.

Brown University, 1984
Brown University, Department of Art. *Children of Mercury: The Education of Artists in the Sixteenth and Seventeenth Centuries.* Exh. cat. Providence, 1984.

Burl. Mag.
The Burlington Magazine (London, from 1903).

Calabi
Calabi, Augusto. *Francesco Bartolozzi, Catalogue des Estampes et Notice Bibliographique d'après les Manuscrits de A. de Vesme, entièrement réformés et complétés d'une étude critique.* Milan, 1928.

Cazort-Johnston
Cazort, Mimi and Catherine Johnston. *Bolognese Drawings in North American Collections 1500-1800.* Ottawa: National Gallery of Canada, 1982.

Cento, 1987
La Pinacoteca Civica di Cento. Catalogo Generale. Bologna: Nuova Alfa Editoriale, 1987.

Colnaghi, New York, 1984
Colnaghi, New York. *Old Master Drawings.* Exh. sale cat. 7 May - 9 June 1984. New York, 1984.

Czére, 1989
Czére, Andrea. *Disegni di artisti bolognesi nel Museo delle Belle Arti di Budapest.* Bologna: Nuova Alfa Editoriale, 1989.

DeGrazia, 1969
DeGrazia, Diane. *Guercino Drawings in the Art Museum, Princeton University.* Exh. cat., Princeton, 1969.

DeGrazia, 1979
DeGrazia Bohlin, Diane. *Prints and Related Drawings by the Carracci Family: A Catalogue Raisonné.* Exh. cat. Washington, D.C.: National Gallery of Art, 1979.

DeGrazia, 1984
DeGrazia, Diane. *Correggio and His Legacy.* Exh. cat., Washington, D.C., National Gallery of Art, 11 March - 13 May 1984. Parma, Galleria Nazionale, 3 June - 15 July 1984. Washington, D.C.: National Gallery of Art, 1984.

Dempsey, 1977
Dempsey, Charles. *Annibale Carracci and the Beginnings of Baroque Style.* Glückstadt: J. J. Augustin Verlag, 1977.

Dempsey, 1980
Dempsey, Charles. "Some Observations on the Education of Artists in Florence and Bologna During the Later Sixteenth Century" *Art Bulletin* 52, no. 4 (1980), pp. 552-69.

Denison-Mules, 1981
Denison, Cara D., Helen B. Mules, and Jane V. Shoaf. *European Drawings: 1375-1825. The Pierpont Morgan Library.* New York: Pierpont Morgan Library and Oxford University Press, 1981.

Detroit, 1965
Cummings, Frederick, ed. *Art in Italy: 1600-1700.* Exh. cat. Detroit: Detroit Institute of Arts, 1965.

Dipinti
Mahon, Denis. *Il Guercino (Giovanni Francesco Barbieri, 1591-1666), Catalogo Critico dei Dipinti.* Exh. cat., Bologna, Palazzo dell' Archiginnasio, 1 Sept. - 18 Nov. 1968. Bologna: Alfa, 1968.

Dirani, 1982-1983
Dirani, Maria Teresa. "Mecenati, pittori e mercato dell'arte nel Seicento. Il *Ratto di Elena* di Guido Reni e la *Morte di Didone* del Guercino nella corrispondenza del Cardinale Bernardino Spada." *Ricerche di Storia dell'Arte* 16 (1982-3), pp. 83-94.

Disegni
Mahon, Denis. *Il Guercino (Giovanni Francesco Barbieri, 1591-1666), Catalogo Critico dei Disegni*. Exh. cat., Bologna, Palazzo dell' Archiginnasio, 1 Sept. - 18 Nov. 1968. Bologna: Alfa, second, corrected edition, 1969.

Emiliani, 1959
Emiliani, Andrea. *Mostra di disegni del seicento emiliano nella Pinacoteca di Brera*. Vol. 1. *I disegni di Brera*. Exh. cat. Milan: Silvana, 1959.

Fairfax Murray
Fairfax Murray, Charles. *The J. Pierpont Morgan Collection of Drawings by the Old Masters Formed by C. Fairfax Murray*. 4 vols. London, 1905-12.

Feinblatt, 1976
Feinblatt, Ebria. *Old Master Drawings from American Collections*. Exh. cat., 29 April - 13 June 1976, Los Angeles County Museum of Art. New York, 1976.

Fischer, 1984
Fischer, Chris. *Italian Drawings from the J. F. Willumsen Collection*. Exh. cat., 14 April - 3 June 1984. Frederikssund, Denmark: The J. F. Willumsen Museum, 1984.

Fischer, 1988
Fischer, Chris. *Italian Drawings from the J. F. Willumsen Collection II*. Exh. cat., 29 June - 14 Aug. 1988. Frederikssund, Denmark: The J. F. Willumsen Museum, 1988.

Freedberg, 1983
Freedberg, Sydney J. *Circa 1600*. Cambridge, Mass.: Harvard University Press, 1983.

Frerichs, 1973
Frerichs, L. C. J. *Italiaanske Tekeningen I: De 17de Eeuw*. Exh. cat., Rijksprentenkabinet, Rijksmuseum. Amsterdam, 1973.

Garas, 1967
Garas, Klara. "The Ludovisi Collection of Pictures in 1633." *Burlington Magazine* 109 (1967), pp. 287-89, 339-49.

Gibbons
Gibbons, Felton. *Catalogue of Italian Drawings in the Art Museum, Princeton University*. 2 vols. Princeton University Press, 1977.

Gilli, 1975
Gilli, E., et al. *L'Ospedale di Cento nei secoli*. Cento: Cassa di Risparmio di Cento, 1975.

Goldner, 1988
Goldner, George, et al. *European Drawings, I. Catalogue of the Collections*. Malibu: The J. Paul Getty Museum, 1988.

Heawood
Heawood, E. *Watermarks. Mainly of the 17th and 18th Centuries. Monumenta Chartae Papyracae*. Hilversum, 1950; reprint, 1986.

Joachim, Microfiche
Joachim, Harold. *Art Institute of Chicago: Italian Drawings of the Fifteenth, Sixteenth, and Seventeenth Centuries*. Chicago and London: University of Chicago Press, 1979.

Joachim-McCullagh
Joachim, Harold and Suzanne Folds McCullagh. *Italian Drawings in the Art Institute of Chicago*. Chicago and London: University of Chicago Press, 1979.

Johnston, 1970
Johnston, Catherine. *Il seicento e il settecento a Bologna*. Milan, 1970.

Johnston, 1973
Johnston, Catherine. *Disegni Bolognesi*. Exh. cat. Florence: Galleria degli Uffizi, 1973.

L.
Lugt, Frits. *Les marques de collections de dessins et d'estampes*. Amsterdam, 1921.

L. Suppl.
Lugt, Frits. *Les marques de collections de dessins et d'estampes: Supplément*. The Hague, 1956.

Lavin, 1980
Lavin, Irving. *Bernini and the Unity of the Visual Arts*. 2 vols. New York: Oxford University Press, 1980.

Libro dei Conti
Guercino's account book. MS. B. 331, Biblioteca Comunale dell'Archiginnasio, Bologna. First published in Jacopo Alessandro Calvi, *Notizie della Vita, e delle Opere del Cavaliere Gioan Francesco Barbieri detto Il Guercino da Cento*. Bologna, 1808; reprinted in Malvasia, 1841, II, 307-44.

Loire, 1988

Loire, Stéphane. "Le Guerchin et la France: quelques tableaux peu connus." *Revue du Louvre,* no. 4 (1988), pp. 307-19.

Loire, 1988a

Loire, Stéphane. "La Circoncision du Guerchin au Musée des Beaux-Arts de Lyon." *Bulletin des Musées et Monuments Lyonnais,* no. 2 (1988), pp. 22-38.

Loire, 1990

Loire, Stéphane. *Le Guerchin en France.* Exh. cat., 31 May - 12 Nov. 1990. Paris: Éditions de la Réunion des Musées Nationaux, 1990.

Longhi, 1926

Longhi, Roberto. "The Climax of Caravaggio's Influence on Guercino." *Art in America* 14 (June 1926), pp. 133-48.

Lurie, 1963

Lurie, Ann Tzeutschler. "Old and Modern Drawings: A Drawing by Guercino." *Art Quarterly* 26 (Summer 1963), pp. 217-33.

Lurie, 1970

Lurie, Ann Tzeutschler. "Guercino's Versions of the Rest on the Flight to Egypt and the Lancellotti Tondo." *Bulletin of the Cleveland Museum of Art* (March 1970), pp. 93-101.

Lynes

Lynes, Mildred Akin. "The Drawings of Guercino in the Dan Fellows Platt Collection, Englewood, New Jersey." Unpublished M.A. Thesis, Institute of Fine Arts, New York University, New York, 1940.

M-T

Mahon, Denis, and Nicholas Turner. *The Drawings of Guercino in the Collection of Her Majesty The Queen at Windsor Castle.* Cambridge: Cambridge University Press, 1989.

Mahon, 1937

Mahon, Denis. "Notes on the Young Guercino: I Cento and Bologna; II Cento and Ferrara." *Burlington Magazine* 70 (Jan. - June 1937), pp. 112-22, 177-89.

Mahon, 1947

Mahon, Denis. *Studies in Seicento Art and Theory.* (Studies of the Warburg Institute, vol. 16.) London, 1947; reprint, Westport, Conn.: Greenwood Press, 1971.

Mahon, 1949

Mahon, Denis. "Guercino's Paintings of Semiramis." *Art Bulletin* 31 (1949), pp. 217-23.

Mahon, 1950

Mahon, Denis. "L'*Eclettismo* e i Carracci: un post-scriptum." *Commentari* 1 (1950), pp. 163-69.

Mahon, 1951

Mahon, Denis. "The Seicento at Burlington House: Some Addenda and Corrigenda, I - Drawings by Guercino." *Burlington Magazine* 93 (Feb. - March 1951), pp. 56-58.

Mahon, 1956

Mahon, Denis. *Mostra dei Carracci. Disegni.* Exh. cat., Palazzo dell' Archiginnasio. Bologna, 1956.

Mahon, 1965

Mahon, Denis. "Stock-taking in Seicento Sudies." *Apollo* 82 (Nov. 1965), pp. 378-91.

Mahon, 1967

Mahon, Denis. *I Disegni del Guercino della Collezione Mahon.* Exh. cat. Bologna, 1967.

Mahon, "Casa Gennari," 1968

Mahon, Denis. "Drawings by Guercino in the Casa Gennari." *Apollo* 88, no. 81 (1968), pp. 346-57.

Mahon, 1981a

Mahon, Denis. "Guercino as a Portraitist and His *Pope Gregory XV.*" *Apollo* 113 (April 1981), pp. 230-35.

Mahon, 1981b

Mahon, Denis. "Guercino and Cardinal Serra. A Newly Discovered Masterpiece." *Apollo* 114 (Sept. 1981), pp. 170-75.

Mahon-Ekserdjian

Mahon, Denis and David Ekserdjian with the assistance of Helen Davies. *Guercino Drawings from the Collections of Denis Mahon and the Ashmolean Museum.* Supplement to the *Burlington Magazine.* Exhibition held at the Ashmolean Museum, Oxford, 29 April - 22 June 1986, and at Hazlitt, Gooden & Fox, London, 15 Oct. - 12 Nov. 1986. Also published separately. *Burlington Magazine* 128 (March 1986).

Malvasia

Malvasia, Carlo Cesare. *Felsina Pittrice.* 2 vols. Bologna, 1678. Ed. cit., second edition, Bologna, 1841.

Mandowsky, 1980

Mandowsky, Erna. *Old Master Drawings. Seattle Art Museum Collection Guide.* Seattle: Seattle Art Museum, 1980.

Marabottini, 1966

Marabottini, Alessandro, ed. *Le Arti di Bologna di Annibale Carracci.* Rome, 1966.

Marangoni, 1959

Marangoni, Matteo. *Guercino. I Grandi Maestri del Disegno.* Milan: Aldo Martello Editore, 1959.

Martin, 1977

Martin, John Rupert. *Baroque.* Icon Editions. New York: Harper & Row, 1977.

Marzocchi, 1984

Marzocchi, Lea. *Scritti originali del Conte Carlo Cesare Malvasia spettanti alla sua 'Felsina Pittrice.'* (Rapporti no. 40) Bologna: Alfa, 1984.

McComb, 1934

McComb, Arthur. *The Baroque Painters of Italy.* Cambridge: Harvard University Press, 1934.

Minneapolis, 1971

Drawings and Watercolors from Minnesota Private Collections. Exh. cat., 13 May - 13 June 1971. Minneapolis Institute of Arts, 1971.

Moir, 1974

Moir, Alfred, ed. *Drawings by Seventeenth Century Italian Masters from the Collection of Janos Scholz.* Exh. cat., 26 Feb. - 31 March 1974, The Art Galleries, University of California, Santa Barbara, and elsewhere. Santa Barbara: University of California, 1974.

Moir, 1986

Moir, Alfred, ed. *Old Master Drawings from the Collection of John and Alice Steiner.* Exh. cat. Santa Barbara Museum of Art, 1986.

Mongan-Sachs

Mongan, Agnes and Paul J. Sachs. *Drawings in the Fogg Museum of Art.* 3 vols. Cambridge, Mass.: Harvard University Press, 1940.

Monuments des Arts, 1829

Pineux-Duval, Pierre-Amaury. *Monuments des Arts du Dessin Chez les Peuples Tant Anciens Que Modernes Recueillis par Le Baron Vivant Denon.* 4 vols. Paris: M. Brunet Denon, 1829.

Neilson, 1972

Neilson, Nancy Ward. *Italian Drawings Selected from Mid-Western Collections.* Exh. cat. St. Louis: St. Louis Art Museum, 1972.

Nijmegen, 1988

Aikema, Bernard and R. D. Kollewijn, et al. *Italiaanse Tekeningen Uit Nederlandse Collecties: 1570 - 1800.* Exh. cat., Nijmegen Museum "Commanderie Van Sint Jan," 1988.

Norfolk, 1950

Norfolk, 1950. *Old Master Drawings, Fall Exhibition, Norfolk Society of Arts.* Exh. cat., Nov. - Dec. 1950. Norfolk, 1950.

Oberhuber, 1977

Oberhuber, Konrad, ed. *Renaissance and Baroque Drawings from the Collections of John and Alice Steiner.* Exh. cat., 18 Nov. 1977 - 15 Jan. 1978, Fogg Art Museum and elsewhere. Cambridge, Mass.: Fogg Art Museum, 1977.

Oberhuber, 1979

Oberhuber, Konrad, ed. *Old Master Drawings. Selections from the Charles A. Loeser Bequest.* Cambridge, Mass.: Fogg Art Museum, 1979.

Ottani, 1965

Ottani, Anna. *Il Guercino. I maestri del colore,* no. 63. Milan, 1965.

Ottawa, 1988

Ottawa, 1988. *Master Drawings from the National Gallery of Canada.* Exh. cat., Vancouver Art Gallery and elsewhere. Washington, D.C.: National Gallery of Art, 1988.

Paris, 1988

Paris, 1988. *Seicento: le siècle de Caravage dans les collections publiques françaises.* Exh. cat., Paris, Grand Palais. Paris, 1988.

Passeri

Passeri, Giambattista. *Vite de' pittori, scultori ed architetti che hanno lavorato in Roma, morti dal 1641 fino al 1673.* Rome, 1772. Ed. cit.: critical edition by Jakob Hess, Leipzig and Vienna, 1934.

Pepper

Pepper, D. Stephen. *Guido Reni.* Oxford: Phaidon, 1984.

Planiscig-Voss
Planiscig, Leo and Hermann Voss. *Handzeichnungen alter Meister aus der Sammlung Geiger.* Vienna: Amalthea, n.d.

Posner, 1968
Posner, Donald. "The Guercino Exhibition at Bologna." Review of *Dipinti* and *Disegni. Burlington Magazine* 110 (Nov. 1968), pp. 596-607.

Reed-Wallace, 1989
Reed, Sue Welsh and Richard Wallace. *Italian Etchers of the Renaissance and Baroque.* Exh. cat. Boston: Museum of Fine Arts, 1989.

Riccòmini, 1969
Riccòmini, E. *Il seicento ferrarese.* Milan: Silvana, 1969.

Righetti Dondini, 1768
Righetti Dondini, Orazio Camillo. *Le Pitture di Cento e le Vite in Compendio di Vari Incisori e Pittori della Stessa Città.* Ferrara, 1768.

Robinson, 1973
Robinson, Franklin W. *One Hundred Master Drawings from New England Private Collections.* Exh. cat. Hanover, New Hampshire: Dartmouth College, 1973.

Roli, 1968
Roli, Renato. *I fregi centesi del Guercino.* Bologna: Pàtron, 1968.

Roli, 1972
Roli, Renato. *Guercino. Collana disegnatori Italiani.* Milan: Aldo Martello Editore, 1972.

Rosenblum, 1962
Rosenblum, Robert. "A New Source for David's *Sabines.*" *Burlington Magazine* 104 (1962), pp. 158-62.

Russell, 1923
Russell, Archibald G. B. *Drawings by Guercino.* London, 1923.

Russell, 1973
Russell, Francis. "A Guercino Footnote." *Master Drawings* 11, no. 3 (1973), p. 271.

Salerno
Salerno, Luigi with the assistance of Sir Denis Mahon. *I dipinti del Guercino.* Rome: Ugo Bozzi Editore, 1988.

Sambon, 1929
Sambon, Arthur. *Les Dessins de Luca Cambiaso et de Gian Francesco Barbieri dit Le Guerchin.* Exh. cat., Paris, Galerie Sambon, 8 - 20 Nov. 1929. Paris, 1929.

Scannelli, 1657
Scannelli, Francesco. *Il Microcosmo della Pittura.* Cesena, 1657; facsimile edition, Milan: Edizioni Labor, 1966.

Southorn, 1988
Southorn, Janet. *Power and Display in the Seventeenth Century.* Cambridge, England: Cambridge University Press, 1988.

Spark, 1949
Spark, Victor D. *Spark Studios. Catalogue of the Exhibition and Sale of the Dan Fellows Platt Collection of Drawings and Water-Colors by Artists from the 17th to the 20th Centuries.* Exh. cat., May - Oct. 1949. New York.

Spear, 1982
Spear, Richard. *Domenichino.* 2 vols. New Haven and London: Yale University Press, 1982.

Spike, 1984
Spike, John. *Baroque Portraiture in Italy: Works from North American Collections.* Exh. cat. Sarasota, 1984.

Stampfle-Bean, 1967
Stampfle, Felice and Jacob Bean. *Drawings from New York Collections, II, The Seventeenth Century in Italy.* Exh. cat. New York: The Pierpont Morgan Library, 1967.

Steinberg, 1980
Steinberg, Leo. "Guercino's *Saint Petronilla.*" In *Studies in Italian Art History* I. *Memoirs of the American Academy in Rome.* Cambridge: MIT, 1980, pp. 207-34.

Stix—Fröhlich-Bum
Stix, Alfred and L. Fröhlich-Bum. *Die Zeichnungen der Venezianische Schule. Beschreibender Katalog der Handzeichnungen in der Staatlichen Graphischen Sammlung Albertina,* vol. 1. Vienna, 1926.

Stix—Spitzmüller
Stix, Alfred and Anna Spitzmüller. *Die Schulen von Ferrara, Bologna, Parma und Modena, der Lombardei, Genuas, Neapels und Siziliens. Beschreibender Katalog der Handzeichnungen in der Staatlichen Graphischen Sammlung Albertina,* vol. 6. Vienna, 1941.

Stone, 1989
Stone, David M. "Theory and Practice in Seicento Art: The Example of Guercino." Unpublished Ph.D. Dissertation, Harvard University, 1989; University Microfilms, Ann Arbor.

Tedeschi
Tedeschi, Martha. *Great Drawings from the Art Institute of Chicago: The Harold Joachim Years 1958-83.* New York: Hudson Hills, 1985.

Thiem, 1978
Thiem, Christel et al. *Sammlung Schloss Fachsenfeld. Zeichnungen, Bozzetti und Aquarelle. . .* Stuttgart: Graphische Sammlung, 1978.

Thiem, 1979
Thiem, Christel. "Unpublished Chalk Drawings by Guercino in the Collection of Schloss Fachsenfeld." *Master Drawings* 12 (Winter 1979), pp. 401-17.

Thiem, 1983
Thiem, Christel. *Disegni di artisti bolognesi dal seicento all'ottocento (della Collezione Schloss Fachsenfeld e della Graphische Sammlung Staatsgalerie Stuttgart).* Exh. cat. Bologna, 1983.

Tuer
Tuer, Andrew White. *Bartolozzi and His Works.* Second edition, revised and enlarged. London: Field and Tuer, 1885.

Turner, 1980
Turner, Nicholas. *Italian Baroque Drawings (from the British Museum).* London: Colonnade Books, 1980.

Turner, 1980a
Turner, Nicholas. "Review of Gibbons, *Catalogue of Italian Drawings in the Art Museum, Princeton University.*" *Art Bulletin* 62 (Sept. 1980), pp. 488-89.

Turner, 1981
Turner, Nicholas. "Some Preparatory Drawings for Guercino's Early Altarpiece of Sts. Francis and Louis of France at Brisighella." *Master Drawings* 19, no. 2 (1981). pp. 164-66.

Turner, 1984
Turner, Nicholas. Review of Bagni, 1983. *Burlington Magazine* 126 (1984), pp. 641-42.

Turner, 1986
Turner, Nicholas. Review of Mahon-Ekserdjian, *Burlington Magazine* 128 (1986), pp. 841-43.

Van Tuyll, 1989
Ackley, Clifford S., Michiel C. C. Kersten, William W. Robinson, and Carel Van Tuyll van Serooskerken. *From Michelangelo to Rembrandt: Master Drawings from the Teyler Museum.* Exh. cat., 10 Feb. - 30 April 1989, The Pierpont Morgan Library and elsewhere. New York: The Pierpont Morgan Library, 1989.

Varriano, 1973
Varriano, John. "Notes on Princeton Drawings: Guercino, Bonfanti, and *Christ Among the Doctors.*" *Record of The Art Museum, Princeton University* 32, no. 1 (1973), pp. 11-15.

Varriano, 1974
Various Authors. *Five Colleges Roman Baroque Festival.* Exh. cat. Includes "Drawings by Guercino and his Followers." Exhibition held at the Mount Holyoke College Art Museum, South Hadley, Massachusetts, 8 April - 3 May 1974. n.p., 1974.

Ward-Jackson
Ward-Jackson, Peter. *Victoria and Albert Museum, Catalogues, Italian Drawings,* Volume II, *17th-18th Century.* London, 1980.

Washington, 1990
Washington D.C., National Gallery of Art. *Selected Baroque Paintings from Italian Banks.* Exh. cat., 26 Sept. - 11 Nov. 1990 and elsewhere. Venice: Marsilio Editori, 1990.

Westin and Westin, 1975
Westin, Jean K. and Robert H. Westin. *Carlo Maratti and His Contemporaries: Figurative Drawings from the Roman Baroque.* Exh. cat., 19 Jan.- 16 March 1975, Museum of Art, The Pennsylvania State University, University Park, 1975.

Wood, 1986
Wood, Carolyn. "Visual Panegyric in Guercino's Casino Ludovisi Frescoes." *Storia Dell'arte* 58 (1986), pp. 223-38.

Zafran, 1979
Zafran, Eric M. *One Hundred Drawings in the Chrysler Museum at Norfolk.* Exh. cat. Norfolk: Chrysler Museum, 1979.

Photo Credits

Photographs have been supplied by the owners of the objects reproduced. We note below the following exceptions and acknowledgements.

Photos generously supplied by Christie's, London: figs. 15b, 16c, 25c, 38a, 40c; Suppl. nos. 169, 171, 220, 221, 229.

Photos generously supplied by Sotheby's, London: Suppl. nos. 204, 223-225, 242.

Photos generously supplied by Sotheby's, New York: Suppl. no. 226.

Reproduced Courtesy of the Art Institute of Chicago: cat. nos. 8, 13, 28, 33; fig. 61a; Suppl. no. 16. Copyright © 1991 the Art Institute of Chicago.

Reproduced by Gracious Permission of Her Majesty Queen Elizabeth II, figs. 31c, 40b.

Color photos by Bob Lorenzson, New York: cat. nos. 19, 34, 44.

FINITO DI STAMPARE
NELLE OFFICINE DI BERTONCELLO ARTIGRAFICHE
IN CITTADELLA/PADOVA NEL MESE DI FEBBRAIO 1991
A CURA DI NUOVA ALFA EDITORIALE IN BOLOGNA